LAWMAKING UNDER PRESSURE

LAWMAKING UNDER PRESSURE

International Humanitarian Law and Internal Armed Conflict

Giovanni Mantilla

CORNELL UNIVERSITY PRESS ITHACA AND LONDON

First published 2020 by Cornell University Press

Library of Congress Cataloging-in-Publication Data

Names: Mantilla, Giovanni, 1981– author.
Title: Lawmaking under pressure : international humanitarian law and internal armed conflict / Giovanni Mantilla.
Description: Ithaca [New York] : Cornell University Press, 2020. | Includes bibliographical references and index.
Identifiers: LCCN 2020006015 (print) | LCCN 2020006016 (ebook) | ISBN 9781501752582 (cloth) | ISBN 9781501752599 (epub) | ISBN 9781501752605 (pdf)
Subjects: LCSH: Humanitarian law—History. | Civil war. | Humanitarian law—Social aspects. | Social pressure—Political aspects.
Classification: LCC KZ6471 .M356 2020 (print) | LCC KZ6471 (ebook) | DDC 341.6/7—dc23
LC record available at https://lccn.loc.gov/2020006015
LC ebook record available at https://lccn.loc.gov/2020006016

Contents

Acknowledgments

Acknowledgments commonly begin with authors reviewing the many debts they have incurred over the course of the years that it takes to write a book. Personally, I have always found the debt metaphor to be a bit too transactional, and hence inappropriate to describe a process more often characterized by intellectual generosity, mentorship, idea sharing, and helpful critical engagement. I bear a huge gratitude to a great many people, and remain humbled and moved by their selfless dedication to helping me improve my work.

The Department of Political Science at the University of Minnesota provided a very friendly and nurturing intellectual environment during six happy years in Minneapolis. In particular, I thank Kathryn Sikkink and Fionnuala Ní Aoláin for being brilliant scholars and kind, wonderful humans—this book could not have been written without their unflailing encouragement. I am equally grateful to Bud Duvall, Ron Krebs, David Samuels, Dara Strolovitch, and Joan Tronto for supporting me throughout, in various capacities. The N. Marbury Efimenco Fellowship funded part of my coursework, while my fieldwork and writing stages were respectively funded through a Compton International Fellowship granted by the University of Minnesota's Interdisciplinary Center for the Study of Global Change and the Robert T. Holt Distinguished Doctoral Dissertation Fellowship in Political Science administered by the University of Minnesota Graduate School. Smaller grants such as the Andrew Dickinson Memorial Fellowship and the Hella Mears Graduate Fellowship enabled me to make shorter but crucial research trips, and an Upper Midwest Human Rights Fellowship granted through the university's Human Rights Center allowed me to spend a summer in New York City interning for Human Rights Watch in 2008. My thanks go to Sara Braun, Karen Brown, Sabine Engel, Catherine Guisan, Hella Mears, David Weissbrodt, and the members of various selection committees for trusting my abilities enough to put money on the line.

After leaving Minnesota I was lucky to hold postdoctoral positions at Brown University's Watson Institute for International and Public Affairs and Princeton University's Niehaus Center for Globalization and Governance. At Brown I especially thank Peter Andreas and Nina Tannenwald for their mentorship during a very productive year. At Princeton I am especially grateful to Helen Milner and Robert O. Keohane for their enthusiasm in my research, their engaging and thoughtful critiques, and their contribution to an interdisciplinary conference on the laws of war in October 2015 (organized jointly with Bob and with my colleague Geoffrey P. R. Wallace).

The Centro de Investigación y Docencia Económicas in Mexico City was a wonderful place to call home for three years. Mark Aspinwall and Lorena Ruano were steadfast department heads and kind supporters in the División de Estudios Internacionales. I warmly thank all my colleagues at CIDE. At Cambridge University I have found a similarly welcoming, stimulating environment. Particular thanks go to Duncan Bell at Christ's College and Jason Sharman at the Department of Politics and International Studies for their mentorship.

This work is also the product of countless friendships in several places. Whether in Bogotá, Cambridge, Minneapolis, Providence, Princeton, Mexico City, New York, or elsewhere around the world, while completing this research I received a constant stream of love and support from many wonderful human beings. For obvious reasons I cannot include everyone here, but I must mention a number of people: Tatiana Acevedo, Catalina Arreaza, Rebecca Bell-Martin, Azer Binnet, Noelle Brigden, Jonas Bunte, Ana Cuesta, Geoff Dancy, Sarah Bauerle Danzman, Dora Marujo Dias, Carlos Andrés Díaz, Carlos Echeverría, Jesús Estrada-Pérez (RIP), Patricia Ferreira, Brandon Fischer, Janice Gallagher, Juan Guerra, Bai Linh Hoang, Elliot James, Michelle Jurkovich, Pablo Kalmanovitz, Denis Kennedy, Esen Kirdis, Amy Lerner, Sandra Ley, Moira Lynch, Emma Stone Mackinnon, T. J. Malaskee, Jerome Marston, Darrah McCracken, Verónica Michel, Adam Mielke, Felipe Muñoz, E. G. Nelson, Katharina Neureiter, Kim Nolan, Mayumi Okuda, Justin Pearce, Angel Camilo Peñaranda, Menaka Phillips, Angela María Restrepo, Javier Rojas, Daniel Rosas, Cesar Rueda, Maria Paula Rueda, Sergio Ruiz, Bret Ryan, Gabriela Sáenz, Natalia Santiesteban, Libby Sharrow, Geoff Sheagley, Paul Snell, Chris Stone, Laura Thaut, Camilo Vargas, and Marcela Villarrazo. Thank you all for the fun, nurturing time spent together; I look forward to more.

The hospitality of several people in Europe, the United States, and beyond was critical for executing this project. In particular, I have my brother Mario Alberto, my cousins Carlos Eduardo and Karin, and my friends Kerstin Feurstein, Julian Sánchez Berbesi, Roberto Sierra, and Aaron Welo to thank. Paola Castaño hosted me several times in Chicago, sharing her space, her colors, and her infectious joy with me every single time.

For invaluable editing assistance as I approached the finish line I thank Molly Biddle, and for his warm and loving support in the final stage of the project, Ashley Walsh.

Dozens of colleagues have read and commented on aspects of this project over many years. I am particularly grateful to Matthew Evangelista, who—essentially unprompted—generously organized a superb book workshop at Cornell University in 2016, summoning the collective brilliance of Neta Crawford, Renée de

Nevers, Isabel Hull, Peter J. Katzenstein, Agnieszka Nimark, Jens Ohlin, Judith V. Reppy, Steven M. Ward, and Anna Wojciuk, among others. The book is undoubtedly better for their incisive reading and feedback. Helen Kinsella has been an enduring intellectual ally and dear friend through the years; I cannot thank her enough. Sandesh Sivakumaran very kindly read the entire manuscript and offered thoughtful, timely advice toward the end of the process. Audiences at several academic conferences since 2012 improved the book's argument and empirics. Michael Barnett deserves very special thanks for being a source of constructive criticism and support for over a decade now.

The staff of various institutions where I conducted archival and library research were instrumental in helping me gather the rich materials on which this book is based—especially Fabrizio Bensi at the International Committee of the Red Cross (ICRC) in Geneva, Anne Liskenne at the Diplomatic Archives of France in Paris (and Nantes), and various individuals at the UK National Archives in London and the U.S. National Archives in College Park, Maryland. The ICRC also granted me permission to consult certain portions of its restricted archives, for which I am very grateful.

Jacques Moreillon, honorary member and former director of principles and law at the ICRC, read most chapters generously and critically, and connected me with many other important knowledgeable persons in or around Geneva. In practice he became an essential informal adviser, and for that my deep gratitude goes out to him. ICRC members François Bugnion and Yves Sandoz likewise showed willingness to speak with me at length (the latter on several occasions) on the issues dealt with here. Dara Kay Cohen and Martha Finnemore kindly read my draft project and provided useful advice. David Forsythe, Sylvie Junod, Frits Kalshoven, and Michel Veuthey all commented on one or a few draft chapters, helping me sharpen my approach and reconsider some views. The Departamento de Ciencia Política at the Universidad de los Andes in Bogotá, Colombia, generously hosted my brief stint as a visiting scholar in January–February 2012. Several individuals in Bogotá, Geneva, and elsewhere generously agreed to interviews for a chapter on Colombia that never made it onto the final version.

Roger Haydon at Cornell University Press was an encouraging, supportive, and patient editor. I immensely appreciate his efforts to see this book through.

I acknowledge the incredibly valuable feedback of the editors and reviewers of *International Organization*, the *European Journal of International Relations*, and the *Journal of the History of International Law*, where portions of research included here (in chapters 1, 3, and 5) appeared as the following articles:

Mantilla, Giovanni. "Forum Isolation: Social Opprobrium and the Origins of the International Law of Internal Conflict." *International Organization* 72, no. 2 (2018): 317–49. Cambridge: Cambridge University Press / IO Foundation.

Mantilla, Giovanni. "The Protagonism of the USSR and Socialist States in the Revision of International Humanitarian Law (IHL)." *Journal of the History of International Law* 21, no. 2 (2019): 181–211. Leiden: Brill.

Mantilla, Giovanni. "Social Pressure and the Making of Wartime Legal Protections for Civilians." *European Journal of International Relations* 26, no. 2 (2020): 443–68. London: Sage.

I thank the publishers of the articles for allowing me to reuse the material.

Lastly, I thank my sister, Maria Angélica, and my parents, Mario Mantilla Ayala and Fabiola Casas Duque, for their love, encouragement, and support of my studies.

LAWMAKING UNDER PRESSURE

Introduction

FAILURE IN PARIS, SUCCESS IN GENEVA

Meeting in Paris on November 29, 1948, state delegates in the United Nations (UN) Third Committee discussed the Draft International (later Universal) Declaration of Human Rights (UDHR) days before its adoption. That afternoon they considered a Cuban proposal to insert as a new human right the right to resist oppression: "Any person shall have the right to offer appropriate resistance to manifest acts of oppression or tyranny."[1] Supportive of the initiative's intent but dubious of the phrasing, Hernán Santa Cruz, the Chilean representative, quickly moved to amend the Cuban text to read, "When a government seriously or systematically violates human rights and freedoms, individuals and peoples are entitled without prejudice to an appeal to the United Nations to resist oppression and tyranny."[2]

The U.S. delegate, Eleanor Roosevelt, then took the microphone to express that "in her opinion, the recognition in the declaration of human rights of the right to resist acts of tyranny and oppression would be tantamount to encouraging sedition, for such a provision could be interpreted as conferring a legal character on uprisings against a Government which was in no way tyrannical." The Cuban delegate, Guy Pérez Cisneros, stood his ground and explained to Roosevelt that his proposal "was not dangerous but expressed a legitimate right which had for its object the independence and sovereignty which the free exercise of human rights should guarantee." He referenced Cuba's liberation struggle from Spain and reminded others that "the speeches of Jefferson, Bolivar, and San Martin" likewise contained this idea.

However, as Johannes Morsink notes, overall the right to resist oppression "was not very popular" in the UN human rights debates of the late 1940s.[3] It had been discussed since 1947 in various *petits comités* which, despite finding in it merit as a general principle, recommended it for inclusion in the UDHR in some subdued form but not as a stand-alone right. In 1948, with the exception of Chile, Cuba, and the Soviet Union (as a last-ditch supporter), all other delegates speaking within the Third Committee found it wanting or inconvenient. The Australians, Belgians, and Ecuadorians politely acknowledged the noble intent behind it but just as quickly denounced it as dangerous, as Roosevelt had done before them. The Australians noted that "the legitimation of the right to resist . . . would necessitate a clear definition of those two expressions. Such a definition would raise very great difficulties: Where did oppression and tyranny begin?" The Belgian delegate asked, "Who would decide what constituted an act of oppression or tyranny?" Ecuador quipped, "How could resistance to oppression be made legal when it was necessarily of an illegal character?" British delegates echoed these concerns.

Ultimately, in the diplomatic environment of the UN Third Committee, the right to legitimate armed resistance against oppression and tyranny met an unremarkable fate, confined to a rarely noted passage of the declaration's preamble and deprived of its status as a human right.[4]

Fast-forward eight months to August 3, 1949, in Geneva. There, the Swiss-organized diplomatic conference revising the Geneva Conventions for the protection of the victims of armed conflict concluded four months of negotiations, including those on an article extending international humanitarian law (IHL), for the first time in history, to internal armed conflict.[5] Of all the topics debated in Geneva in 1949, reportedly no other issue gave rise to "such a long discussion and to such a detailed and exhaustive study," as Soviet delegate Platon D. Morosov admitted before expressing full support for the extension and setting forth an ambitious USSR proposal on the matter.[6] The Soviet text failed, but an article did emerge nonetheless. It is now better known as Article 3 common to the Geneva Conventions (Common Article 3, or CA3), which binds parties to "armed conflicts not of an international character" to observe certain humanitarian rules and limits as a matter of codified international law. Since its inception, CA3 was hailed as revolutionary, and it has slowly become a bedrock rule of the modern legal humanitarian order, underpinning the law of armed conflict, international criminal law, and, arguably, the so-called Responsibility to Protect.[7]

These vignettes are telling. On their face they suggest that in the late 1940s a majority of states were eager, or at least willing, to grant international humanitarian guarantees to all those caught in the crossfire of organized internal violence, including wounded fighters and civilians, no matter their political allegiance. At the same time, Chile and Cuba aside, states appeared largely unprepared to concede that "legitimate" revolt or rebellion against oppression should be enshrined as a human right.

Why? Certainly, differing outcomes from two topically similar debates may have to do with important differences of substance (humane conduct and protection *in bello* versus a human right *ad bellum*) and particularly, from the perspective of states, with diverse assessments of appropriateness and risk.[8] Yet the controversies around both innovations resembled each other so starkly during their respective contemporaneous diplomatic debates that one may at least suggest that something else *beyond substance* was at play, and perhaps crucially so: the politics of process and procedure.

Process and procedure in Geneva markedly differed from those in Paris months earlier. In Geneva, unlike Paris, the International Committee of the Red Cross (ICRC) had forcefully thrown its weight behind the extension of the Geneva Conventions to internal conflict, presenting it early on as an "essential" postwar innovation alongside the renewal of the rules governing interstate conflict. Drawing on its nearly century-long experience in legal and practical humanitarianism and later on its efforts during the Spanish Civil War (1936–39), by the mid-twentieth century the ICRC possessed tremendous practical knowledge and normative authority to influence the agenda of legal revisions and motivate concern behind modifications and additions.

Likewise, in Geneva, unlike in Paris, most delegations from smaller and mid-size European and Latin American countries expressed early and strong support for the idea of humane treatment for all amid internal conflict (many of them citing their own historical experience), giving the issue great urgency and downplaying, also early on, the sovereignty concerns of more powerful states—especially Britain, France, and the United States. Therefore, in Geneva, the idea of "humanizing" internal conflict had not been prejudiced in early meetings as a more or less noble afterthought but amplified and endorsed in conference settings that included delegations from nearly every participating state.

Finally, in Geneva, unlike in Paris, the issue of internal conflict had been quickly and fiercely caught in Cold War politicization, with a Soviet bloc publicly dressing itself in humanitarian garb, pointedly castigating the conservative stance of its allegedly more liberal-democratic Western foes, and casting vociferous pressure upon the few but powerful Western skeptics that remained. Together these political and procedural factors appear to have hugely influenced the diplomatic process behind CA3, in contrast with the failed human right to resist oppression, altering the social dynamics within the negotiating room in Geneva and generating sufficient pressure for the adoption of a landmark controversial legal rule.

This book develops the argument that the politics of *social pressure*, especially those enacted and channeled in processes and procedures of multilateral codification, matter decisively for the making of international law. Substantively, I focus on the historical development of the rules of IHL for internal conflict, which began to gestate in the mid-nineteenth century but were only codified decades later and ultimately have changed the normative fabric of world politics.

The origins and negotiation of the law of internal conflict have surprisingly not yet been theorized or sufficiently historicized, even though some of these international rules (especially CA3) are now considered essential "laws of humanity," being deployed to good effect in prominent controversies, including that regarding the conduct of the United States in Afghanistan.[9] Moreover, despite a wave of excellent revisionist international and global histories of international human rights law,[10] far less attention has been paid to IHL (or the law of war, or the law of armed conflict, as it is variously known).[11] Particularly, the detailed political genealogy of human rights' wartime sibling,[12] the international law of internal armed conflict, remains untold and unduly obscure, leaving open some essential questions about its sources, its development, and their consequences. As I shall explain, this silence is regrettable not only because of the law's arguably intrinsic importance but because its development mirrors the transformation of international society and global politics over the last century and a half, and as such should be of great interest to scholars of International Relations (IR), law, and history.

Curiously, this gap in our knowledge about the deeply contentious history of this branch of international law also coexists with growing academic and policy interest in internal conflict and atrocity. Many knowledgeable scholars of international law and IR, not to mention the general public, still ignore the existence of these rules. Some years ago, while dining with a group of colleagues after an academic workshop, one of them asked me the usual question, "So, what do you do?" Excitedly, I answered that I researched the international rules governing internal armed conflict. I received a bewildered look, followed by, "Wait, there *are* international rules for internal conflicts? Who knew!" In fact, internal conflict is an arena long regulated by international law, as the international lawyers and advocates who rely on these rules to persuade or cajole states and nonstate actors to follow through well know.

This book asks why and how states, commonly concerned with their sovereignty—particularly regarding internal security affairs—have adopted legally binding international rules to constrain their ability to counter organized violence within their borders.

Intuitive answers are unhelpful. Take the international law of interstate conflict by way of contrast. Theoretically, there are good reasons why governments may have chosen to create international rules to regulate wars with one other. For instance, as James Morrow contends, states may have plausibly turned to international law to introduce legal clarity about expected battlefield behavior, thereby reducing useless cruelty.[13] States' strategic interest in bringing about reciprocal restraint can serve as a baseline (albeit neither complete nor time-invariant) explanation for the existence of IHL for international conflict.

A reciprocity hypothesis, however, does not travel easily to the IHL for internal conflicts. Unlike in war between states—which despite their differences in material power, ideology, and interests generally see each other as legal equals—in internal conflict governments generally tend to view armed opponents as illegitimate actors undeserving of legal protection and likely unwilling or unable to return it in kind. Historically, states have indeed perceived IHL for internal conflicts as more beneficial (politically and militarily) to rebels than to themselves.

A quick overview of historical hurdles illustrates this point. "On no earthly account can I admit any thought or act hostile to the old Government," pithily declared the Russian delegate, General Nicholas Yermolov, in 1912 while discussing a proposal for an international treaty legalizing the impartial provision of humanitarian aid amid internal conflict. Quoting the words of General William Tecumseh Sherman during the U.S. Civil War, Yermolov declared that "any offer of services, direct or indirect, of Red Cross Societies to insurgents or revolutionaries could not be conceived as more than a violation of friendly relations, as an 'unfriendly act,' likely to encourage and foster sedition or rebellion in another country."[14]

Thirty-seven years later, in 1949, British diplomat Robert Craigie forcefully called upon other state delegations to dismiss the idea of regulating internal conflict via international law because doing so "would appear to give the status of belligerents to insurgents, whose right to wage war could not be recognized."[15] France and the United States sided with Craigie.

Fast-forward now to 1974 when, while facing a proposal to regulate national liberation struggles as international conflicts under IHL, British and U.S. delegates lamented the damage this would cause to "the structure of The Hague and Geneva Conventions [involving] the need to reconstruct the whole of humanitarian law."[16] At the same diplomatic conference, delegate after delegate from Third World states took a stand at the podium against the creation of (more) IHL rules for internal conflict, claiming they might trespass on state sovereignty and threaten their stability,[17] essentially legalizing neoimperialist intervention.

In 1995 the UN International Law Commission, charged with drafting the text that would become the Rome Statute creating the International Criminal Court (in 1998), decided to "set its sights low" and exclude provisions dealing with atrocities committed in internal conflict, fearing states' backlash to a potentially radical encroachment on sovereignty.[18] And in 2008 international legal expert Jonathan Somer concluded that it was "quite likely that if states were to convene today in order to draft Common Article 3 . . . nothing would come of the effort."[19]

As this litany of dire reactions shows, the idea of creating international rules for internal conflicts time and again has clashed against a key *Grundnorm* of IR: state sovereignty. Despite cumulative, well-publicized atrocity, the notion that governments should draw up and commit to humanitarian standards of restraint and protection faced an uphill political battle, yet it was, on occasion, codified into law.

How did this occur?

My answer in this book can be summed up in a single term: *social pressure*. Concretely, I identify a two-stage pattern. The first stage is characterized by *normative pressure* deployed by specific actors or "norm entrepreneurs" that galvanized atrocious events to place the issue of new legal rules on states' agenda. Beginning in the mid-nineteenth century, this process took several decades, featured diverse and surprising protagonists, and its success was far from preordained; obstacles and opponents abounded. This book's empirical chapters document these obstacles in detail, with special emphasis on the reactions of liberal empires Britain, France and the United States, as well as the means and conditions under which they were overcome.

In the second stage, I demonstrate the crucial role that another mechanism of social pressure that I label *forum isolation* played during the actual multilateral negotiation of specific rules for internal conflict. In 1949 and in 1974–77, the negotiation of rules dealing with internal conflict and national liberation, respectively, pitted unwieldy majority coalitions of "proregulation" states against a handful of powerful opponents which, finding themselves isolated in a diplomatic corner while being mired in status and reputational politics internationally, felt compelled to acquiesce to the new rules to save face and prevent perceived political damage. My wager is that, absent the overwhelming, combined weight of international social pressure channeled by diplomatic procedure, it is unlikely that the international rules governing various forms of internal conflict would have survived negotiation in 1949 and the 1970s.

Yet the story behind the legal codification of international rules for internal conflict is not a simple, happy one of obstacles overcome. As this book demonstrates, socially pressured codification came at a price both in 1949 and 1977. On the one hand, yes, powerful state recalcitrants ultimately acquiesced to the overwhelming pressure placed on them to accept (or at least not to obstruct) the creation of controversial new international rules for internal conflict. Yet invariably their acquiescence was grudging, and they remained unconvinced of the merits of legal change. Unpersuaded but under sociopolitical duress, those skeptical state delegates then devised a strategic, backstage response: they would accept formal legal change but would ensure, through subtle textual moves, that the negotiated rules would be created in such a way that they would have a hard time being applied in practice. The politics of rule origins can help explain, in part, the mixed record of legal influence held by IHL for internal conflict.

Legal Primer

First things first. What are the rules of IHL for internal conflict? Treaty-based IHL for internal conflict emerged in 1949 and was expanded in 1977. The first and most important rule in this field remains CA3, which binds parties to respect and guarantee the humane treatment of the wounded, the sick, the detained, and noncombatants "without any adverse distinction" and to uphold prohibitions addressing a few of the most gruesome acts committed during armed conflict, including violence to life, mutilation and cruel treatment, torture, hostage taking, and summary judgment.[20]

In 1977 states concluded the negotiation of two other treaties: the Additional Protocols (APs) I and II to the Geneva Conventions. Additional Protocol I (API) governs interstate as well as national liberation war.[21] Additional Protocol II (APII) regulates internal conflicts that meet certain demanding criteria, essentially those resembling fully fledged civil wars.[22] APII extends CA3 particularly in the legal protection of the civilian population, civilian objects, and medical transports from the dangers of hostilities. It also protects children and expands the list of prohibited acts to include terrorism and slavery, for instance.[23]

In strict legal terms, of the two APs, only APII is formally recognized as relevant to internal or "noninternational" conflicts because, though one might intuitively describe "national liberation" as a form of internal violence, the political process behind the protocols' negotiation succeeded in legitimating it as a form of international conflict. This book does not take the strict legal view and analyzes the politics behind the inclusion of national liberation war in API as well as the negotiation of APII.

The design of these legal instruments varies in important ways. CA3 features no definition of internal conflict, contains no formal requirements to regulate its application, and does not require reciprocity from armed nonstate actors to apply. The APs in contrast either require reciprocity from the nonstate actor or contain conditions to narrow legal applicability. APII does not refer explicitly to "parties to conflict" and, unlike CA3, it does not firmly stipulate the ability of the ICRC to lend its services amid conflict.

International Law as Compromise

This book engages the development of the humanitarian rules for internal conflict as a contentious, historically conditioned, collective process of political *compromise* via international law.

While the assertion that international law is a political compromise seems uncontroversial, it is curiously one with which theorists of IR and law have not fully grappled and whose consequences are still not consistently appreciated.[24] As Richard Bellamy, Markus Kornprobst, and Christine Reh have noted, although the term compromise is "widely used across all major subdisciplines of Political Science . . . its frequent mentions notwithstanding, the systematic study of compromise remains surprisingly underdeveloped."[25] Compromises, Reh notes, "are not based upon a synthesis of positions . . . [and] as such, [they are] unlikely to be equitable, optimal or stable agreements."[26] Standard views in IR theory tend to downplay the production and fragility of compromise in exchange for declaring one or another causal factor / mechanism (power, strategic choice and bargaining, or persuasion, to name some) as the best explanation for a legal outcome.

But what is a compromise? And what kind of compromise is IHL governing internal conflicts? I define compromise as a *collective political achievement* shrouded in the powerful mantle of international law. And it is my view, based on the research presented here, that the international law in this area is a particular type of compromise: a socially pressured compromise, achieved partially through face saving.

As Reh notes, quoting Richard Bellamy and Martin Hollis, compromises are "packages 'many of the components of which . . . [negotiators] would reject if taken in isolation.'"[27] Per force, then, a compromise is collective; it involves mutual concessions among at least two actors and contains within it varying, perhaps asymmetric degrees of (dis)satisfaction for the involved parties. Collective concession making implies only that no actor can single-handedly call the shots or literally "lay down the law." As Philip Allott has memorably put it, "A treaty is a disagreement reduced to writing. . . . The eventual parties to a treaty enter a negotiation with different ideas of what they want to achieve. Negotiation is a process for finding a third thing which neither party wants but both parties can accept."[28] Negotiators engage each other in political debate, follow decision-making procedures, and if need be, make concessions to produce an outcome.

This does not, however, mean that all participants in a negotiation concede to the same degree or explain why and how concessions are made.[29] Concessions and compromise may be made or extracted via a variety of tactics, one of which, highlighted here, is social pressure.[30] Participants' dissatisfaction with a legal outcome can take several forms, including public statements of intent but also interpretations that are not expressed but which can nonetheless strongly impact the measure of agreement underlying a negotiation or codified rule and its performance. This is why, for instance, international legal scholars have sensibly begun to differentiate between "thin consent" and "thick consensus" in the production of international law.[31]

Overall, to capture this complexity—the stakes, process, and reasons behind the origins of international legal agreements—I argue that we need to approach international lawmaking as

- an international diplomatic practice riven with power, interest, and values amid sociopolitical hierarchies
- a site of political struggle, though not one necessarily beholden to the materially powerful
- a process that is historically situated and deeply contextual
- in modern IR, at least, a fairly well structured and institutionalized procedure[32]

Importantly, I contend that, given their nature as compromises, the results of multilateral lawmaking are momentary *achievements*, not in the vernacular sense of "progressive development" but pragmatically, as settlements of political struggle through law, which despite being codified nevertheless remain subject to intense contestation.[33]

In what sense is IHL for internal armed conflict a socially pressured, face-saving compromise?

Social pressure, the theoretical protagonist of this book, is underpinned by a social-psychological microfoundation: *opprobrium*, or "shame." Opprobrium-based mechanisms, particularly shaming (or "naming and shaming"), are now commonly used to explain outcomes in world politics.[34] At their core they rely on the claim that state actors, like individual persons, are vulnerable to social-psychological pressures.

How does opprobrium matter for the process of legal emergence examined here? Put simply, sovereign states might never have agreed to introduce and adopt humanitarian rules for internal conflicts without the operation of social opprobrium. As I demonstrate throughout this book, "norm entrepreneurs" of various kinds were doubtless fundamental for placing the idea of regulation on states' agenda. But once negotiations opened and state groupings positioned themselves toward them in public multilateral forums, it was the shame that came from diplomatic *isolation* cast upon skeptics—with its perceived consequences for their international standing and social reputation—that pushed through to their acceptance the controversial proposals that now constitute this branch of international law.

Take the case of CA3. As mentioned, in the mid-1940s, following World War II but also the Spanish Civil War, states debated for the first time the merits of "humanizing" internal conflict. Under Red Cross stewardship, a subset of smaller powers from continental Europe, Latin America, and Scandinavia declared their support for this idea in the prenegotiations stage while other, more powerful, states such as the United States and the empires of Britain and France expressed doubts. Their key concern was that accepting international standards for internal conflicts might legitimate and empower rebels and unilaterally bind governments to respect insurgent armed groups without a reciprocity assurance. The British and French, which still retained colonies the world over, were particularly flummoxed. Unable to extricate the idea of including internal conflicts in the Geneva Conventions during prenegotiations, both empires came armed to the diplomatic conference with instructions to nix it. They harbored the hope that their sovereignty-protecting views would echo broadly.

Yet once in Geneva, these otherwise influential European empires hit a social wall. Their recalcitrance was not widely shared and, facing an unwieldy majority of states that defended the idea of humanizing internal conflict, they found themselves nearly alone in their deep skepticism, with a socialist bloc furiously pointing fingers of scorn at them. Cornered and embarrassed, the British and French delegates then shifted to deception tactics which would help them save face and salvage their self-interest. They achieved this by taking part in the drafting of what eventually became CA3, inserting within it ambiguous language which they read in a narrow manner but that was more generously interpreted by their proregulation peers.

Although the historical details behind pressured codification varied slightly in the two major episodes of rule making I study here—in 1949 and in 1974 through 1977—this is the core political dynamic that I identify in this book: the mobilization of international opprobrium upon a few government skeptics and those skeptics' strategic face saving via legal (drafting) moves. The codified international rules that resulted, normatively important though they became, ultimately crystallized fundamental tensions between humanitarianism and state sovereignty. Such contestedness has arguably characterized, to a large degree, their fate in practice.

Importantly, and as chapter 1 will further elaborate, the production and effectiveness of social pressure hinge on broader international historical conditions and political struggle. In a macroscopic vein, I highlight certain changes within international society, and especially its expanding membership and institutional structure (punctuated by war, between states and within them), as well as varying international social contests over legitimacy, hierarchy, and order, which since the early twentieth century have characterized world politics. These macrotransformations and factors, I argue, served both as the historical conditions of possibility for legal transformation in the field of the laws of war, and as the sources of political contestation that ultimately tilted the balance toward the acceptance of legal rules for internal conflict during diplomatic negotiations.

Contributions

Theoretically, this book contributes to a new generation of IR scholarship embedding historical sociology and social psychology (sometimes together) within international law and norms theorizing. This includes research on ontological security, stigmatization, stratification, and status and hierarchies in world politics.[35]

I am greatly indebted to these new theoretical strands. As mentioned, social pressure operates upon state diplomats because it taps on to key status anxieties at particular historical moments—notably, when the prevailing hierarchy is in flux or under dispute.[36] Although IR scholars have long drawn on social psychology, and arguments about identity and standing have proliferated, few have applied social psychological insights specifically to understand multilateral negotiation processes while making efforts to connect them to the heterogeneous, fraught, and hierarchical nature of international society in the twentieth century.[37] Even fewer among them have paid sufficient attention to the "backstage" dynamics of global lawmaking that I demonstrate here to be essential for grappling with the nature, promise, and limits of international law.

This book also contributes to revitalized debates among international historians, legal scholars, and political theorists about the origins and development of international law, the institutions of international society, and the practices of global governance.[38] In particular, there has been a veritable explosion of new histories of international human rights. Excellent, deeply researched works by Roland Burke and Steven L. B. Jensen, to name only two, have become instant classics, documenting and emphasizing, as I do here, the importance of previously obscured factors and actors in the emergence and evolution of human rights law (especially Third World and socialist states' protagonism) and the productive influence of the Cold War and decolonization as political engines of normative and legal dynamism.[39] This book echoes Jensen's interest in what he terms "negotiating universality"—that is, the fraught collective construction of international standards of appropriate conduct.[40] This book's argument is, in fact, an effort to theorize such universality from an IR standpoint.

Within IR itself, the English School and constructivism have always held a deep interest in historical explanation and sociological theorizing. Ongoing work of this sort—for instance, on the globalization of international society—is particularly congenial to my interests, as it takes seriously the effects of the transformation of international society upon the dynamics and outcomes of international legitimation and legalization, including the operation of imperialism, nationalism, and civilizational standards in the late nineteenth century, as well as twentieth-century decolonization and Cold War social competition.[41] These transformations were fundamental for the emergence and operation of important international rules, of which political contestation and the normative contestedness are among the essential and often neglected ingredients.

The book's final core contribution is to the field of international law. In describing the emergence and negotiation of IHL for internal conflict, I address enduring puzzles among international lawyers about the meaning of the law.[42] For example, to this day little is known regarding the origins of the ambiguous expression "armed conflict not of an international character," which determines CA3's scope of application. That this outcome was a compromise has always been clear, yet the behind-the-scenes political process that produced it and its protagonists' motives and intentions have remained obscure. How, despite their material power and fierce opposition, did Western states come to accept the legitimation of national liberation war via API? And why has API never become applicable to national liberation conflicts? Primary material from multiple archives allows me to clarify these issues to an important degree. To the extent that puzzlement over the meaning of parts of the law remains to this day, this book is important both to historical and contemporary legal debate.

1

SOCIAL PRESSURE IN INTERNATIONAL LAWMAKING

Historically, states have paid rebels few niceties. International doctrines existed for centuries to elicit restraint in war *between* states, yet older customary international law said little about internal war, and what it said was not commonly taken seriously as binding. And while one can point to historical cases of governments mired in internal war that proposed and signed good conduct agreements with insurgents, states long neglected or refused to create similar international rules for internal conflicts, even after the modern era of law of armed conflict treaties began in 1864–65.

This long historical trend began to change in the twentieth century. Since 1949, states have codified binding international humanitarian law (IHL) standards encouraging battlefield restraint and protection in various forms of armed conflict occurring within their borders.[1] The central legal instruments of this kind are Common Article 3 (CA3) and the Additional Protocols (APs).[2]

The emergence of international rules governing battlefield conduct during internal conflict is a startling outcome in world politics. Why would states choose to subscribe to international laws limiting their means to fend off—even squash—a rebellion, inviting commentary, critique, and accusation from international audiences? Since the international law of internal conflict strikes at the very core of state sovereignty, one of the basic institutions of modern international relations (IR), its historical adoption constitutes a real puzzle for scholars of IR, history, and law.

Although from our vantage point international concern about internal atrocity is commonplace and the legal means to eradicate it seem integral to the contemporary normative order, the regulation of internal armed conflict has been invariably controversial among states. A strict desire to preserve state sovereignty for a long time advised against it. International society's great powers, especially Western liberal empires, opposed them fiercely. And even the leading nonstate organization in the field of practical and legal humanitarianism, the International Committee of the Red Cross (ICRC), hesitated for decades to endorse their creation. Yet despite adverse historical precedents and powerful state opposition, under certain conditions codified international legal standards eventually emerged to address atrocity in internal armed conflict.

If the existence of these standards itself is puzzling, so are the timing of their codification and their design. CA3 and the APs both emerged in politically convoluted times (1949 and the 1970s) marked by Cold War contention, Western fears of contagious communist rebellion, and imminent or ongoing (and sometimes violent) decolonization. What could have driven states and fragile empires to commit to international legal standards at these precise times, considering the political and military risks they implied (including legitimating and being obliged to show restraint toward communist and colonial insurgents)?

Regarding their design, some of these standards were designed without clear safeguards for states against rebel nonacceptance or noncompliance. Famously, CA3 lacks a condition of rebel reciprocity, binding states unilaterally regardless of their nonstate opponent's attitudes. Additional Protocol II (APII), for its part, neglects explicit mention of the armed nonstate actors to which it applies. Also conspicuously, Additional Protocol I (API) includes a large list of military and humanitarian obligations that national liberation groups should legally try but might perhaps hardly be expected to apply, seemingly placing the legal burden on states' shoulders only.

Existing theoretical arguments on the emergence and negotiation of international rules cannot explain the origins and design of IHL for internal armed conflict. These humanitarian standards were not created for instrumental or functionalist reasons, due to generalized humanitarianism, or through great-power imposition. Instead, as I explain in this book, they were born out of a long and tortuous political process of *social pressure*.

This chapter presents a theoretical framework to understand this process of rule emergence and codification. I develop a two-stage argument. The first stage addresses the process through which the humanitarian legalization of internal conflict became an issue of international concern. I explain how and why the principal "norm entrepreneur" behind IHL, the ICRC, initially hesitated for several decades to push for treaty-based legalization of internal conflict and, eventually, after repeated civil war atrocity and bottom-up activist pressure, fought to place it on states' legal agenda.

The second stage addresses the diplomatic negotiation of specific legal rules and instruments. I foreground the importance of a specific mechanism of social pressure—*forum isolation*—during legal codification processes, amid international political contests among states for status and social reputation.

The outcome of this long process of rule emergence, characteristic of a heterogeneous international order riven by political diversity, attachment to sovereignty, and growing rhetorical commitment to "humane" legal internationalism, is one of political, moral, and legal *compromise*. This is to say that, over time, with much difficulty but with important successes, a fraught body of humanitarian rules emerged over the twentieth century to temper internal atrocities, imperfectly but indelibly chipping away at stringent notions of state sovereignty.

Four Arguments about International Lawmaking

IR scholars have developed important theoretical constructs to explain why and how international rules emerge. Characteristically, they make at least four types of arguments: realist, rational institutionalist, domestic-political, and liberal constructivist.

The *realist* argument insists that powerful states make and break the rules as they wish; rule making is treated as an exercise in great-power politics or, in a critical-theory formulation, as domination.[3] Presumably, then, powerful states may have at various points in world history found it convenient for whatever selfish reasons, to draw up international law for internal conflict, imposing their views on other states.[4]

In contrast, *rational-institutionalist* arguments commonly highlight the utility of international rules as devices that states use to achieve common goals; rule making for states is a functional, cooperative endeavor.[5] Following this logic, one may think that states indeed found it useful to create international law for internal conflict, maybe in an attempt to "level the battlefield" with rebels and elicit reciprocity.

Domestic politics arguments generally come in two flavors: they point to the *interests* or the *identity* of states, or both, to explicate states' desire to create international rules; rule making occurs either to further the instrumental goals of a subset of societal actors or to enshrine the identity and values shared by the states that make the law.[6] In this view, interest groups within states might have lobbied their governments to make these international standards, perhaps with the instrumental goal of preventing future atrocity at home or contain negative humanitarian externalities. Alternatively, states embracing prohumanitarian sentiments (liberal democracies, most likely) may have coalesced internationally to create these rules.

A traditional *constructivist* argument would highlight the moral and deliberative origins of rules; indeed, in a prominent model of international norms dynamics, new norms emerge because entrepreneurs work hard to persuade others of their value. Advocates' persuasive, reasoned argumentation generates new norms that often later crystallize into law.[7] Accordingly, we may expect that morally motivated actors historically lobbied and persuaded their peers, even the recalcitrant ones, getting them to accept new rules to humanize internal conflict.

In this book I approach these venerable lines of argument critically. Notice two traits shared by them. First, according to each at the end of a lawmaking process there would appear to be more or less clear winners and losers. Powerful states, rational-strategic states, moral entrepreneurs, or domestic interest and value groups could in principle be identified and given credit as victors over weaker, stubborn, or recalcitrant peers and actors. Second, for each theory, the predominant reasons and ways in which agreements are struck should be readily discerned and traced back to one favored factor and negotiation dynamic: relative power (coercion), cooperative calculation (functional bargaining), domestic lobbies ("intergovernmentalism" or "ideational coalition building"), or moral and reasoned argument (persuasion). And at the end what we encounter as outcome is either an imposition, a contract, or a norm which may or may not diffuse more broadly, pending formal signature and ratification.

While these four views carry heuristic power and are appropriate to explain certain cases or aspects of international cooperation and lawmaking, they must be adjusted to account for the complexity of the case at hand and beyond. In my view, by shaping the puzzle of rule creation around a preferred factor, each of these standard theoretical arguments in fact unnecessarily smooths over the underlying tensions, contestation, and resistance that characterize the process of global lawmaking.

I recognize that the four arguments just described are probably better conceptualized as ideal types since, in practice, most scholars of international law, norms, and cooperation understand that the empirical reality of agreement making is far murkier. Put otherwise, we know that embedded in most international agreements there are shades of material power, instrumental interest and calculation, and ethical and moral considerations. The best applied scholarship acknowledges it. Yet it remains true that IR scholars continue to rely on these ideal-type arguments to adjudicate between "correct"—indeed, "better"—theories, well despite commendable calls for "eclectic" theorizing.[8]

I proceed differently here. My theoretical goal in this book is to offer an argument which takes as its basic premise the notion of international law as a *com-*

promise and formulates a complex, historically grounded model that combines and takes into account actor sociability, rationality, and power, moving us away from visions of international lawmaking as imposition, bargaining and exchange, interest- or identity-furtherance, or persuasive success.

Making these conceptual moves arose as a necessity as I evaluated the empirical evidence gathered for this project. Simply, I could not otherwise have captured the history and the nature of the rules of IHL for internal conflict. These are international rules which emerged not because powerful states wanted them, and yet those states played a crucial role in their making. Certainly some morally motivated actors (including some states) were at the forefront of their codification, and this mattered tremendously. Yet advocates' sheer persuasiveness or moral outrage was not always or alone decisive in rule adoption. As I explain, states' domestic interests and identities were prevalent forces, yet they often went *against* rule creation or operated in counterintuitive ways. Finally, instrumental coordination as a shared motive for rule making here was not only largely absent, but when it was expressed (in seeming attempts to make the law more "credible"), it was introduced as means to hinder the law's application, not to enhance it. Above all, the ghost of legitimating and empowering rebels through the creation of the law worked to spoil instrumental reasoning. At the same time, social pressures mobilizing international opprobrium and the perceived fear of delegitimation via status or reputational damage facilitated the rules' adoption and shaped their design.

Why a Historical Approach Is Necessary

This book is as much a history of IHL for internal conflict as it is a theoretical effort to understand its origins. Why is a strongly historical approach necessary?

Bluntly stated, I view international law as a product of politics in historical context.[9] Modern diplomatic codification is by now an old political institution, dating back at least to the mid-nineteenth century.[10] Yet despite the persistence of certain diplomatic practices and their gradual institutionalization through the years,[11] global politics have changed markedly, and the politics and procedure of international codification too have undergone important transformation.

On the one hand, at the broadest level, structural social and material shifts have altered world politics over the last century and a half. Examples abound: Imperialism was once an accepted institution in world politics, though not so anymore (at least not formally), despite enduring imperialist impulses and practices.[12] The international society of states (the society that makes international law) is no longer dominated by Europe or the West as it was from the nineteenth century until the world wars, even though certain European states might still fancy themselves great powers and retain outsize influence.[13] Humanitarianism, too, has changed from being a concern of Christian peoples toward other (white) Christians, to a concern about the welfare of all human beings experiencing atrocity or emergency,[14] again at least as a matter of international rhetoric and legal norms. Nonstate and transnational actors now figure prominently in the practice and remaking of international order.[15]

These and other world political changes mean something for the practice (and study) of international lawmaking. Indeed, some of the conditions enabling the social pressures I identify were made possible only through historical change, especially in the post–World War II setting. These include major postwar impulses to address current (and cumulative) atrocity; states' postwar anxieties about increasing or maintaining international status, even predominance; and decisive claims making by newly empowered postcolonial states in a global international society. As noted, international social and material hierarchies have at least partially changed in terms of their main protagonists, rank order, and substantive content, also producing a shift in states' preoccupations and in the production of international opprobrium. Changing institutional practices and procedures of codification since the early twentieth century—from the use of rules of unanimity, to reliance on majoritarian voting and consensus norms, to the universal participation of states under legal equality—have similarly altered codification processes in consequential ways.[16] Since the late 1970s, the practice of treaty codification in the law of armed conflict has somewhat dissipated and become outpaced by customary international law arguments and the jurisprudence of international tribunals, altering the politics, focus, and protagonists of legal development in ways not easily grasped by ahistorical perspectives.

Therefore, if we wish to understand the evolving political dynamics underlying the emergence and development of any given international institution or law, we simply cannot assume away a transformed historical context.

Social Pressure

The central theoretical protagonist of this book is the concept of social pressure. Social pressures are ubiquitous, and sometimes consequential, in international politics. Especially since the publication of Margaret E. Keck and Kathryn Sikkink's watershed work on the "naming and shaming" strategies of transnational advocacy networks, the conceptual language of shame has found a place in IR theory.[17] Although scholars of IR have by now written a lot about the importance of a variety of social pressures to understanding relevant aspects of world politics, reference to social pressure in IR, specifically, long seemed circumscribed to explaining one key puzzle: state conformity with international rules or norms. Only in the last decade has scholars' theoretical focus on social pressure decidedly expanded beyond compliance—for instance, to the context of decision making within international organizations (such as the European Union), international policy diffusion through ranking dynamics, or the making of international order through stigmatization.[18]

This book builds on this important work and develops it by focusing on the operation of social pressure as a lever for international legal emergence and codification. We have established models to explain how issues become international "problems" meriting regulation—what one might call international *agenda setting*. Yet, with few exceptions, the detailed construction of international law within diplomatic settings has not been studied by scholars interested in social pressure. Further, as I will detail, the existing work on international negotiation that does pay attention to social influences proceeds without sufficient attention to the historical context and importance of interstate social competition over status and social reputation within a fractured and hierarchical international community.[19] Also rare is the furnishing of dispositive evidence of the incidence and influence of social pressures upon lawmaking, and actor reactions to that social pressure, both of which are prominent in my account.

Definitions

Social pressure can be defined as a form of attempted, nonmaterial influence by some (source) actors upon other (target) actors, designed or tending to force the target's hand (conduct) to accord with a social expectation. The microfoundation of social pressure is opprobrium, or shame.

Social pressure can take multiple forms. It can become manifest in and is most commonly theorized as explicit *shaming* acts, such as boycotts by activist groups alleging unethical or illegal behavior on the part of states or corporations.[20] It can involve politicians calling each other out as hypocrites for saying one thing and then doing another as a means to sway voters' attention and support. Social pressure can also operate more subtly, as when an actor fears in advance that taking a particular stance will bring it derision for appearing out of step with public opinion or with its public image and thus refrains and recalibrates its actions.

Put conceptually, opprobrium invariably triggers pressure upon an actor through the revelation of a *broken social expectation*, whether it be public inconsistency between an actor's words or deeds and its professed self-identity; nonconformity with group identity or conduct; or an actor's breach of a prior public statement or commitment.[21]

Social expectations are thus manifold; they can come from established or enshrined norms or law, from shared opinions within one's in-group, or from an actor's own perception of its social self vis-à-vis various others. They can also follow from unexpected or shocking events that appear to compel action.

In politics the exertion or mobilization of opprobrium via social pressure normally carries important consequence; it can brand certain behaviors and discourses as illegitimate and help enforce social conformity by singling the shamed actor out as a social culprit, potentially tainting its social reputation or downgrading its status vis-à-vis relevant others.[22] Because both status or standing and reputation are directly tied to actors' self-esteem, political actors may react to effective or expected opprobrium via cognition (as politically costly) and emotion (as anxiety inducing).[23]

Social pressure, I should be clear, is *attempted influence*, which may or may not alter another actor's behavior; that is to say, it operates conditionally. Whether pressured actors end up acquiescing to it *depends primarily on who they are and what they perceive to be at stake* in the revelation of breach. This perception, in turn, hinges crucially on who exerts the pressure, what the actors' prior relationship is, how, when and where pressure is enacted, and of course, who the perceived audience or public is. This means one must delve into the content, process, protagonists, and context of given episodes of pressure politics in order to ascertain the combination of factors producing them and making them work.

Throughout this book I pay special attention to the agents and recipients of pressure and the context in which pressure is produced and mobilized. *Context* refers both to the broader political environment in which pressure occurs, but also to the institutional platform, or forum, which channels it. Put differently, the pressure politics I study here necessitate not only a propitious historical circumstance but also a dedicated, particular forum utilized by savvy political actors to influence others' decisions amid legalization. The combination of these elements does not invariably produce the outcome—my argument is not deterministic—but in creating steep pressure connected to something greater than the specific rule at hand—that is, to international politics—it increases the chances that those put under pressure will acquiesce, albeit grudgingly and strategically.

The Framework

How did the regulation of violence during internal conflict become an issue of international concern? What explains the codification process, design, and adoption of the international humanitarian rules dealing with internal armed conflict?

I answer each of these questions in order. To explain international agenda setting I draw upon existing constructivist theorizing in IR regarding the emergence of legal norms, adding new insights and some necessary nuance. Next, I theorize the codification process behind the instruments of IHL for internal armed conflict, highlighting the politics of social pressure that, I argue, explain their contested design and their face-saving adoption.

Phase One: Normative Pressure about Internal Conflict

The international rules on the conduct of war between states were among the first to be codified into treaty law in the modern era. Starting in 1856, states (mostly European empires at first) began to promote multilateral declarations and binding treaties to induce restraint among and humanitarian protection for soldiers, prisoners of war, and, belatedly, civilians.[24] Internal conflict, however, was conspicuously absent from interstate debate on wartime rules until around 1912 and failed to become regulated internationally until 1949, even though various forms of "internal" atrocity raged the world over throughout this entire period. What explains the law's silence on internal conflict for nearly a century of codification? How did states finally accept consideration of internal conflict as a worthy issue to legislate?

Because neither states nor interest groups within states were the instigators behind the international regulation of internal war, I begin with the IR approach to international norm emergence that is most explicitly open to nonstate agency: constructivism. Famously central to dominant constructivist explanations of normative change is the pressure work of so-called norm entrepreneurs, or issue "champions." These are motivated actors—from individual activists, to nongovernmental organizations, advocacy networks, and officials at intergovernmental organizations or within states—who busy themselves with promoting change by pushing to (re)formulate new rules of appropriate behavior.[25] A robust IR research program has developed over the last two decades demonstrating the role and efficacy of norm entrepreneurs as change agents.

But how do actors become champions of an issue? How do entrepreneurs choose which issues to focus on? When do they succeed or fail? Theories of norm entrepreneurship and advocacy networks cite a host of potential explanatory factors from issue characteristics (the nature or value of an issue) to the context (the environmental "incentives and constraints") in which norms entrepreneurs operate.[26] Other work has examined relations between actors within the same advocacy network, or "network structure" (the relations between issues, actors within a network, and partnerships within networks), that help configure entrepreneur preferences for change advocacy.[27]

At issue in this book is an early case of norm entrepreneurship in the modern era: that of the ICRC and its work to help create and expand the international law of armed conflict. I focus explicitly on the ICRC because since its origins in the mid-nineteenth century until about the 1960s it remained the main guardian and promoter of IHL and the go-to organization to which states deferred on the advancement of humanitarian law.[28]

As will be elaborated on in chapter 2, upon its founding in 1863 the ICRC soon faced the question of internal atrocity. In debating what to do, it chose a specific path: to engage in practical humanitarian aid work to alleviate internal atrocity while steering clear of proposals to regulate such situations via international law. The ICRC maintained this approach until 1921. Why was this route taken? Why did the ICRC not forcefully promote the legal humanization of internal conflicts from the outset?

I maintain, first, that the elements of the international social context in which the ICRC operated in the mid-nineteenth century limited its ability to take up the cause of internal conflicts forcefully. By "social context" I mean not a material opportunity structure but broader international (European) norms and institutions constitutive of state sovereignty at the time, and especially growing military nationalism and imperialism, as well as enduring antirevolutionary politics. I argue that this social context likely prevented the ICRC from singling out internal conflicts as an issue for states to "humanize" through binding law. For it to have done so would have meant to challenge the very fabric of international order at the time.

I connect the macrocontextual (or top-down) dimension with two bottom-up organizational constraints: the ICRC's need for survival and its risk-averse internal culture. Chapter 2 demonstrates that the ICRC, respected though it was from the beginning, faced important hurdles in its early years which threatened its position as a humanitarian broker and locked a certain conservatism inside it. A young organization in the 1860s, the ICRC saw its legitimacy challenged when other groups positioned themselves as alternatives to it, with the backing of key states. Although unsuccessful, organizational competition alerted the ICRC to the need to "pace" itself and not push controversial proposals which might trigger state backlash. Adding to this, lackluster respect for the 1864 Geneva Convention in its major initial testing ground (the Franco-Prussian War of 1870–71) gravely imperiled the ICRC's legitimacy and raison d'être: IHL itself.

How were these obstacles overcome? One the one hand, I argue that *generational change* was necessary for the ICRC to fully embrace new controversial issues in IHL; by the 1920s, new leaders had eventually come along who were less burdened with (or shaped by) past concerns. In addition, its initially shaky organizational stability was eventually secured. As decades went on, the ICRC's primacy in the field of legal humanitarianism during armed conflict became unquestioned.[29]

Finally, the international social context also changed, driven partly by repeated major civil war atrocity and the slow decay of formal imperialism, particularly after World War I. But changes both within the organization and outside it did not automatically necessitate a turn to internal conflict. Instead, persistent *normative pressure* from actors on the ground was critical to convince the ICRC's changing leadership that internal atrocity was a cause that it should vigorously adopt. I examine the role of on-the-ground advocates, especially national Red Cross and Red Crescent societies and concerned individuals suffering hardship from civil conflict and revolution at this time, to "convince" the ICRC (and the international Red Cross movement) that international humanitarian rules were necessary to placate internal atrocity.

Phase Two: International Codification—Forum Isolation and Covert Pushback

Once on the table, with the ICRC and the International Red Cross on board, how did the humanitarian regulation of internal conflict go from aspiration to legal rule? As noted, multilateral codification is complex and features a plethora of relevant, potentially causally relevant factors. Yet as I have argued, IR analyses often miss an important dimension to lawmaking: dynamics of social pressure between states, and coalitions of states vying for superior status internationally. The Cold War, for instance, was a political contest fought not only via proxy war but through diplomacy in international forums devoted to making, debating, and interpreting international norms and law.[30] Decolonization, too, was an international social and diplomatic struggle, as much as a set of "domestic" wars of self-determination.[31]

I identify a specific type of social pressure: that which occurs between state delegations that form a majority coalition vis-à-vis a minority, both leading up to negotiations *and* during them. Majority and minority social group dynamics among states, I argue, can activate a distinct form of social pressure during diplomatic intercourse, which I term *forum isolation*. I argue that forum isolation—along with the strategic, deceptive response it elicits, which I label *covert pushback*—together explain the ultimate adoption and design of CA3 in 1949 and API in 1977. The absence of this dynamic likewise explains the divergent design of the other relevant instrument, APII.

By forum isolation I refer to the act of standing in (near-)absolute minority during diplomatic negotiations; to find oneself literally in a proverbial diplomatic corner. Forum isolation is one among a larger battery of mechanisms of social pressure, all of which have opprobrium, or shame, as their microfoundation.[32]

This deserves some clarification. Shaming is simply the act of exposing a behavior or a position to connote public illegitimacy. It is akin to Frank Schimmelfennig's mechanism of "rhetorical entrapment" because both mobilize opprobrium by revealing an actor's inconsistent conduct or practice *in light of* a prior declaration of commitment or support for a standard of legitimacy.[33] "Stigmatization" is more demanding. According to Rebecca Adler-Nissen, it involves "the co-occurrence of . . . labeling, stereotyping, separation, and status loss and discrimination." Additionally, for stigmatization to be effective, the target must accept "the moral authority of the stigmatizer" as well as her claims.[34] Finally, "social influence" is, in Alastair Iain Johnston's classic formulation, a sort of umbrella concept encompassing various opprobrium microprocesses which, following social identity theory, operate according to in- and out-group dynamics. Distinctively, Johnston asserts, "only groups *whose approval an actor values* will have . . . influence."[35]

Forum isolation works differently. It certainly involves shaming, but by adding a nearly physical dimension (in the act of publicly "cornering" an actor) it sharpens and multiplies its intensity. The threat of a public vote, or of having their isolated position made evident on the public record, appears especially grave to diplomats.

Moreover, unlike shaming and rhetorical entrapment, forum isolation does not rely on an explicit prior commitment or support for a standard of legitimacy. Rather, it *engages actors' identities directly*, activating anxieties over a revealed inconsistency between values and deeds (the breach of a social expectation) and connecting that inconsistency to broader international *status struggles*.

Forum isolation is also not stigmatization. It is indeed (a threat of) outcasting, yet it requires neither the harshness implicit to the acts of labeling, stereotyping, and discrimination, nor does it require the target's acceptance of the "moral authority" of the stigmatizer. In this sense, forum isolation is arguably more short-lived and superficial, allowing the target to "manage" opprobrium and to react strategically while still feeling the burn of social pressure.

Finally, unlike Johnston's notion of "social influence," forum isolation goes beyond peer or in-group pressure to theorize the powerful opprobrium that comes from being placed in an *utter, near-universal minority*. My crucial claim here is that diplomats as social actors will not invariably or easily dismiss out-group pressure, and that such pressure will in fact work powerfully when it forms part of a majority that also includes peers.[36]

This last insight finds support in a growing line of social psychological research.[37] Several theories exist that study majority/minority group relations, including so-called conversion, objective consensus, and convergent-divergent approaches. They all start from the same baseline—particular effects inhere in majority/minority group relations—but diverge on some aspects, especially on how to characterize the level of cognitive processing (simple or elaborate) and the type of outcome (sincere or superficial) of majority influence attempts. An additional line of work ("self-categorization" theory) brings back social identity theory in- and out-group dynamics into studies of majority/minority relations, arguing that "it is the perceived social and self-categorical relationship between the source and the target, rather than fixed, reified qualities of majorities or minorities, that determines the course of the influence process."[38]

Four insights from these various theories are relevant here. First, majority pressure combines both normative and informational qualities. It conveys a sense of appropriateness and "objective" correctness (though the respective dominance of each varies according to social actors' prior relationship, and the minority's existing position on the issue at hand.) Second, majority pressure generates comparison-based reactions where public and private stances may diverge; as Robin Martin and Miles Hewstone note, "because agreement is derived from a need for consensus and not from a change in understanding of the issue, it is most likely to be manifest at a public level."[39] Third, the *content* of the majority position, especially how much it engages the minority's identity and self-interest, will varyingly influence the level of cognitive processing (the "elaborateness" of the reaction) of the minority; the more it contradicts the minority position, the less the minority will simply accept it. Similarly, when in-group peers (which form part of a majority) adopt an unexpected attitude, those in the minority are expected to experience stress and engage in reasoning that tries to resolve the conflict of views and reduce the dissonance.[40] Fourth, and perhaps most simply, the social psychological literature also suggests that once they emerge, the majority and minority can themselves become the new in-group and out-group, respectively, inciting pressures to conform.

Despite lingering debates among social psychologists, these insights provide theoretical and empirical support for my argument on forum isolation as a mechanism of social pressure. Consistent with them, I argue that isolated diplomats were compelled to accept a controversial majority view but did so with a view to save face *and* protect their interests. This also means that, unlike theories of "acculturation," my argument hinges not on mimicry or well-established "cultural scripts" of appropriate action but on social pressures that are mobilized in majority/minority dynamics in public negotiations.[41]

A Political Condition: Status Struggle

Why and when exactly might forum isolation matter in international politics? Standing outside a majority or consensus is not always or necessarily a bad thing; indeed, sometimes it becomes a badge of honor.[42] I argue that under certain political and institutional conditions, multilateral codification can provide an ideal platform for social pressure via forum isolation.

The analytical connection to status is crucial. Like opprobrium, status has become a crucial concept in international politics. Jonathan Renshon defines it as "standing or rank in a hierarchy," which, Renshon and colleagues note, informs "patterns of deference and expectations of behavior, rights and responsibilities."[43] Status carries important political meaning: states care about where they stand in a global hierarchy relative to others.[44] This is essential; because status is inherently comparative, states sometimes compete over it.[45] Particularly, states that perceive themselves to be "underplaced" in a given hierarchy or who face a "shake-up" of the received hierarchical order may develop status *concerns* and engage in material or ideological struggles with others, considering whether to maintain or upgrade their current position or to degrade or dislodge others.[46] Opprobrium, sharpened through isolating dynamics of majority pressure, exerts special political and social-psychological pressure on diplomats, because it sharpens and invites negative comparisons with concrete, competing "others" threatening an actor's perceived rank in an international hierarchy. In this book I focus on the status struggles of the post–World War II period which, as chapters 3 and 5 will show, deeply pervaded the reconstruction of world order, including the remaking of IHL.

Institutional Conditions

I propose that in multilateral codification a configuration of three institutional conditions are more likely to induce opprobrium via forum isolation: universal participation with a one state, one vote procedure; decision making by (or in the shadow of) majority vote; and publicity. These three conditions are all identifiable a priori, yet in my framework, they prove politically consequential as they enable a contingent political phenomenon: the formation of majority (or supermajority) coalitions which mobilize opprobrium and sharpen it via forum isolation.

Negotiations embodying the principle and procedures of sovereign equality (universal participation and a one state, one vote system) are especially hospitable to the opprobrium-via-isolation dynamic for three main reasons. First, as *universal* processes, such negotiations and the decisions they produce tend to enjoy greater legitimacy internationally relative to "club" membership institutions with weighted voting, which preserve power disparities.[47] Second, and related, in enabling the equal participation of all or most existing states in decision making, they allow for a *numerical advantage* that checks material power asymmetries and open doors to conflictual dynamics in a heterogeneous international society.

Third, because universal membership forums tend to be seen as especially legitimate and authoritative, they limit recalcitrant states' "outside options" by raising the social (and material) costs of exit.[48]

In general, the threat or use of a public (roll call) vote can be especially forceful, because it clearly demarcates supporters from opponents. Yet the universality of the forum adds special pressure: as noted, voting in a minority (or alone) against the rest of the world involves the special risk of universal outcasting, even more so if it threatens to unequivocally expose the gap between an agent's deed and its professed, deeply held values, especially with regard to issues framed in strong moral or "civilizational" terms.

Finally, for opprobrium to operate via forum isolation, actors must anticipate or experience the negative reaction of a given valued audience or *public*. My argument hinges on felt or anticipated embarrassment from both internal (inside negotiations) and external audiences. External audiences comprise mainly various sites of public opinion, whether domestic, foreign, or international. Given diplomats' expectation that holding a minority position will draw the public spotlight on them as uniquely retrograde or deviant—potentially provoking national and international embarrassment—they are more likely to feel the "social heat" and pressure of their superiors for change in instructions. In chapters 3 and 5, I cite evidence demonstrating the role of various perceived publics by diplomats facing social pressure during the codification conferences of 1949 and 1974–77.

Of course, not all states are vulnerable to opprobrium on all issues at all times, and not all may "give into" isolation in negotiations. A blanket assertion that "isolation = opprobrium = acquiescence" is unpersuasive, and indeed, as noted, sometimes states do seem to react to isolation and shaming proudly. IR scholars have now begun to more carefully explore varying state responses to and the scope conditions of opprobrium-based mechanisms.[49]

It is not my aim in this book to formulate and test a general framework, which demands a different research design. My initial wager, based on the findings presented here, is that universal diplomatic conferences summoned to codify international law via one state, one vote procedures; allowing for majoritarian voting; and garnering some degree of public attention provide the best platform for forum isolation amid negotiations.[50]

Covert Pushback

The final part of my argument theorizes the *reaction* of the delegations experiencing social pressure. I argue that forum isolation produces face-saving acquiescence and compromise, not a change in underlying preferences or interests.

That is, isolated actors compromise in order to contain social pressure, prevent status damage, and salvage their strategic interests, which run counter to the rule under negotiation. To achieve these joint goals, they pursue discreet or subterfuge methods which, without blowing their cover, weaken the language of the law.[51] In the cases of CA3 and API, the isolated delegations accomplished this through the use of ambiguous language in key parts of the texts, and via the insertion of "antidotes" elsewhere in the law, both carefully calculated moves to complicate the application of rules they did not want in the first place.

These claims contrast with rational-institutionalist work on the design of international law and with constructivist work that emphasizes persuasion through argument.

On the one hand, the operation of covert pushback establishes an obvious link between the making and design of international law with its performance. Prominent institutionalist work in IR, for example, explains variation in the degree of precision in international law as the product of states' cooperation-enhancing rational choices.[52] My framework and findings challenge this approach by demonstrating that social concerns with status and reputation—not simply rational calculation—can directly influence international legal design, and that states can use imprecision to *undermine* the applicability of law rather than to improve it.[53]

Do diplomatic argument and persuasion play a role in my framework? Diplomacy is primarily (though not exclusively) talk, and what relevant actors say, and how they argue it, matters greatly. Yet if we define persuasion as "changing how someone thinks or what they believe," then not all diplomatic argument has persuasive effects.[54] At least in the episodes of multilateral codification I study, diplomacy is argument-based *conflict* and *contestation* over what (and whose) values or beliefs should be enshrined in international law.[55] In them the (re)ordering of the "international community" through rules is precisely what is at stake. And it is a struggle because having one's values and ideas enshrined as international law is considered a political achievement that grants some actors superiority over others; it is, in other words, a hierarchical legitimation contest through global lawmaking.

2

NORMATIVE GATEKEEPING (1863–1921)

The modern international law of armed conflict originated in the mid-nineteenth century. Beginning in 1856, a flurry of international initiatives emerged to introduce legal restraint and humanitarianism into interstate conflict through declarations and treaties. However, aside from some marginal debate, nineteenth-century international lawmaking formally ignored internal conflicts. This remained the case until 1921, when an initial International Red Cross resolution was adopted.

How did the idea arise that international law should address violence in internal conflict? Why did that idea not gain traction during the late nineteenth century, the original high point for the international regulation of armed conflict?

In this chapter, I address the history and politics of international debate in this area until 1921. Understanding this early history is crucial for the rest of the book. By investigating the lack of discussion or clear proposals regarding humanitarian conduct in internal conflict during this period, this chapter highlights the elements that later appeared as necessary to generate the social pressure essential to rule making. In particular, this refers to the importance of norm entrepreneurs who forcefully seize on the creation of new rules and who bring and promote such rules in public forums, rallying others around a common cause. Simply, until 1912, no government came forward with proposals to extend humanitarianism into internal conflict despite the atrocity seen in various places around the world in the second half of the nineteenth century and early twentieth century, including in Europe. Perhaps more curiously, until 1921, no nongovernmental actor defended the idea that atrocity in internal conflict should be ameliorated through international rules.

Normative silence on this issue is unsurprising if we consider exactly who international law's main gatekeepers were at this time: anxious European absolutist monarchies, enthusiastic colonial empires, and nationalist republics. But what of other actors? It seems puzzling that the ICRC—which emerged in 1863 as the central nongovernmental organization dedicated to making war humane—*did not* press especially hard for the formulation of binding legal rules for internal conflicts, even as it was practically occupied with alleviating their horrors. Why?

The answer, I argue, lies in the international social context in which the ICRC operated, as well as in the ICRC's own institutional politics. On the one hand, the norms of sovereignty prevailing in Europe in the second half of the nineteenth century—namely, antirevolutionary norms, reinvigorated imperial colonialism (and racism), and growing military nationalism—militated against the emergence of legal proposals regarding internal conflicts, which could have emboldened and benefitted domestic revolutionaries and anticolonial resistors.[1]

In turn, a series of early organizational challenges provoked (or reinforced) the ICRC's reluctance to confront prevailing sovereignty norms, an attitude which became institutionalized among and even personified in its original membership. Challenges ranged from competition by other would-be humanitarian organizations, to the First Geneva Convention's discredit ensuing from gross noncompliance seen during the Franco-Prussian War of 1870. I observe that in addition to weakening the ICRC's standing as a humanitarian broker, these early setbacks likely cemented a certain conservatism within the committee's small group of leading figures, particularly in its president, Gustave Moynier, which in general quelled the ICRC's enthusiasm for proposals dealing with new binding rules, including those on internal conflict. Overall, governmental discretion regarding what treatment to accord to rebels and civilian populations in those conflicts ruled during the nineteenth century, with humanitarian initiatives remaining localized and haphazard.

This chapter is divided into three sections. The first section discusses the legacy of traditional customary law regarding various forms or levels of violence occurring between state borders. The second section addresses the ICRC's evolving attitudes and practical action toward internal atrocity since its creation. The third and final section takes us all the way through 1921, analyzing interstate debate about early proposals at international conferences on the humanization of internal conflict. As will be shown, specific conditions and pressures after 1912 generated incremental changes in both state and nonstate concerns, spurring their combined norm entrepreneurship. Nevertheless, in the early twentieth century, structural constraints continued blocking the emergence of binding humanitarian law to moderate internal violence, and initial resolutions set precedents that shaped later debates.

Customary Legal Debates before the Nineteenth Century

International customary doctrines (e.g., proclamations or ideas about standards not consigned in multilateral treaty documents) promoting restraint in internal conflict had existed for centuries. Legal historians trace the origins of debates among political theorists about the nature and participants of internal conflicts to Plato's *Republic*, written around 380 BCE, and to Cicero's writings four and a half centuries later. According to Stephen Neff, political thought since this early period has consistently tried to differentiate between "true" wars against "worthy" enemies and conflicts with bandits or brigands.[2] "Real" enemies were those with clear internal lines of authority and with some claim to territory, wealth, and popular legitimacy. War was to be waged according to certain rules of good conduct, such as respect for prisoners of war (POWs). Lesser conflicts, in contrast, could be waged violently and dealt with expediently, according to the local criminal laws. Notable legal publicists and political commentators of the sixteenth and seventeenth centuries, including Francisco de Vitoria and Hugo Grotius, agreed with this view, usually locating civil strife in the second, criminal, category.[3]

This position did not change until the mid- to late eighteenth century, when emerging liberal contractualist ideas began to ferment in western Europe, slowly legitimating claims for representative government.[4] The notion that a revolt against sovereigns could potentially be justified if they did not perform their duty to protect their subjects seems to have provided a crucial conceptual change that enabled a more sober assessment of internal strife.[5]

This shift is reflected in the thought of Swiss legal scholar Emerich de Vattel, who in his *Law of Nations* (1758) introduced a triad of distinction between types of internal strife: rebellion, insurrection, and civil war. This taxonomy proved influential. According to Vattel, rebels were usually few in number and acting in a disorganized manner, waging an unlawful revolt against sovereign authority; they were to be treated as criminals. Insurrectionists, for their part, had some type of just cause that motivated them, including combating repression by their sovereign, but did not aim to overthrow the ruler altogether. Only when those in arms sought to bring down the central government could one speak of a civil war proper, which in Vattel's view pitted two parties against one another as if they constituted distinct societies.[6] Importantly, it was also only this "higher" state of internal strife that according to Vattel activated the application of humanitarian principles: "It is very evident that the common laws of war, those maxims of humanity, moderation and probity . . . are in *civil wars* to be observed by both sides."[7]

Historically, then, entitlement to good treatment between combatants has been entwined with questions of status recognition and claim to legitimate authority, two issues that have persistently riddled debates on the regulation of internal conflicts.

Vattel's proclamation about the application of humane rules in the context of civil war was far from constituting a broader normative belief or an international rule shared by statesmen at the time. Instead it seems that his opinion was quite novel. Legal scholar Lindsay Moir notes that "toward the end of the eighteenth century there had been a distinct move toward the application of the laws of warfare to internal conflict, but this was based almost exclusively on the character of the conflicts and the fact that both [interstate and internal war] were often of a similar magnitude, *rather than any overriding humanitarian concern to treat the victims equally*."[8] However, the decision of whether to apply the customary doctrines of war was essentially at states' own discretion, and they seemed happy to continue treating internal uprisings as criminal.[9] Moreover, it tended to be third-party states that seriously confronted the question of whether to afford recognition rather than states directly facing armed opposition.

Nevertheless, Vattel's attention to the varied nature and intensity of armed challenge appeared to resonate among the legal publicists of the time, leading to the gradual carving out within traditional customary international law of three corresponding conflict categories: rebellion, insurgency, and belligerency. These three categories replicate almost verbatim the distinctions explained earlier. *Rebellion* was thought to cover small uprisings that could be dealt with through regular local measures; international rules had simply no import to quell it. *Insurgency*, for its part, involved a higher—and still undefined—level of hostilities and organization, and its recognition triggered a few rights and responsibilities by parties to the conflict vis-à-vis each other as well as foreign countries. (The inability to set a clear "hostility threshold" would also plague rule making in this area up to the present day.) International responsibilities to foreign third parties were chiefly related to economic matters at sea, such as the insurgents' duty not to blockade ports or their right to search suspicious vessels in order to prevent supplies coming from abroad from reaching their opponents.[10] According to Stephen Neff, recognition of insurgency meant that captured opposition fighters could be given POW status by the government they opposed instead of simply being treated as criminals. This was not a formal, obligatory legal provision but a humanitarian one, granted by states on an ad hoc basis. State recognition of insurgency rarely came in explicit form. Despite this, it appears that for commentators at the time, insurgency status could be triggered automatically without a declaration once a few criteria were met: the armed challengers occupied some concrete portion of territory over which they exercised sovereignty, and they conducted hostilities under an organized corps with clear leadership and in accordance with the customs of war.[11]

The third and "highest" level violent nonstate groups could "graduate to" was *belligerency*, which, when recognized, was taken to mean that a full-scale civil war was taking place and hence that both parties should be treated in the same way as those in an interstate war. The benefits attached to belligerency went further than those of insurgency status, because the former activated a fuller body of neutrality norms that had to be respected by the foreign state granting the recognition.[12] Simply, it constituted the most sophisticated legal mechanism that states could use to show restraint toward their internal armed challengers. It legitimated the opposing party as "state-like," a status that afforded both wartime rights and duties to the belligerent party.

Prominent occasions of belligerence recognition by third states exist. Britain recognized it in the Greek independence struggle against the Ottomans in the 1820s, and later in Portugal in 1828, Trieste in 1848, and, perhaps more importantly, during the U.S. Civil War in 1861.[13] Yet notwithstanding these important cases, recognition of belligerence appears not to have been a predominant practice.[14] Although in theory certain "objective" criteria existed that triggered it, embattled states were not under any obligation to recognize belligerency and rarely did so. When they did, it was usually third states that stood to enjoy some commercial or legal benefit, particularly if trade took place with insurgent-dominated ports. Third states also afforded recognition if they explicitly wanted to materially support and give political legitimacy to an internal struggle occurring in another state, sometimes citing a humanitarian motive.[15]

Importantly, as Moir asserts, "the laws of war were *not* automatically applicable to internal armed conflicts in the nineteenth and early twentieth centuries."[16] Only in a few cases during the nineteenth century did the states directly concerned sign ad hoc accords with rebels to guarantee mutual respect for certain restraints in civil wars. Reciprocity was a key motivation in these bilateral agreements. Two prominent examples are the Swiss Civil War in the 1840s, and at least twice in Colombia, in 1820 and in 1860–61.[17]

Without a doubt, the most crucial precedent in the history of the written laws of war arose during the Civil War through the famous Lieber Code, which constituted the first-ever formal written codification of such rules endorsed by a government in modern times.[18] Ironically, although it originally was conceived as a manual setting out standards for conduct in internal armed conflict, outside the Civil War the Lieber Code became instead a model for the regulation of interstate war.

Francis Lieber was a Prussian-born academic who immigrated to the United States. He had also had direct experience on the battlefield during his youth and became known for his teachings on the customs of war. In 1860, on the brink of the Civil War, Lieber wrote a document entitled *Guerrilla Parties Considered with*

References to the Laws and Usages of War at the request of Major General Henry W. Halleck, the general in chief of the Army of the United States.[19] General Halleck solicited Lieber's opinion on the grounds that "the rebel authorities claim their right to send men, in the garb of peaceful citizens, to waylay and attack our troops, to burn bridges and houses, and to destroy property and persons within our lines. They demand that such persons be treated as ordinary belligerents, and that when captured they have extended to them the same rights as other prisoners of war; they also threaten that if such persons be punished as marauders or spies, they will retaliate by executing our prisoners of war in their possession."[20] Lieber's twenty-two-page response parsed through the differences between guerrillas and several other rebellious agents, including freebooters, marauders, brigands, partisans, free corps, spies, rebels, conspirators, and robbers. Curiously, however, he conducted this survey in reference to the context of external invasion or occupation but, explicitly, not of civil war. In the closing paragraphs he declared,

> I do not enter upon a consideration to their application to the civil war in which we are engaged, nor of the remarkable claims recently set up by our enemies, demanding us to act according to certain rules which they have signally and officially disregarded toward us. . . . The application of the laws and usages of war to wars of insurrection or rebellion, is always undefined, and depends upon relaxations of the municipal law, suggested by humanity or necessitated by the numbers engaged in the insurrection. . . . Neither of these topics can occupy us here, nor does the letter prefixed to this tract contain the request that I should do so.[21]

President Abraham Lincoln and General Halleck were apparently preoccupied with the lack of knowledge of the laws of war displayed by the thousands of new, young army volunteers.[22] Hence, a year after the publication of his original pamphlet, Lieber was appointed along with three other experts to write a broader code regulating the conduct of government forces during war.[23] The resulting document was adopted by President Lincoln as the official instruction manual for the Union's troops and dubbed General Orders 100, *Instructions for the Government of Armies of the United States in the Field*.[24]

Most importantly for our purposes, the Lieber Code contained a full section on "insurgency, civil war, [and] rebellion," which was missing from the paper he had written a year earlier. The code's treatment of these matters was modest (eleven articles out of a total of 157.) It provided definitions that mirrored the differences between insurgency and belligerency offered by Vattel. Similar to the prevailing legal doctrine, Lieber proclaimed the possibility that humanitarian provisions such as POW status could be extended toward rebels but did not specify other concessions. Lieber also seemed preoccupied with clarifying that a government's gesture to give humanitarian concessions to rebels "neither proves nor establishes an acknowledgement of the rebellious people, or of the government which they may have erected, as a public of sovereign power."[25] Governmental and military anxieties around the legitimation of rebels through legal recognition have a long trajectory.

Despite decisively influencing mid-nineteenth-century efforts to regulate war between states, the Lieber Code neither constituted nor generated movement toward an international treaty to humanize civil conflict. That idea remained unrealized until 1949.

The Birth of the International Law of War

Discussions about humanizing war through international agreements began to brew in Europe around the mid-nineteenth century. Various developments served as background conditions for this movement: not only a humanitarian ethos but also a growing enthusiasm for international law in Europe, the introduction of compulsory military service by increasingly nationalistic states, and the rising visibility of war atrocities through public reporting on the subject.[26]

Actual international regulations of warfare among states began to crystallize in the 1860s through the efforts of nonstate and state actors. The year 1863 saw the creation of what became the ICRC in Geneva.[27] ICRC-inspired rules have since concerned principally the alleviation of harm to war victims, a category initially reserved for wounded and sick combatants and later expanded. A few years later, certain European states, especially the Russian Empire, began spearheading multilateral meetings to craft international instruments to regulate the use of weaponry and legitimate behavior between combatants, of which the 1899 and 1907 Hague Peace Conferences became the critical examples.

This "division of concern" between victim protection and warfare regulation over time gave rise to two bodies of international law: the "humanitarian" Geneva lineage shepherded by the ICRC and the state-driven "military" Hague tradition mostly concerned with the conduct of hostilities and the means and methods of war. Although to the contemporary eye this may seem like an artificial, even puzzling distinction, it was deeply felt and maintained by states for almost a century, only to be overcome after intense pressure and fierce governmental resistance in the 1960s and 1970s.

The credit for bringing about the first-ever international agreement for humanizing interstate war, the First Geneva Convention in 1864, goes to the ICRC.[28] This organization was created by five Christian Swiss men as a platform to champion a set of humanitarian ideals for mitigating the horrors of war.[29] Although

ICRC cofounder Henry Dunant, a Genevan businessman, was not the first person to spouse a belief in the need to alleviate war atrocity, he became its most effective and dedicated agitator when, upon witnessing the horrors of the Battle of Solferino in 1859, he wrote a moving manifesto, *A Memory of Solferino*, and paid out of his own pocket to publish and circulate it among many of the key political and intellectual luminaries of the European world.[30] His opus depicted war horrors, notably the helpless fate of wounded soldiers, with impressive skill, and its prose made it a sensational success, turning him into a sort of instant celebrity. The book drew praise from most quarters on the Continent, from notable French figures such as Victor Hugo and Ernest Renan to the Swiss military hero, General Guillaume-Henri Dufour, who went on to be part of the Committee of Five that made up the original ICRC.[31]

Another recipient of the book was Gustave Moynier, a respected and well-connected Genevan philanthropist and lawyer, who was similarly moved with Dunant's narrative and became enthusiastic about making it a reality. At the time, he presided over the Geneva Society for Public Welfare, an organization founded in the 1820s that "brought together high-minded Genevan pietists, men of affairs who sought to improve both the moral and the material lives of the common people." Other Genevan notables were invited by Moynier to form part of the Committee of Five, possessing medical skills to further back team credibility; along came Dr. Théodore Maunoir, a "distinguished surgeon who had been twice president of the Geneva Medical Society, [and who] possessed both a lengthy experience in medical philanthropy and an awareness of developments in the English-speaking world that others lacked." Maunoir in turn enlisted Louis Appia, his "protégé" and then president of the Geneva Medical Society, who also held a respected record of publications on wartime medical care.[32]

With their collective talents, contacts, and resources, Appia, Dufour, Dunant, Maunoir, and Moynier were well placed to act as brokers of the nascent humanitarian spirit by tapping into their links to high-level political figures.[33] Dunant's oeuvre also came equipped with concrete proposals, making the enterprise more amenable to realization. Dunant had four specific ideas: (1) to organize relief societies of principled volunteers who would succor the military wounded and sick *during interstate war*; (2) these societies would be formally recognized by governments and armies as legitimate providers of aid on the field; (3) their members would be identified and protected by a universally accepted emblem; and (4) this commitment could ideally be sanctioned as an international principle in the form of a convention.[34]

Together these ideas constituted the initial agenda of the ICRC. Dunant and his colleagues were able to organize two conferences in 1863 and 1864, and from the latter emerged the First Geneva Convention, protecting sick and wounded soldiers during interstate war on land.[35] As will be seen later, this would become the standard procedure of humanitarian rule making for the ICRC: first, calling for "unofficial" meetings that served to socialize ideas, gather feedback, and produce working drafts that did not constitute formal commitments, and second, liaising with the Swiss government to summon diplomatic conferences where state delegations held treaty-making powers.

Beyond humanitarian rules, the creation of the ICRC in 1863 propelled the emergence of the broader Red Cross movement that survives today, which operates as a complex network of actors at the domestic and international levels. The ICRC sits in Geneva as an independent Swiss-registered, nongovernmental organization with the ability to regulate itself and to guide international legal humanitarian debate in addition to many other activities of protection and to the soft "enforcement" of the law through quiet diplomacy. National societies of the Red Cross (and the Red Crescent and Red Crystal) are organizations that gather volunteers and rely on state approval and state funding, and—to varying degrees—remain beholden to governmental authority.[36] Since the early years of the Red Cross movement, the ICRC has balanced decentralized authority by retaining and upholding the right to recognize new societies and by fostering continued dialogue among the various Red Cross entities through events known as the International Conferences of the Red Cross.[37] These periodic gatherings have also constituted an essential forum for the development of international humanitarian law.

For over three decades, the First Geneva Convention remained the only international binding war-related convention. Yet while the ICRC was the nongovernmental precursor, there were other actors in its midst with similar goals. For reasons still subject to debate, imperial Russia became an active convener of interstate meetings to discuss agreements about peace, disarmament, and legal moderation in war in the second half of the long nineteenth century.[38] At the behest of the Russians, a conference met in St. Petersburg in 1868 which issued a declaration to ban explosive and incendiary bullets, the first example of a formal international weapons ban and a source of future, more expansive commitments.[39] In 1874 a conference was organized in Brussels by Russian czar Alexander II to examine a draft protocol on the laws and customs of war inspired by the Lieber Code and to expand the regulations of the means and methods of war initiated earlier in Saint Petersburg. Although the participating states at the Brussels Conference were willing to sign but not ratify the document, its standards soon made their way into a military manual issued in Oxford in 1880 at a meeting of the Institute of International Law (IIL), an organization interested in the progressive development of international law.[40]

The Oxford manual, however, was conceived as a model for voluntary domestic incorporation, not as a multilateral treaty. It was not until 1899, in the context of an international peace conference at the Hague organized by imperial Russia, that the nonbinding precedents laid earlier, especially on the conduct of hostilities, and weapons, were extended and made into international treaty law. A second Hague conference, held in 1907 with American and Russian backing, revised and complemented the agreements from 1899.[41]

What about Internal Conflicts?

Since internal conflict was not considered at any of these interstate or Red Cross events, and no international instrument dealt with the subject,[42] one might conclude that—the Lieber Code aside—the atrocity of internal conflict had failed to generate international concern among rule makers, including the ICRC.

In fact, at the very founding meeting of the ICRC in 1863, questions were raised about the application of humanitarian provisions to civil conflict.[43] Dunant's *Memoires* and meeting minutes reveal that "after lengthy discussion the committee [thought] that it might be better and wiser to limit itself solely to thinking about the question of voluntary care in the context of the struggles *between* great powers and only to European Wars."[44] Moynier appears to have clarified in 1864 that, "in case it needs to be said, we are not referring here to civil wars; international law is not applicable to them."[45] The reason for excluding civil wars was presumably one of institutional strategy: the committee should have a clear, limited focus on what might be plausibly attained. The extension to other types of war was not precluded on principle; rather, the ICRC founders presumably felt that once the Red Cross idea had taken root and experience had accrued, it could grow in other directions.

Thirteen years later these relatively shy positions on internal conflict had seemingly undergone radical transformation. In 1876, Moynier wrote, "That the wounded are insurgents. . . . . Is that reason not to take them into account? Evidently not, since the motivations of the Red Cross are exclusively humanitarian and detached from politics." He added,

> The affirmative would not be in any doubt if the Convention was involved only with reciprocal agreements between the governments adhering to it, as would be the case of a commercial treaty or a postal convention. But the Geneva Convention is more than that. There is nothing to be found in its text that limits its effects to the contracting parties; on the contrary, all its articles are worded in general terms as if they were the expression of rules to be observed not only in relations between the signatories themselves, but in all circumstances. It is a kind of humanitarian profession of faith, a moral code which cannot be compulsory in certain cases and optional in others.[46]

Why this change of heart? Simply put, internal conflicts ravaged in the immediate years after the ICRC's creation. Table 2.1 presents a list of the internal wars in which the ICRC or national Red Cross societies were involved during the first three decades of existence.

The ICRC was confronted with the cruelty of quickly erupting civil conflicts, prompting changes to its initial mission statement. Note that table 2.1 includes some minor uprisings and revolts short of insurrection and civil war. This confirms that since its early years, ICRC practice did not conform to the distinctions between different levels of conflict set out by the received customary international norms and, perhaps unwittingly, broke new ground.[47]

Early on, the ICRC refrained from directly attempting to operate on the ground unless it had been invited to do so by a legitimate local actor. Instead, respectful of sovereign, nonintervention norms, the ICRC preferred to encourage the national Red Cross society, if one existed, to take charge of relief provision.[48]

The first instance of ICRC "indirect" influence occurred during the Third Carlist War in Spain (1872–76). Upon the request of the Spanish Red Cross Society,

TABLE 2.1. List of Internal Conflicts with Red Cross/ICRC Involvement, 1868–1882

COUNTRY	YEARS	CIVIL WAR, INTERNAL TROUBLES, OR VISITS TO POLITICAL PRISONERS IN INTERNAL TENSIONS?	WHO INTERVENED?
Turkey (Candia Revolt)	1868	Troubles (insurrection)	National society (Italy)
Austria (Dalmatia)	1869–70	Troubles (insurrection)	National society (Austria)
Borneo	1870	Troubles (insurrection)	National society (Batavia)
France (Paris Commune)	1871	Troubles (insurrection)	National society (France)
Spain (Carlist War)	1871	Civil war	National society
Spain (Carlist War)	1874	Civil war	National and foreign societies
Turkey (Herzegovina)	1875	Civil war	National societies, foreign societies, the ICRC
Argentina	1880	Unclear	National society
South Africa (Transvaal)	1880	Troubles (insurrection)	National society
Turkey (Bosnia)	1881–2	Troubles (insurrection)	National society
Egypt (Arabi-Pacha)	1882	Troubles (insurrection)	Unclear

Sources: Jacques Moreillon, *Le Comité International de La Croix-Rouge et La Protection Des Détenus Politiques* (Geneva: Institut Henry Dunant, 1973); Gustave Moynier, *La Croix Rouge: Son Passé et Son Avenir* (Paris: Sandoz et Thuillier, 1882); ICRC, *Manuel Chronologique Pour l'Histoire Générale de la Croix-Rouge, 1863–1899* (Geneva: Imprimerie I. Soullier, 1900); Pierre Boissier, *From Solferino to Tsushima* (Geneva: Institut Henry Dunant, 1985).

the ICRC extended its good offices, encouraged combatants to observe the First Geneva Convention, and offered moral and intellectual support, particularly to the idea that relief workers should be granted neutrality and that they should not be treated as insurgents by the government for providing aid. Eventually the Carlist insurgents decided to set up their own relief society, La Caridad, and with the official Spanish Red Cross set up a liaison office in Paris.[49] Moynier himself managed most of these contacts directly from Geneva.[50] Importantly, in this case, the ICRC also sent appeals to the other national Red Cross societies for the channeling of aid to Spain and agreed to publish constant updates on all these developments in the organization's bimonthly journal, the *Bulletin International des Sociétés de Secours aux Militaires Blessés*.[51]

The experience of the Carlist War is representative of ICRC operations in these initial instances, during which it acted largely by combining moral pressure, publicity, and the mobilization of practical help. The outcome of this collaboration seems to have been a happy one, as eventually both parties to that conflict issued orders against executing prisoners and the wounded and permitted the flow of aid from other Red Cross societies.[52]

Yet "success" in Spain was soon dampened by dire news arriving in 1875 about the violence in Bosnia-Herzegovina and Bulgaria during their uprising against the Ottoman Empire. Indeed, the Balkan uprisings seem to have provided the crucial moral shock that led the ICRC to publicly change the position it had held a decade earlier. According to Pierre Boissier, "in Bulgaria, particularly, the rising was put down by Turkish irregulars, known as Bashi-Bazouks, with appalling cruelty. A terrible tale of torture and massacre, claiming over 30,000 victims, soon reached a horrified and indignant Europe." The ICRC eventually realized that the duty of the movement was "crystal clear: take action, regardless of the nature of the conflict."[53]

ICRC action was careful and controlled, however. First, as in Spain, it saw itself as unable to enter internal conflicts without express invitation. In the case of the Balkan Wars, the committee could not easily appeal to the Ottoman Red Crescent Society, which, due to the recent passing of its founder, was moribund. Second, the ICRC understood the international politics of the conflict; it suspected that the uprisings had been fostered by Austria and Russia and had to exercise caution since it risked upsetting two crucial Red Cross partners. (This danger also precluded asking the Red Cross societies of the neighboring countries to intervene.) Eventually the ICRC chose a partial, safer solution: upon receiving a plea for help from Montenegro (a neutral country during that war) to cope with the refugees that had reached its territory, the committee was pleased to organize its very first delegation and to act in partnership with the newly formed Montenegrin Red Cross Society. As Jacques Moreillon notes, this set a double precedent for the ICRC; it had for the first time decided to help the civilian *victims* of internal conflicts, going beyond its initial mandate of tending to wounded and sick *combatants*. The circumstances had evidently forced the committee to devise creative ways of dealing with an internationalized civil war without politically upsetting its key protagonists.[54]

Beyond political barriers to action, the performance of the Red Cross movement in the midst of internal conflict was marred by a long list of practical hurdles: poor means of transportation and communication, meager financial and medical resources held by national Red Cross societies, ignorance or denial of its existence by insurgents, and sheer antagonism by governments that reneged on their prior commitment to the First Geneva Convention.[55] Internal conflicts of varying intensity clearly presented the movement with extraordinary challenges. In all, however, it can be said that the committee definitely went beyond the initial expectations it had set for itself in 1863–64.[56]

Beyond practical help and moral influence, how did the ICRC view the prospects of formulating rules for internal conflict? In 1882 Moynier reflected that "in the absence of written precepts [for such conflicts], which we agree are delicate and difficult to formulate *a priori*, the Red Cross did not always show felicitous inspiration, given the diversity of cases that it encountered. In our opinion, it sinned by abstaining too often, because it either did not feel protected enough by the laws of war or because political considerations exert more influence over it than they should."[57]

Moynier curiously found himself both underlining the importance of formulating legal rules *and* foreclosing the chance of attaining them. In the same book, he almost solemnly declared that "it is time to regularize the way in which the Red Cross conducts itself vis-à-vis intestine wars, just as we have done with international wars. One does not see why it would not extend its obligations in the former case as in the latter."[58] Did the ICRC heed Moynier's own advice and move in this direction?

Certainly, as I have shown, the organization did not ignore the issue nor remain aloof in practice. In his book Moynier formulated the practical "national Red Cross first" approach it had followed until then as a potentially generalizable procedure for relief action in internal conflicts.[59] Yet these principles fell short of the rules the organization had proposed earlier for interstate war.

There was also opportunity to debate the topic in the context of the periodic international conferences of Red Cross societies, which, as mentioned earlier, constituted a critical forum for the socialization of new humanitarian principles. For reasons that are still unclear, sometime in the 1870s the Belgian Red Cross submitted to the ICRC the following question for consideration at the next meeting of national societies: "In the case of insurrections, is there occasion to send relief to insurgents before they have been recognized as belligerents?"[60] At the time, the customary procedure was for the ICRC to divide the various questions it had collected among the different member Red Cross societies, which would prepare a brief report for presentation.[61]

In October 1883, the ICRC tasked the French Red Cross Society with responding to the question on relief to insurgents. Such a request likely stirred controversy among the French since they had only a decade earlier dealt with the revolutionary uprising of the Paris Commune of 1870, during which the rebels had not only denied recognition to the French Red Cross but also attacked it. Unsurprisingly, the Count of Beaufort, head of the French Red Cross Society, responded politely but negatively to Moynier, declaring in a private letter that "given the diversity of circumstances in which this [voluntary assistance to insurgents] can become manifest, it does not seem to us to be amenable to a search for general rules or conclusions of principle which guide the practice of the Red Cross in the future."[62]

Moynier appointed the Dutch Red Cross Society as the new rapporteur on the question,[63] which came back with a set of proposed principles that in essence codified the practical experience the Red Cross had garnered until then. The Dutch report, however, was only submitted to the third conference, to be held in Geneva in 1884, and (seemingly for reasons of time) it did not come up for discussion.[64] The proposal carried over to the Fourth International Conference of the Red Cross in 1887 where it died a strange death after being mysteriously "withdrawn" by its own authors before discussion, without further explanation offered on record or in private.[65]

Given these failed attempts by national Red Cross societies, the question resurfaces: Why did the ICRC, despite singling out the lack of clear humanitarian rules as the most important blocking factor for the pursuit of its work in civil wars, stop short of mobilizing states around that cause? Why did it embrace practical action but not *legal* change?

I argue, first, that key normative structures shaping sovereignty and world politics at this time were patently inimical to the idea of codifying international rules for internal conflict, constraining ICRC entrepreneurship. Second, at the organizational level, soon after the signing of the First Geneva Convention the ICRC's initial legitimacy was challenged by a set of threatening setbacks that likely reduced its willingness to place new legal issues on states' agenda. A risk-averse conservatism seems to have become institutionalized within the organization, compounding the colonial, racist mind-set of its president, Gustave Moynier. These factors only receded slowly once a new generation of ICRC leaders emerged around 1915.

Sovereignty Norms at the End of the Nineteenth Century

Since its creation, the ICRC has always been a strange creature, acting both through and upon state sovereignty. In the nineteenth century, the institution of sovereignty was characterized by intense antirevolutionary norms and, from the middle of the century onward, by the aggressive expansion of Western, imperial, colonialist practices in non-Western territories particularly in Asia and Africa.[66] As David Strang notes, "In the hundred years between 1780 and 1880, new colonies were formed at the rate of five a decade. Between 1880 and 1910, new colonies were formed at four times this rate, or twenty per decade. The pace of colonial formation slowed after 1910, as the number of candidates for colonial imperialism declined."[67]

Thomas Biersteker and Cynthia Weber have called our attention to "the constitutive relationship between state and sovereignty; the ways the meaning of sovereignty is negotiated out of interactions within intersubjective identifiable communities; and the variety of ways in which practices construct, reproduce, reconstruct, and deconstruct both state and sovereignty."[68] The colonial practices of European states mentioned earlier reflected and reproduced a world that was not a universal society of formally equal and sovereign states.[69] According to Strang, "Europeans resuscitated pre-Westphalian forms of divided sovereignty like the protectorate and compromised the internal authority of nominally sovereign states like China. Western powers received tribute as suzerain states in Asia and Africa and paid it as well. Settler colonies like the British Dominions developed complete mixtures of formal dependence, internal self-government, and international personality."[70] Michael W. Doyle notes that imperial control was "a system of interaction between two political entities, one of which, the dominant metropole, exerts political control over the internal and external policy—effective sovereignty—of the other, the subordinate periphery."[71]

This larger context, I argue, was patently less than conducive to the type of legal regulation of the internal affairs of the western European states that were the ICRC's core audience. Drafting, signing, and ratifying a formal, binding treaty that would impinge upon the interests of these powerful states in such a critical way, with language that could potentially empower these mostly non-Western (and mostly nonwhite) subjects, was probably not a viable route for the ICRC to take. Highlighting the Western/non-Western civilizational and racial divide is crucial here because, as noted, it was precisely the countries in Africa and Asia that were the target of Western imperialism during this period and whose changes in sovereign control were at stake. Moreover, international law, including the laws of war drawn up in Geneva and the Hague, reflected the "standard of civilization" of the time, founded upon the constructed cleavages between civilized states and uncivilized peoples.[72]

How does this relate to the ICRC more directly? It has been widely documented that, visionary as Henry Dunant, Gustave Moynier, and company were in the domain of humanitarianism, they bore shared traits with what one could call the social episteme of the time.[73] Prior to becoming a remarkable humanitarian, Dunant was since his youth a convinced Bonapartist who believed that France, led by Napoleon III (whom he is quoted as having called "the successor to Romulus" and "the new Cyrus"), had been tasked with "reconstituting" the Holy Roman Empire. A few years before *A Memory of Solferino* appeared, Dunant's *opera prima* had been "an impressive in-quarto of 46 pages . . . decorated with the Imperial arms" titled *The Restoration of the Empire of Charlemagne* and dedicated to "His Majesty Emperor Napoleon III."[74] In fact, it was while chasing Napoleon in order to deliver him this book that Dunant found himself in Solferino and witnessed the impressive horrors of the battlefield.

For his part, Moynier, who has elsewhere been referred to as a "dedicated colonialist,"[75] was a supporter of the view that the Red Cross "should extend itself only to those parts of the world that were becoming westernized." ICRC historian Pierre Boissier further concedes that "while he did not relegate all colored men to the ranks of 'the savages or barbarians,'" Moynier remained convinced (in 1873) that "'the races which have a civilization, but a civilization different from ours' [did] not have the moral standards or philosophy that are compatible with the Red Cross."[76]

The mid- to late nineteenth century was also the time in which military nationalism gained strong western European roots, something to which the Red Cross movement was not impervious.[77] John Hutchinson puts it quite bluntly when he claims that "between 1880 and 1906, the Red Cross was transformed from an institution that owed its first allegiance to the idea of civilization to one that, by its actions as well as its words, wholeheartedly supported the aggressive nationalism and militarism of the period." Hutchinson notes, "The basic direction of this evolution was set at the Geneva Conference in 1884, when, at the behest of the Italian central committee, two fundamental propositions were discussed and approved: that 'the Red Cross owes the military sympathy and deference in peacetime, and absolute obedience in wartime; while the state owes the Red Cross protection, in the form of laws that will assure its special position as an institution recognized by the state.'" He adds, "It is fair to say that greater rapport between national Red Cross Societies and the military was an almost universal phenomenon in the period from the 1880s to 1914 and that the dominant feature of this closer relationship was the planned integration of the Red Cross into the wartime military-sanitary arrangements of each country."[78]

Respect for nonintervention at a time of both growing colonialist and nationalist practices exerted inhibiting effects on the decisions of the ICRC.[79] Even ICRC historian François Bugnion has characterized the action of the committee in internal conflict during the late nineteenth century as having "narrow limits" and toeing a cautious line which the organization "considered necessary to ensure that any action it took was not seen either as unacceptable interference in the internal affairs of a country or a National Society, or as a bias toward one side or the other."[80]

Organizational Setbacks

In addition to broader normative factors, in its early decades the ICRC faced important challenges which likely curbed its enthusiasm for humanitarian legalism. Critics already existed who questioned the notion that voluntary humanitarian relief should substitute for states' responsibility, picking up the military's slack and lowering the cost of war.[81] Yet by the late 1860s states raised the complicated issue of regulating the ICRC's structure, the role of the national societies during peacetime, and the relationship between the national societies and the ICRC. The Prussian government was enthusiastic about broadening the domain of action of the Red Cross by suggesting that national societies could train nurses to care for the sick poor while "on break" from war. This vision was not shared by other states, as most feared it would amount to financial, technical, and moral overstretch. The ICRC was also ambivalent about assuming peacetime responsibilities and remained averse to external designs on its own affairs.[82]

Important dissent also came from within the movement, as when the French National Red Cross suggested in 1867 that ICRC headquarters should move from Geneva to Paris. Although the idea did not gain traction in the end, the French remained a thorn in the ICRC's side for some time. They put a damper on a project to extend the First Geneva Convention to war at sea, for example, threatening to withdraw support. In response, Moynier became anxious that an attempt to embellish the original treaty would bring the whole edifice down, writing "such a result, would be disastrous, because it is of paramount importance to preserve the unity of this European understanding, so quickly and so auspiciously formed, even if it means sacrificing part of the hoped-for reforms."[83] And though four additional articles on sea warfare were eventually drafted and circulated among states, they did not receive enough ratifications to enter into force.

Perhaps the biggest blow faced by the ICRC during its first decade went straight to the heart of its earlier success: the gross noncompliance (or repeated violation) by governments of the First Geneva Convention during the Franco-Prussian War of 1870. While the Prussian Army seemed to have been much better equipped to respect the rules it had signed, the French were reportedly in "disarray" and unable to keep an eye out on abuses of the Red Cross emblem by alleged volunteers who were actually just using it to deflect war levies and violence.[84]

The balance sheet after the Franco-Prussian War was at best unflattering. Moynier's earlier assumption—that no government would violate its commitments willingly for fear of embarrassment—proved naive. Shortly thereafter he became convinced that "enlightened self-interest" to avoid being judged by the "court of public opinion" was not a strong mechanism to prevent abuses, and that legal punishment was needed.[85] Yet with the war being so recent, Moynier decided to take a public discussion of wartime violations off the agenda for the upcoming Third International Conference (originally scheduled for 1872 but delayed until 1884), afraid of creating strains within the movement and between two crucial members, France and Prussia. This, however, upset other European countries that wanted to see it discussed. To make matters worse, word of "plotting" against the Geneva Convention also surfaced around this time; Austria and France expressed their discontentment with it and willingness to replace it with other measures. In short, as David P. Forsythe wryly notes, "the Red Cross idea almost perished during the Franco-Prussian war."[86]

I suggest that this backlash likely led Moynier and company to prioritize the ICRC's organizational survival and elicited a defensive attitude which discouraged them from further legal expansion. Indeed, as Hutchinson notes, by 1884 the ICRC had surely learned that "there were clear limits to what could be achieved and had decided not to risk further the displeasure of the powers, lest the gains of 1864 be lost in the process."[87]

Conservativeness and pragmatism were not new factors for the ICRC, however; they are better understood as a birth trait that deepened over time. As Boissier's anthology suggests, since its very founding the ICRC was well aware that if it hoped to pursue its agenda with some degree of success, it had to be strategic and "play with the players"—that is, with states—and convince *them* to change the rules of the game.[88]

Efforts toward Regulation beyond the ICRC

Beyond ICRC thought and practice, it appears that the broader (albeit still small and largely European) society of international legal scholars held a similarly conservative view regarding proposing international humanitarian rules for civil conflicts. The IIL (of which Moynier was a member) took up the issue of internal armed conflict in its meetings in 1898 and 1900. There, despite some debate on the matter, IIL members failed to do more than to formalize the customary doctrine of belligerence concerning the neutral role and conduct of third states. Humanitarian considerations during combat proved controversial. One IIL member is quoted as saying, "The IIL is a scientific association which must rigorously stay outside the realms in which the political passions of the day are aired. . . . This proposal, to me, seems to have a character of political actuality that is too pronounced. . . . I suggest that the project be momentarily set aside as inopportune."[89]

This conservative view elicited opposing replies. A few members felt that the institute should aspire to shed light precisely on this type of controversial legal issues. Others insisted that distinctions should be made between "constitutional or dynastic insurrections, which we must condemn, and insurrections against a tyrannical or oppressive governments, which are legitimate."[90] Another group sought to exclude "noncivilized" countries from the purview of application of the eventual norms.

In the end, the rapporteur of the meeting opposed these contentious opinions, for fear that narrowing down the field of application and denying some insurgents their rights "would discharge them from their attendant obligations. Instead of limiting the field of application, we should instead extend it."[91] The controversies were ultimately resolved by extricating the subjective political considerations from the official language, opting instead for technical/factual criteria. As such, the two ensuing nonbinding declarations firmly strengthened the norms of nonintervention and said very little about humanitarian considerations.[92] Like the customary law of the time and the Lieber Code written a half century earlier, they carefully stressed that showing humane treatment to rebels did not amount to recognition of belligerent status.

How these debates related to the ICRC's own thinking is not entirely clear. Although Moynier was honorary president of the IIL, at the ICRC he retained his independence. One instance, however, may serve to illustrate how Moynier, despite leading an organization that championed legal (not only practical) change, remained extremely sensitive toward questions that might disturb state sovereignty and compromise the neutrality of the Red Cross in internal armed conflicts, emulating the IIL's own "prudence" on the matter.

In October 1895, before the Cuban revolutionary uprising against colonial Spain transformed into the Spanish-American War (1898), American Red Cross (ARC) president Clara Barton privately wrote to Moynier referring to an application she had received from a recent acquaintance, a medical doctor and Spanish Red Cross member by the name of A. J. Díaz, who was reportedly very active in providing relief to victims of the uprising in Cuba. Díaz believed that acting as a member of the ARC (in addition to the Spanish Red Cross) would enable him to carry out relief operations more effectively, prompting him to approach Barton for official admission.[93] Unable to decide on an issue that in her view touched indirectly on international law, Barton deferred to Moynier, who opined that Díaz should seek to work with his Spanish compatriots only, adding, "If this does not suffice for him, and he wishes to accede to your [Red Cross] Society, this cannot be, it seems to me, but for a hidden political motive and in hopes that this new status will enable him to [treat] insurgents. From the humanitarian viewpoint this would certainly be a happy outcome, but I think it would be regrettable to set such a precedent, i.e., to associate one person to two different Red Cross Societies . . . in a civil war during which susceptibilities are overexcited." For this reason, Moynier advised Barton to turn Díaz's request down, adding, "Mr. Díaz's zeal could be usefully employed to produce an entente between the Spanish government and the Cuban insurgents toward the reciprocal observation of the laws of war and especially of the Geneva Convention. This would be . . . the surest way of achieving his goals."[94]

This vignette illustrates the points made here about the ICRC's modus operandi. Moynier's simultaneously cautious and principled response to Barton served to guard his organization's interest and to show respect toward prevailing norms while still displaying a commitment to the diffusion and application of humanitarian precepts in war. Regarding internal armed conflicts, Moynier appears to have seen the organization's role as that of an intermediary working within strict sovereign, neutral bounds with a duty mostly limited to exerting moral influence that left the difficult politics to others.[95]

Into the Twentieth Century

Almost since its inception the ICRC opted to participate in internal conflict relief but refrained from forcefully advocating the codification of international legal rules. I have argued that broader normative structures in Europe at the time (antirevolutionary norms, the dramatic rise of imperialism, and budding nationalisms at home), as well as its diminished standing as a humanitarian broker and the attendant conservative pragmatism it may have elicited among its core members, all probably prevented it from taking a decisive legal approach to such a politically charged issue. The similarly conservative opinion on this topic of other international legal experts did not help to move this agenda forward but instead reified the normative status quo.

By the 1890s a tense international context, however, quickly propelled state and pacifist groups' interest in the prevention or moderation of interstate war. Arms races between European powers threatened the balance of power. Tensions were also brewing at home for many European countries as traditional political institutions coped with the social consequences of rapid industrial growth. Against this background, and in a matter of years, Czar Nicholas II championed the First International Hague Peace Conference in 1899, a gesture soon followed by the United States, which, on the heels of two recent conflicts of its own (in Cuba against Spain, and while invading the Philippines), proposed a second conference, eventually convened by the Russian czar in 1907. Although the governments that gathered at the Hague were largely concerned with codifying rules for the conduct of hostilities and the methods of combat, some among them also wished to revise the First Geneva Convention and to adapt it to maritime warfare (a task left pending decades prior). These external pressures forced the ICRC to shake off its conservatism toward updating existing law. Its plans were preempted, however, by Nicholas II when he circulated his proposal to meet at the Hague.[96]

Given the public prominence that the upcoming Hague Peace gathering had attained, Swiss/ICRC plans were put on hold. There was uncertainty and nervousness as to how the 1899 Hague Conference would approach the First Geneva Convention, perhaps lowering the standards attained before. Yet it seems that with the influence of the Swiss delegate, governments agreed that its revision should occur not at the Hague but at a separate "special" event be held to that purpose under the aegis of Switzerland. The 1899 Hague Conference adapted the First Geneva Convention rules to maritime warfare, but the most important issue—safeguarding the integrity of the original accord—was left in the hands of the ICRC, which steered a revisions process that culminated in 1906.[97]

In all these discussions, however, the issue of internal armed conflict remained conspicuously absent. Other less controversial and comparatively neglected issues had started to take precedence—notably, increasing the legal protections for POWs. The Hague Conferences took important steps toward regulation in this area, but there remained glaring gaps related to implementation that the ICRC, with some hesitation, declared it could endeavor to fill.[98]

The new century found the ICRC accepting new normative and operational tasks in less controversial subjects, reducing the odds that internal conflicts might take on greater relevance. Moreover, the ICRC's conservative organizational culture remained largely unchanged. As ICRC historian André Durand has noted, "at the beginning of the twentieth century, the ICRC was obviously in no hurry to change its composition, since no new members were appointed for sixteen years, from 1898 to March 1914."[99] The original generation led by the aging Moynier continued running the organization, and the passing of the torch to a younger generation would not be completed until the 1920s and 1930s. Generational persistence plausibly operated as a reproductive mechanism that furthered the inherited reluctance of the ICRC to tread on the waters of formally regulating humanitarianism in internal conflict.

Putting Internal Conflicts on the Agenda: The ARC's 1912 Proposal

It was not the ICRC, but a government and its national Red Cross society that eventually attempted to fill the legal gap on internal conflicts. In 1912, the United States, acting as host to the Ninth International Conference of the Red Cross in Washington, DC, drafted a report and a proposal for creating the first-ever international agreement on the provision of humanitarian relief during civil war and internal disturbances.[100] Although it failed to crystallize, this initiative triggered the first public discussion of the topic among government diplomats and constituted a springboard for future efforts at regulation.

The United States proposed to formally allow the extension of humanitarian relief to the sick and wounded victims from all sides (state forces, insurgents, and noncombatants), expressly permitting a foreign Red Cross to offer its services to another country's government or Red Cross society when faced with internal conflict. Relief offers would be directed at the war department of the recipient state, would have to be approved by it, and would have to be tendered following the humanitarian precepts governing the First Geneva Convention.[101]

The origins of this initiative are not well known.[102] It is prima facie consistent with the expansionist—indeed, imperialist—impulse of U.S. foreign policy during the Progressive Era.[103] At the same time, as François Bugnion asserts, "The American Red Cross report was remarkable in that it managed to reconcile the interests of the victims, Red Cross freedom of action, and the rights of the parties to the conflict. The sovereignty of the government was amply protected."[104] And nothing in the language of the draft agreement smacked of obvious imperialism.

What motivated the American delegation to extend this proposal? The original invitation sent by the American Red Cross to member states, national societies, and the ICRC did not include civil war on the agenda, and no state had suggested adding it, either. Its inclusion on the agenda seems to have come in April 1912, one month before the conference started. The International Relief Board, a subagency of the American Red Cross, was requested to prepare a study on the conduct of national Red Cross societies in foreign civil wars. This report was researched and later presented at the ICRC meeting by Joshua Reuben Clark Jr., a graduate of Columbia Law School who had been appointed assistant solicitor in the U.S. Department of State in 1906.[105] According to his biographers, when the Mexican Revolution erupted, Clark had already served as close counselor to the secretary of state and to President William Howard Taft. One of the areas Clark promoted was humanitarian relief to victims of the revolution. A fervent Mormon, he may have been concerned with the large numbers of Mormon victims in Mexico. Historians have also noted that the problems caused by the "embittered rivalries of competing factions" (in the words of Foster Rhea Dulles) over Red Cross aid after the overthrow of the Díaz regime in 1911 led the State Department to make efforts to clarify the delicate issue.[106] More generally, the American Red Cross proposal may have been trying to legalize its expanding humanitarian operations in internal conflicts.[107]

On the other hand, given Clark's work as legal adviser and diplomat for the U.S. government before and after 1912, drafting legal justifications for repeated interventions by the American government in Latin America and defending the private interests of Americans residing there, there is reason to suspect that his proposal on Red Cross aid in internal conflict concealed ulterior motives.[108]

Whatever its origins and intent, this proposal came to naught. The representative from imperial Russia, General Nicholas Yermolov, fired the opening shot by declaring that "in no case or manner could the Imperial government become a contracting party to or even a discussant of any agreement or vow on this topic," and that "given its political gravity," in his opinion "it should not be opened to discussion in a Conference of exclusive humanitarian and pacifist nature."[109]

In a shrewd rhetorical move, Yermolov cited the words of General William Tecumseh Sherman during the U.S. Civil War: "On no earthly account can I admit any thought or act hostile to the old Government." The Russian general went further, asserting that "any offer of services, direct or indirect, of Red Cross Societies to insurgents or revolutionaries could not be conceived as more than a violation of friendly relations, as an 'unfriendly act,' likely to encourage and foster sedition or rebellion in another country."[110] France and Italy agreed, with the former declaring that this was patently a "governmental question, and a government cannot see revolutionaries as belligerents." To this—and given that at the time Latin America showed a great concentration of internal conflicts—the Italian representative, General Luigi Ferrero, added that the topic was "too local" and "special" and as such unworthy of general discussion at an international conference.

Clark defended his proposal by highlighting its humanitarian character and the many safeguards it included—especially the fact that it allowed states to accept or decline offers for foreign relief. He clarified that in no circumstance would relief provision indicate a recognition of belligerence upon insurgents. Indeed, most states sitting in Geneva seemed to be concerned with legally legitimizing potential revolutionaries—a recurrent worry, as we have seen.

Moreover, Clark scolded Russia's Yermolov for his conservatism, reminding him that the conference was primarily a meeting of Red Cross societies, not of governments, and as such airing ideas and projects to advance the humanitarian mission was completely appropriate. Clark also cited the American Red Cross's prior experience in relief provision to both sides of internal conflict. And in response to Yermolov's audacious reference to the U.S. Civil War, Clark reminded the audience of the humanitarian work of the U.S. Sanitary Commission, which provided care to wounded and sick members of both the Union and Confederate Armies.[111]

Notably, not all states were as fiercely opposed to the idea as the Italians or the Russians. The British representative warned against it apparently not on principle but due to the security difficulties it entailed, mentioning the Paris Commune. China suggested that relief to insurgents could be domestic but not foreign, fearing an implicit recognition of belligerence. Greece supported the idea of principles for allowing relief once an internal conflict had reached civil war proportions and once rebels had been implicitly or explicitly recognized as belligerents. Only Argentina, Cuba, Switzerland, and Uruguay supported the U.S. proposal; Cuba had in fact come to Washington with its own proposal for legitimating domestic relief, only to see it rhetorically lumped in—and eventually dismissed—with the U.S. project.

Despite some moderation, it is clear from the debates that most states in the room were either dubious or overtly against the idea of legitimizing humanitarian relief provision in civil conflicts. The political motives behind rejection are not hard to ascertain: a mix between risk aversion among the imperiled European powers and states' broadly shared fear of legitimizing rebels through international principles.

The ICRC played a notoriously demure role in the 1912 discussion. Gustave Moynier had died in 1910, so it was his successor, Gustave Ador, who now presided over the organization and over the conference. Interestingly, in his interventions on this subject, Ador appeared to actually side with the skeptics—for instance, when he acquiesced to the idea that these were "personal matters relating to the particular situation of certain countries, but which could not give rise to a voted resolution by the Conference." For the ICRC this seems like a disappointingly unenthusiastic attitude. Yet in the end Ador recognized that the topic remained on the agenda and that "it is very likely that in a few years this question will have been advanced and may be resolved in a different manner than it was today."[112]

Ador was right. "More than time," explains Bugnion, what was needed was "precedent."[113] One might add, more and more atrocious precedents. Over the next few years, several Red Cross societies and the ICRC itself would garner additional fresh experience in war relief efforts. These experiences led to advances at the following International Conference of the Red Cross Societies.

New Shocks: Russia and Hungary

First came the Russian Revolution in 1917. The crumbling of the Russian Empire, and with it the Russian Red Cross Society, one of the most distinguished and able of the societies existing at the time, raised new challenges for the humanitarian mission of the ICRC. In January 1918 the Soviet Council of People's Commissars confiscated the property of the Russian Red Cross and announced a plan to reorganize it. Alarmed, the ICRC appointed a Swiss delegate in Petrograd to deal with the rapidly changing situation. Much to the ICRC's surprise, however, the Soviet response was welcoming. A declaration signed by Premier Vladimir Lenin himself stated that Soviet Russia remained committed to the Geneva Convention, as well as to "all other Conventions and international agreements relating to the Red Cross," and that the Russian Red Cross would continue to be active in assisting and helping prisoners of war.[114] Action followed words, and a special committee for POWs and refugees was set up in Moscow. A parallel committee had been formed by the ICRC representative there, Édouard Frick, and formed by Red Cross societies from neutral countries such as Denmark, the Netherlands, Norway, Sweden, and Switzerland.[115] These combined efforts reportedly provided considerable political, material, moral, and medical help to political detainees, interned children, refugees, and prisoners of war in need of repatriation.[116]

The situation in Hungary was equally perplexing. In March 1919 communist revolutionary Béla Kun unseated the government of President Mihály Károlyi, and though the coup d'état had been bloodless, the new government threatened to punish by death any contravention to it—a clear affront to humanitarian values. In addition, Hungary represented a crucial point of passage for the repatriation of POWs scattered through the region after World War I, and so securing its presence there was key for the ICRC.[117] Luckily, in Hungary, the ICRC and the national Red Cross were again given all assurances by the communist government of their neutral status and of respect for their humanitarian work. This allowed the ICRC representative in Budapest to conduct visits to many political detainees for some time, the first such visits for the ICRC.

Béla Kun, however, retracted his lofty promises when the head of the Italian military mission in Budapest offered protection to captured rebels. Italy, according to Kun, could not consider as combatants "armed gangs who, in the interests of the counter-revolution, massacre women and children and want to exterminate the Jews."[118] Kun's hardened position was short-lived, however, and his revolution ended with Romania's invasion in late July 1919. Concerned now with ensuring good treatment of the former communist revolutionaries and other prisoners of war, along with offering some relief for the awful conditions experienced by the broader population, the ICRC eventually stayed in the country until 1922.

According to the ICRC's report of activities between 1912 and 1920, the Hungarian and Russian efforts finally proved the value of the "indispensable role of the Red Cross in a civil war."[119] Indeed, as we will see, new nonbinding rules emerged in 1921 on the heels of these recent experiences.

However, archival evidence suggests that this change of mind was neither automatic nor necessarily a product of the ICRC's own reflection. In a letter as late as January 1919, the committee expressly refused to support the idea of organizing international relief for civil war victims, not just in Europe but worldwide.

Instead of enthusiasm, the ICRC channeled the skeptics from the 1912 conference by declaring that "one cannot conceive of organized action that applies to those types of wars, provoked by reasons in which a foreigner should not intervene." Moreover, in the ICRC's view, "civil war is very different to ordinary war; it is not subject to the laws and customs of war. It comes in many forms in different localities and countries, following the character of the nation in which it reigns. One can hardly see how one could subject it to such an organization."[120] Following decades-old practice, the ICRC reiterated that only the national Red Cross of the concerned country could provide relief to the combating sides. The letter ended by suggesting that the ICRC nevertheless found the idea "interesting" and that it would consider how to execute it. Hence, despite the practical efforts led by its representatives on the ground, the ICRC back in Geneva remained cool toward the idea of regulating civil wars even after the bloody Russian Revolution had wound down. "Learning" from recent traumas had not been as automatic as official histories seem to imply. What happened then?

My research points, in particular, to the dedicated correspondence directed to the ICRC by a former member of the (old) Russian Red Cross, Georges Lodygensky, who after the fall of the tsarist empire had taken refuge in Geneva but continued to be in communication with different Red Cross organizations on the ground in revolutionary Russia. Clearly anxious to facilitate concrete aid provision to victims, Lodygensky authored two reports detailing the profound need for a coordinated Red Cross in civil wars given the critical humanitarian challenges present all over his country. The ICRC, seemingly impressed by his work, published these reports in its quarterly journal.[121] Importantly, Lodygensky was convinced that the ICRC had to take the issue of internal conflicts more seriously by creating its own permanent special unit devoted to civil war relief and coordination and by promoting legal studies to achieve the formalization of international Red Cross collaboration in such conflicts. He submitted these ideas directly to ICRC president Gustave Ador and to others on Ador's staff in personal meetings in May 1920.

This time, faced with extensive and dedicated research, the ICRC finally acquiesced. Ador himself replied to Lodygensky, recognizing his brave perseverance and promising to "hasten the juridical and diplomatic examination of the questions raised by the intervention of the International Red Cross in civil wars."[122] Ecstatic, Lodygensky replied within three days, and over the next two months, he sent to the ICRC his thorough vision of both the theoretical and practical aspects of project, built upon the multiple recent experiences of various national societies in conflicts in Estonia, Hungary, Mexico, Portugal, Russia, and Turkey.[123] Lodygensky's writings became key for the debate on the topic at the upcoming conference, and he was directly invited to participate as representative of the "old" Russian Red Cross.

These historical vignettes allow me to extend my argument regarding the persistent reluctance of the fundamental moral entrepreneur in the area of humanitarianism to promote formal international mechanisms of civil war relief. In particular, they illustrate the point that atrocity trauma requires active and persistent mobilization to lead to prompt a rethinking of old attitudes and policies.

A Concrete First Step: Legitimating International Red Cross Access to Civil Wars

The experience from then recent civil wars, embedded within the broader collective horror following the abuses committed in World War I, did make an impression on several national Red Cross societies. In preparation for the next International Conference of the Red Cross, and likely in response to Lodygensky's missives, the ICRC asked the national societies to submit reports with their views on the topic. Eight of them responded positively: Finland, Germany, Italy, Poland, Portugal, Turkey, Ukraine, and, through the person of Lodygensky, the "old" Russian Red Cross. As Kimberly Lowe notes, "The dissolution of the Russian, Austro-Hungarian, and Ottoman Empires catapulted numerous societies from a state of wartime mobilization into the throes of civil war and revolutionary troubles. These first-hand experiences of civil violence infused the 1921 debate with a new urgency."[124]

These reports were unequivocal in affirming the need of applying the Geneva Convention to internal conflicts and the crucial role the ICRC should play in them.[125] Although priority of action continued to be given to *domestic* Red Cross societies, the reports recognized that whenever these were unable to operate, the ICRC or foreign Red Cross societies should have a right to help. Exact proposals varied, with the Turkish Red Crescent suggesting that foreign societies and the ICRC should enjoy a type of "extraterritoriality" and neutral status in the context of civil wars. Others emphasized that the neutrality and independence of a national Red Cross operating in a country experiencing regime change should be guaranteed. Notably, these reports all suggested that states should observe the laws of war toward rebels, even if these rebels were not formally recognized as belligerents. This included giving humane treatment to captured combatants, similar to that of POWs.

Fifty national societies, some of them accompanied by government delegates, attended the Tenth International Conference of the Red Cross, taking place in

Geneva in 1921. Underlying its urgency, the topic of civil war was given its own commission of ten members, Commission III. In 1921, however, the speakers reporting directly on this subject were national societies' representatives, not government delegates—a factor that very likely colored the debates and helps explain why they stood in such stark contrast to those of 1912.[126] This time most societies agreed that there should be some sort of agreement to authorize Red Cross relief in civil wars. As Lowe notes, "As conceived by the conference, the right to humanitarian assistance ascribed to all men by virtue of their suffering and was granted by a moral authority superior to the state. The last three years had made it clear that 'today, after the fall of the three empires the most strict in their defense of autocracy, there is no longer any government that could refuse the Red Cross the right to help the rebels as well.'"[127] Participants insisted that, beyond insurgents, *all* victims of internal conflicts should be entitled to humanitarian aid.

Consistent with these pleas, a resolution was eventually adopted making Red Cross operations in internal conflicts legitimate. Codifying past practice, the national Red Cross societies of countries facing internal conflicts were assigned a primary role and were encouraged to remain neutral and independent. More importantly, the resolution also authorized the national societies to request outside Red Cross assistance, to be channeled via the ICRC. The ICRC, however, had to make sure the receiving government agreed with such help, and in case of state refusal, it was entitled to make this reluctant attitude public. The committee was also called to take over the task of humanitarian assistance if a government or a national Red Cross society was dissolved during a civil war.[128]

An additional step was taken in 1921.[129] Through the insistence of Georges Lodygensky, the conference added a statement in the resolution condemning the practice of hostage taking, and suggesting that political detainees captured during civil war should be treated humanely. Yet with regard to this addition, the German Red Cross representative succeeded in amending textual references to rebels as "belligerents" and "prisoners of war," arguing that such language might prematurely legitimate an uprising in its early stages and deprive a government of its legal ability to quell it. ICRC president Ador empathized with this concern, noting that "if a revolution breaks out . . . for example if communist parties declare themselves against the government and seek to overthrow it, it is difficult to consider these revolutionaries, these rebels, as prisoners of war and to treat them with all the benefits of The Hague Convention offers to prisoners."[130]

This exchange reveals two crucial points. First, it reinforces the theme developed in this book about the anxieties felt not only by states but also by the Red Cross, regarding the risks of legitimizing insurgents through the use of legal categories that enhanced both their status and their prerogatives. Second, with regard to the specific political context of the time, it brings to light a latent concern among many of the participating national Red Cross societies in 1921 with potential communist revolutions. The idea of humanizing internal conflicts through the provision of aid to all victims may well have been uncontroversial by then, yet since many of the possible beneficiaries in future uprisings might be of communist stripe, those debating in Geneva wished to exert caution so as *not* to legitimate them by inadvertently granting them the legal character of belligerents.[131]

As a result, one can conclude that even though in 1921 recent civil war atrocities may have begun to do away with the persistent sovereign risk aversion toward the provision of humanitarian aid during internal conflict, political fears provoked by a feared application of the principles to communist rebels limited humanitarian legalism even in nonbinding form. That the German Red Cross representative felt at liberty to express this concern publicly suggests that this was a concern shared more broadly, perhaps by the majority of representatives. This dynamic of modifying the language of the sanctioned rules to avoid their application in undesirable circumstances repeated itself in subsequent debates about rules for internal conflicts in 1949 and the 1970s.

The 1921 resolution was doubtlessly important. In practice it served to legitimize the work that the ICRC, as well as a few national Red Cross societies, would perform in a variety of civil conflicts between 1921 and 1949, as will be detailed in subsequent chapters. Moreover, as we will see, it laid a crucial precedent, opening the door to eventual legally binding developments. That said, the resolution's relevance was also limited. It constituted a nonbinding statement obtained not at a diplomatic conference of state delegations with treaty-making power, but at a meeting of the international Red Cross movement. It may well have been seen as "quasi-law" by the ICRC and national Red Cross societies, but it did not constitute binding law upon states. Second, while it legitimated humanitarian relief in internal conflicts, it also stopped short of expressly banning the resort to inhumane acts (except for the Lodygensky proposal, which condemned them). In other words, even if its spirit pointed toward legitimating the idea that extant rules for interstate war should also apply in internal conflicts, it did not effectively regulate combatant behavior during internal war, which would take decades to occur. As such, it appears that even if the Red Cross was now convinced of its right to humanitarian *action* in internal conflict, it still wavered on the idea that international *law* should regulate it.[132]

3

SQUARING THE CIRCLE

Creating Common Article 3 (1921–1949)

Internal conflict finally came under the purview of international humanitarian law (IHL) in 1949 through the codification of Article 3 common to the Geneva Conventions (Common Article 3, or CA3). CA3 changed international law: It became the very first *binding* international legal rule to protect the victims of armed conflicts occurring within states' borders; the Universal Declaration of Human Rights, adopted just months prior in December 1948 by the United Nations (UN) General Assembly, was a non-binding document, or "soft law."

In terms of its substance, CA3 enshrined a list of principles that tackled the most frequent abuses inflicted upon wounded and captured persons in internal conflicts, including death, torture and other forms of cruel and degrading treatment. Moreover, CA3 added fair trial safeguards that offset the traditional (criminal) treatment given to rebels under domestic treason laws. And although CA3 lacked a comprehensive set of protections for civilians amid internal hostilities, it laid a bedrock of humanitarian guarantees for them. Finally, CA3 encouraged the parties to conflict to come to special agreements and expand their mutual commitments as they saw fit, implicitly recognizing that states and rebels could negotiate accords on equal footing. Its expansiveness quickly led to its popular characterization as a "convention in miniature," an expression initially used by a Soviet delegate in 1949 to (derisively) compare it to the broader protections states had built for interstate conflicts, but later re-signified positively by the Red Cross to highlight the broad coverage it actually permitted in practice.[1]

As Jean Pictet of the International Committee of the Red Cross (ICRC) anticipated already in 1948, incorporating internal conflicts in the Geneva Conventions would constitute a "veritable squaring of the circle," welding into palatable legal form humanitarian concern and the safeguarding of states' domestic security.[2] Why and how did states manage to square the proverbial political and legal circle through the creation of CA3?

I argue that the adoption of CA3 was the product of a two-step process characterized by *normative pressure* and social pressure via *forum isolation*. First, I illustrate how despite the normative inroads made in 1921, ICRC action in practice was often hindered by government refusal to admit its services or to show humanitarian restraint in internal violence. These setbacks had an important effect since, in demonstrating the inadequacy of nonbinding instruments, they eventually allowed the ICRC to press for binding rules. A new wave of civil war atrocity was key for slowly generating a shared interest among a majority of states to include humanitarian protections for internal conflicts in the Geneva Conventions.

Yet to say that some states were either willing or pressured to entertain the idea does not mean that codifying a legal rule on internal conflict was a foregone conclusion. There remained steep barriers, the most important of which was the attitude of some powerful states that had a direct stake in the outcome—especially Britain and France, which feared the application of IHL in their colonies. The second half of this chapter demonstrates that intense public and private pressures blocked the dismissal of the idea of humanizing internal conflicts, "tamed" delegates pushing for high conditions of application, and through forum isolation activating opprobrium concerns about status and social reputation, compelled British and French accommodation to the "proregulation" majority view.

The context in which the multilateral negotiations of 1949 took place was crucial; by 1949, Britain and France were war-beaten powers struggling to retain their international standing. After World War II, both quickly began to lose their legitimacy and effective authority in Africa and Asia due to an international moral crusade and various uprisings in support of the principle of self-determination. The early Cold War contest between competing liberal and socialist ideologies accentuated these global political status struggles, and anticolonialism in particular gave the Soviet Union a powerful public argument—if for propaganda reasons—against liberal-democratic, imperialist Western countries. The Soviets put humanitarian arguments against colonialism to good use during the negotiation of the Geneva Conventions. In addition, the openness of most other participant delegations to accept the idea of humanizing civil wars combined with Soviet rhetoric pushed colonial and other less radical Western skeptics against the political wall.

In the end, although privately unpersuaded about the wisdom of the idea, isolated British and French delegates realized that continuing to oppose a humanitarian idea embraced by a diplomatic majority in Geneva would be socially costly inside and outside the negotiating room. Citing direct diplomatic evidence of these felt social pressures, I show that these states became isolated and were compelled to modify their position and accommodate.

Yet forum isolation did not exert unilateral effects. Instead, in a move that I label *covert pushback*, France and the United Kingdom decided to take the reins of the drafting process to craft a version that simultaneously pleased them, as well as "the humanitarians" in the room, while also neutralizing more extreme alternatives. To do so the colonial powers shaped a key portion of the text to read ambiguously—the "definition" of the internal conflicts to which the rule would apply—hoping that such ambiguity would later allow them to avoid its implementation in practice. The initial skeptics took pains to see their version of the text adopted, even letting an opportunity to delete the provision go by the wayside. This counterintuitive attitude can only be explained through attention to the social aspects of the negotiations. Indeed, in 1949, France and the United Kingdom understood that the balance of opinion supported the creation a humanitarian rule for internal conflicts. Preempting the adoption of a different, unpalatable text, they stood by their draft. Ultimately, despite some very important insertions of protective content, theirs was the version that emerged as CA3.

ICRC and Red Cross Intervention in Internal Conflicts, 1921–1938

The nonbinding resolution (XIV) adopted in 1921 allowed the ICRC to lend its humanitarian services in a number of internal conflicts and other cases of domestic instability, including those in Upper Silesia (1921–23), Poland (1924), Montenegro (1924), Italy (1931, through the National Red Cross), Austria (1934), and Spain (1936–39).[3] On the whole, however, that resolution performed less well than its drafters and the ICRC had hoped. A few countries declined Red Cross action, arguing that an internal conflict was either not occurring or had ended and that those held were being treated in accordance with domestic laws. This was the case in the Soviet Union (1921–22 and 1926–27), the Irish Free State (1922–23), Lithuania (1937), and Nazi Germany (1933–45). A failed ICRC attempt to offer help during the Rif War in northern Morocco (1920–26) also suggested that colonial powers thought their protectorates were outside the scope of application of the 1921 resolution.[4] In all cases, historical evidence confirms that the ICRC seems to have been greatly frustrated by these failures of access, being particularly well aware of the dire situation in which political detainees found themselves throughout these countries.[5]

None of these internal conflicts, however, seem to have had more impact on the ICRC and the Red Cross movement than the Spanish Civil War, which for three years pitted the incumbent Republican side against the Nationalist insurrectionaries led by General Francisco Franco. Although ICRC involvement in Spain was heavy and saw some important successes, the atrocity balance sheet was, in the end, seriously distressing.[6]

At the outset of the war, the Republican government forcibly reorganized the Spanish Red Cross.[7] The Nationalist rebels, for their part, created their own Red Cross committee based in Burgos, and it was unclear what this duality would mean for their relations with the ICRC. The ICRC decided to communicate with both Red Cross organizations on the basis of the 1921 resolution. Luckily, both recognized the ICRC's moral authority and replied positively to a request to allow its channeling of foreign Red Cross assistance. Further, they committed to supporting ICRC delegates on the ground in the creation of information agencies for civilian prisoners and prisoners of war (POWs). Finally, each accepted the fact that the ICRC would be working with the other.

These commitments allowed the ICRC to widely extend its operations in Spain. By the end of 1936 it had reportedly sent nine delegations to various regions of the country. As André Durand notes, "In the Spanish War the International Committee did its utmost to extend its operations as much as it would have done in an international war, since the conflict increasingly took on an international character."[8] ICRC operations comprised a variety of important areas: basic relief, aid to national Red Cross societies, protection of the Red Cross emblem, prison visits, assistance to prisoners, establishment of lists, news provision, exchange and evacuation of persons, and aid to civilians. Humanitarian need was staggering. By the end of the war, the committee's News and Tracing Service had reportedly sent 5,025,843 family messages, including incoming and outgoing notes.[9] The ICRC also endeavored to remind both combating sides of existing IHL and strived to have them sign limited humanitarian agreements on the basis of reciprocity, chiefly for prisoner exchange as well as for the evacuation of the elderly, the sick, women, and children.

As extensive and crucial as this assistance was, the situation during the war remained utterly precarious. Both sides engaged in gruesome practices and many prisoners, civilians, or combatants were executed or held captive.[10] A state of belligerence was never recognized between the parties, so the laws and customs of interstate war did not become applicable. Republicans and Nationalists also failed to reach ad hoc agreements for restraints on specific acts of violence, such that "the conflict was characterized by a callous disregard for the laws and customs of war and humanitarian principles."[11]

Given the extent of the ICRC's involvement and the cruelty of the war, the conflict constituted a watershed for the eventual development of the rules for internal conflicts. As ICRC historian François Bugnion notes, the war "highlighted the serious problems resulting from the absence of legal rules applicable to civil wars and showed how difficult it was, during actual hostilities, to reach agreements between belligerents to limit the violence and protect the victims. . . . In the final analysis, the Spanish Civil War underscored the need to draw up, in peacetime, legal rules applicable to civil wars."[12]

By the mid- to late 1930s the ICRC realized that commitments bearing force of international law had to be put in place for internal conflicts. It knew, however, that this could only be done by summoning a diplomatic conference of states, which seemed like a distant thought given the brittle political context of the time. Political tension included not only the war in Spain but also the winds of broader international conflict in Europe. In the meantime, as a way of framing its own aspirations, the ICRC decided to prepare a study on the topic in preparation for the upcoming Sixteenth International Conference of the Red Cross, scheduled to take place in 1938 in London.

The Yung Report and the Sixteenth International Conference of the Red Cross, 1938

Walter Yung, a member of the ICRC and its Legal Commission, was in charge of the study. Explicitly based upon recent Red Cross experience, the report sought to elaborate upon and clarify the resolution approved in 1921, particularly in areas that had previously gone unidentified, such as prohibiting reprisals against civilians or facilitating their evacuation from war zones. Interestingly, Yung's report distinguished between three different types of internal conflict (minor troubles, grave troubles, and civil war) and proposed diverse types of protection for each.[13] Although this categorization is reminiscent of the different levels of internal conflict considered under traditional customary law, Yung's report made no meaningful reference to received doctrines of belligerence.

Rather, his typology responded to the humanitarian difficulties the ICRC had faced in the 1920s and 1930s, particularly to states' refusal of foreign Red Cross aid because a civil war allegedly did not exist. A prior tendency to lump together different forms of internal violence under the composite notion of civil war in hope that states would allow equal protections across varying levels of violence had proved unhelpful. Consequently, drawing those differences would become essential in debates about creating and applying humanitarian rules in internal conflicts.

Predictably, Yung's report argued that Red Cross action was legitimate in all three situations. As before, initial relief would be the responsibility of the national Red Cross societies, including during "minor" troubles, while foreign assistance by the ICRC or another national Red Cross would be justified amid major troubles or a civil war. The only real difference for Yung was that outside intervention favoring captured rebels during minor troubles seemed unrealistic; hence, there the domestic criminal code should be expected to apply. Yung also drafted specific guidelines for Red Cross and ICRC action, restating and expanding their ability to provide aid to victims.

In addition, Yung's report explicitly recognized the fact that until then the basis for ICRC intervention in internal conflict was not formal international law but stemmed from resolutions adopted by the International Conference of the Red Cross. This confirms that the ICRC had become aware of this "hard law" gap, which proved crucial moving forward. To address it, Yung's report enclosed a detailed draft resolution with detailed humanitarian safeguards for wounded and sick fighters, POWs, political prisoners, and noncombatants. The 1921 resolution had included some language to this effect, but Yung now went further by including several provisions drawn from the legal instruments that until then only applied to interstate war. Finally, the draft resolution clarified that none of the humanitarian provisions it contained should be taken as explicit recognition of a state of war or belligerence. Disclaimers to neutralize the legitimization of rebels continued to be essential for securing governmental acceptance of any humanitarian rules for internal conflicts and represented the only intersection between older doctrines of recognition and newer "nonpolitical" humanitarian norms.

The ICRC sent the report and the draft resolution in advance to all national societies of the Red Cross. As Bugnion explains, "This prompted the Spanish Red Cross to produce a document on the same subject. In it, the Spanish Red Cross unreservedly endorsed the Committee's conclusions, and emphasized the need for close co-operation between the ICRC and the National Society of a country engaged in civil war."[14] Yung's work and the Spanish Red Cross response were debated at the Sixteenth International Conference of the Red Cross, which took place in London in 1938. Held within the smaller Legal Commission, the discussion quickly collapsed when an American delegate asked for clarification as to whether the ICRC resolution was to apply only to the Spanish case or to all future civil conflicts.[15] A Portuguese representative responded that it might not be appropriate to discuss generalized standards at exalted times (read: during wartime) and that the ICRC should continue to "study" the topic for later consideration.

Delegates from France, Germany, and Italy agreed with this sentiment; this was not surprising given the antirevolutionary and fascist politics in those countries prior to World War II. Now at the forefront, the ICRC defended its proposal by reiterating that it needed a solid basis upon which to operate in this type of conflict. A Greek delegate agreed, but noted that any norms set at this point could only be of moral, not legal, character. For their part, Belgian, Chinese, and Egyptian representatives decried this attitude and highlighted the humanitarian nature of the initiative. In the end, the French delegate admitted that it was not really against debating the issue and that the ICRC should indeed have a moral basis for its action, but noted that, given the possibility of different interpretations, the topic should be left to expert international jurists.[16]

Given these pressures to delay, the ICRC acquiesced. Only a short resolution emerged from the Sixteenth Conference recalling the terms of the 1921 resolution, commending the ICRC and other Red Cross societies for their "spontaneous" actions during recent civil wars, and requesting that the ICRC and the national Red Cross societies "endeavor to obtain" respect for the humane treatment of the wounded and the sick, POWs, medical personnel and stores, political prisoners, noncombatants, and children, among others. The resolution also encouraged the ICRC to continue studying the issue of Red Cross protection during civil war and to report its work at the next International Conference of the Red Cross,[17] which only took place once World War II concluded.

A Long Road to CA3

The astonishing cruelty committed during World War II, particularly against civilians and POWs, made evident the need to strengthen the existing legal norms regulating international armed conflict.[18] The Spanish Civil War had a similar demonstration effect with regard to internal conflicts.

Four different treaties eventually emerged from the Diplomatic Conference of Geneva in 1949. The first three were "updated" versions of older conventions: (1) the Convention for the Amelioration of the Condition of the Wounded and Sick in Armed Forces in the Field; (2) the Convention for the Amelioration of the Condition of the Wounded, Sick and Shipwrecked Members of Armed Forces at Sea; and (3) the Convention Relative to the Treatment of Prisoners of War. The fourth, the Convention Relative to the Protection of Civilian Persons in Time of War, was a brand-new agreement with safeguards for civilians living in occupied territory or as "enemy" civilians in belligerent countries.[19] This last treaty was a major innovation; in contemporary debates about IHL it is often forgotten that until 1949 no specific covenant existed that offered detailed safeguards to protect noncombatants. And although the text of that convention ignored some crucial areas (such as restrictions on the conduct of hostilities), the step taken in 1949 laid an important foundation.[20]

In February 1945 the ICRC issued a first memorandum to the "Big Five" (China, France, the Soviet Union, the United Kingdom, and the United States) laying out an agenda to revamp the conventions.[21] At this time the Swiss organization especially wished to ascertain whether the major powers shared an interest in revising the law. Civil war was not explicitly mentioned.

In the meantime, the ICRC organized a new gathering of the Red Cross movement, the first since the prewar Sixteenth International Conference of 1938. The Red Cross movement had been expanding since the early decades of the twentieth century to look less European/Western. In 1900 there were thirty-seven recognized national Red Cross societies, most of them in Europe.[22] By 1926, with the breakup of the Austro-Hungarian, Ottoman, and Russian Empires and the associated entry of various new states into the system, the number of national societies had risen to fifty-two.[23] Additionally, between 1900 and 1945, various former colonies had attained full or partial independence, while Latin American national Red Cross societies had multiplied over time and become more active participants at the international conferences. By the end of World War II, the movement counted sixty-four member societies.[24] The attendance of national societies to the international conferences had also popularized: at the 1912 international conference, thirty-five national societies were present; forty-nine attended in 1921, and fifty-six in 1938. By the 1940s a plurality of smaller European, Latin American, and "other" (African, Asian, and Middle Eastern) states offered important counterpoints to major Western powers in humanitarian discussions. (For lists of attendance at key meetings between 1912 and 1949, see table 3.1.)

Forty-nine national Red Cross societies were represented at the 1946 Preliminary Conference of National Red Cross Societies for the Study of the Conventions and of Various Problems Relative to the Red Cross in Geneva discussing possible updates to the conventions.[25] The ICRC's Jean Pictet put the issue of civil war on the table from the outset during debates about the Wounded and Sick Conventions.[26] In addition, the Norwegian and Yugoslavian Red Cross societies mentioned it as a necessary reform in their reports to the conference.

The initial ICRC proposal was cautious. It suggested that only the general humanitarian principles rather than all treaty provisions of the convention should apply in civil wars and under the condition that the "adverse" party respected them in return. This type of conditional reciprocity, whereby one party can declare itself unbound by a commitment if the other party is shown not to comply, is fairly uncommon in international law nowadays and had since the 1929 POW

TABLE 3.1. Comparison of Attendance at Key Meetings, 1912–1949

1912	1921	1938	1946 (NATIONAL SOCIETIES ONLY)	1947 (GOVERNMENT EXPERTS ONLY)	1948	1949 (GOVERNMENT DELEGATIONS)
Argentina (RC)	Argentina (RC)	Afghanistan (G)	Argentina	Australia	Afghanistan (G)	Afghanistan
Austria-Hungary (RC+G)	Armenia (RC)	Albania (RC+G)	Australia	Belgium	Argentina (G)	Albania
Belgium (RC+G)	Australia (RC)	Argentina (RC+G)	Austria	Brazil	Australia (RC+G)	Argentina
Bolivia (G)	Austria (RC)	Australia (RC+G)	Belgium	Canada	Austria (RC+G)	Australia
Brazil (RC+G)	Brazil (RC)	Belgium (RC+G)	Brazil	China	Belgium (RC+G)	Austria
Bulgaria (RC)	British India (RC)	Bolivia (RC+G)	Bulgaria	Czechoslovakia	Bolivia (RC)	Belgium
Canada (RC+G)	Bulgaria (RC+G)	Brazil (RC+G)	Canada	France	Brazil (RC+G)	Bolivia
Chile (RC)	Canada (RC)	Bulgaria (RC+G)	Chile	Greece	Burma (RC)	Brazil
China (RC+G)	Chile (RC)	Canada (RC)	China	India	Canada (RC+G)	Bulgaria
Cuba (RC)	China (RC)	Chile (RC+G)	Colombia	Norway	Chile (RC+G)	Burma
Denmark (RC)	Colombia (G)	China (RC+G)	Costa Rica	New Zealand	China (RC+G)	Byelorussia
Dominican Republic (G)	Czechoslovakia (RC+G)	Colombia (RC+G)	Cuba	Netherlands	Colombia (RC+G)	Canada
El Salvador (G)	Denmark (RC+G)	Costa Rica (RC+G)	Denmark	Poland	Costa Rica (RC+G)	Chile
France (RC+G)	Dominican Republic (G)	Cuba (RC+G)	Ecuador	South Africa	Cuba (RC)	China
Germany (RC+G)	Dutch Indies (RC)	Czechoslovakia (RC+G)	Egypt	United Kingdom	Denmark (RC+G)	Colombia
Greece (RC+G)	Ecuador (G)	Danzig (RC)	Finland	United States	Dominican Republic (RC+G)	Costa Rica
Italy (RC+G)	Estonia (RC)	Denmark (RC+G)	France		Ecuador (RC)	Cuba
Japan (RC+G)	Finland (RC)	Dominican Republic (RC+G)	Greece		Egypt (RC+G)	Czechoslovakia
Mexico (RC+G)	Georgia (RC)	Ecuador (RC)	Guatemala		Ethiopia (RC+G)	Denmark
Norway (G)	Germany (RC+G)	Egypt (RC+G)	Haiti		Finland (RC+G)	Ecuador
Persia (G)	Greece (RC+G)	Estonia (RC)	Hungary		France (RC+G)	Egypt
Peru (G)	Haiti (G)	Finland (RC+G)	India		Greece (RC+G)	El Salvador
Portugal (RC+G)	Hungary (RC+G)	France (RC+G)	Iraq		Guatemala (RC+G)	Ethiopia

Russia (RC+G)	Italy (RC+G)	Germany (RC+G)	Iran	Haiti (RC+G)	Finland
Serbia (RC)	Japan (RC+G)	Greece (RC+G)	Ireland	Iceland (RC+G)	France
Siam (G)	Latvia (RC)	Guatemala (RC+G)	Italy	India (RC+G)	Greece
Spain (RC+G)	Lithuania (RC)	Haiti (RC+G)	Liechtenstein	Iran (RC)	Guatemala
Sweden (RC+G)	Mexico (RC)	Hungary (RC+G)	Luxembourg	Ireland (RC+G)	Holy See
Switzerland (RC+G)	Netherlands (RC)	India (RC+G)	Mexico	Italy (RC+G)	Hungary
Turkey (RC+G)	New Zealand (RC)	Ireland–Eire (G)	Norway	Japan (RC)	India
United Kingdom (RC+G)	Norway (RC)	Italy (RC+G)	New Zealand	Lebanon (RC)	Iran
Uruguay (G)	Panama (G)	Japan (RC+G)	Netherlands	Liechtenstein (RC+G)	Ireland
United States (RC+G)	Persia (G)	Latvia (RC)	Panama	Luxembourg (RC+G)	Israel
Venezuela (G)	Poland (RC)	Lithuania (RC+G)	Peru	Mexico (RC+G)	Italy
	Portugal (RC+G)	Luxembourg (RC+G)	Poland	Monaco (RC+G)	Lebanon
	Romania (RC+G)	Netherlands (RC+G)	Portugal	Netherlands (RC+G)	Liechtenstein
	Russia (RC-Old)	New Zealand (RC+G)	Romania	New Zealand (RC+G)	Luxembourg
	Serbia (RC+G)	Nicaragua (RC+G)	Siam	Nicaragua (RC)	Mexico
	Siam (RC+G)	Norway (RC+G)	Sweden	Norway (RC+G)	Monaco
	South Africa (RC)	Panama (RC+G)	Switzerland	Pakistan (RC+G)	Netherlands
	Spain (RC)	Papal State (G)	Czechoslovakia	Papal States (G)	New Zealand
	Sweden (RC+G)	Paraguay (RC)	Turkey	Paraguay (RC+G)	Nicaragua
	Switzerland (RC+G)	Peru (RC+G)	South Africa	Peru (RC+G)	Norway
	Turkey (RC)	Poland (RC+G)	United Kingdom	Philippines (RC+G)	Pakistan
	United Kingdom (RC+G)	Portugal (RC+G)	United States	Portugal (G)	Peru
	Ukraine (RC)	Romania (RC+G)	Uruguay	Siam (RC)	Portugal
	Uruguay (G)	Siam (RC+G)	Venezuela	Spain (RC+G)	Romania
	United States (RC)	South Africa (RC+G)	Yugoslavia	Sweden (RC+G)	Spain
	Venezuela (RC)	Spain–Nationalist (RC)		Switzerland (RC+G)	Sweden

(continued)

TABLE 3.1. (continued)

1912	1921	1938	1946 (NATIONAL SOCIETIES ONLY)	1947 (GOVERNMENT EXPERTS ONLY)	1948	1949 (GOVERNMENT DELEGATIONS)
		Spain–Republican (RC)			Syria (RC+G)	Switzerland
		Sweden (RC+G)			Turkey (RC+G)	Syria
		Switzerland (RC+G)			South Africa (RC+G)	Thailand
		Turkey (RC+G)			United Kingdom (RC+G)	Turkey
		USSR (RC+G)			United States (RC+G)	Ukraine
		United Kingdom (RC+G)			Uruguay (RC+G)	USSR
		United States (RC+G)			Venezuela (RC+G)	United Kingdom
		Uruguay (RC)				United States
		Venezuela (RC+G)				Uruguay
		Yugoslavia (RC+G)				Venezuela
34	49	59	48	16	56	59

Note: RC = Red Cross/Red Crescent national society; G = government delegation.

Sources: American Red Cross, Neuvième Conférence Internationale de La Croix-Rouge, Washington, DC (Washington, DC: American Red Cross, 1912); ICRC, Dixième Conférence Internationale de la Croix-Rouge tenue à Genève du 30 Mars au 7 Avril 1921, Compte Rendu (Geneva: ICRC, 1921); ICRC, Sixteenth International Red Cross Conference, Report, London, 1938 (Geneva: ICRC, 1938); ICRC, Report on the Work of the Preliminary Conference of National Red Cross Societies for the Study of the Conventions and of Various Problems Relative to the Red Cross, Geneva, July 26–August 3, 1946 (Geneva: ICRC, 1947); ICRC, Report on the Work of the Conference of Government Experts for the Study of the Conventions for the Protection of War Victims, Geneva, April 14–26, 1947 (Geneva: ICRC, 1947); ICRC, Seventeenth International Red Cross Conference, Stockholm (Geneva, 1948); Federal Political Department of Switzerland, Final Record of the Diplomatic Conference of Geneva of 1949, vol. 1 (Bern: Federal Political Department of Switzerland, 1963).

Convention been limited in the framework of IHL, yet in 1946, the ICRC felt its inclusion might make the idea of civil war protections more acceptable to states.

Records show that in 1946 the national Red Cross societies felt more adventurous than the ICRC. Representatives of the Belgian Red Cross and Iranian Red Crescent in fact suggested inverting the conditional reciprocity clause so that parties to conflict would automatically be expected to apply the principles of the convention *unless* they explicitly announced otherwise. (For the main textual formulas considered between 1946 and 1949, see table 3.2.) The rationale here was that "civilized" states (and insurgents aspiring to "civilized" statehood) would feel compelled to respect the law and find themselves unable to publicly oppose noble humanitarian norms. This was a clever use of civilizational language against the military interest of powerful states and empires and already signaled the broader international politicization of the issue, more fully realized later.

Importantly, participants at the 1946 conference did not see the benefit of defining with precision the types of internal conflicts to which eventual rules would apply. The Egyptian and Iranian societies felt that simply referring to "armed conflict" would suffice, since that allowed for broad coverage across violent situations whether internal or between states. Other societies in attendance were in tacit or explicit agreement. Finally, participants suggested that the *entire* text of the Wounded and Sick Conventions, not just their underlying principles, should apply to internal conflicts.[27] Another commission debating revisions to the POW Convention came to similar conclusions.[28]

These initial debates were encouraging for the project of humanizing internal conflicts. The ICRC had achieved more than it asked for in terms of both the scope and substance of the provisions, and none of the participating National Red Crosses rejected the measure—quite the opposite. (State representatives were not present at this meeting, helping to explain this "generosity.") And as noted, national Red Cross societies were entertaining the *full extension* of the Wounded and Sick Conventions and the POW Convention to internal conflicts, not a specific "tailor-made" article (like the eventual CA3) to be devoted to them. That idea would emerge later.

States' Reactions to the Revisions Process in General

By the fall of 1946, France, the United Kingdom, and United States had all begun debating internally on how to react to the ICRC proposals and whether to participate in preparatory meetings. Whereas France and the United States soon welcomed the idea of revisions, the United Kingdom hesitated. The U.S. military had reportedly tried to follow the conventions during World War II, and while it had generally found them useful, it had faced a number of challenges that it wished to

TABLE 3.2. Various Formulas for the Inclusion of Internal Conflicts in the Geneva Conventions, 1946–1949

MEETING	WORKING TEXT ON INTERNAL CONFLICTS	NOTES
1946 (Preliminary Conference of National Red Cross Societies)	"In the case of armed conflict within the borders of a State, the Convention shall also be applied by each of the adverse parties, unless one of them announces expressly its intention to the contrary."	This was the text produced at the meeting.
1947 (Conference of Government Experts)	"In case of civil war, in any part of the home or colonial territory of a Contracting Party, the principles of the Convention shall be equally applied by the said Party, subject to the adverse Party also conforming thereto."	This was the text produced at the meeting.
1948 (Seventeenth International Conference of the Red Cross, "Stockholm formula")	*For the Wounded and Sick Conventions:* "In all cases of armed conflict not of an international character which may occur in the territory of one or more of the High Contracting Parties, each of the adversaries shall be bound to implement the provisions of the present Convention. The Convention shall be applicable in these circumstances, whatever the legal status of the Parties to the conflict and without prejudice thereto." *For the POW and Civilians Conventions*, the following phrase was inserted: "subject to the adverse party likewise acting in obedience thereto."	This was the text produced at the meeting.
1949 (Diplomatic Conference)	See Stockholm formula for Wounded and Sick Conventions above, but add: (1) government recognition of belligerence of rebels; and (2) rebels should present characteristics of a state: an organized military force under the direction of a civil authority, control of territory, governmental functions over a population, explicit and actual compliance with the laws and customs of war, and the means of enforcing the Geneva Conventions. Protecting Powers were only authorized by special agreements.	First Working Party text.
	"In the case of armed conflict not of an international character occurring in the territory of one of the High Contracting Parties, each Party to the conflict shall be bound to apply, as a minimum, the following provisions: 1. Persons taking no active part in the hostilities and those placed *hors de combat* by sickness, wounds, captivity or any other cause, shall be treated humanely in all circumstances and without any discrimination. To this end, the following acts are and shall remain prohibited with respect to the above-mentioned persons: a) violence to life, in particular murder of all kinds, mutilation, cruel treatment and torture; b) taking of hostages; c) outrages upon personal dignity, in particular, humiliating and degrading treatment; d) the passing of sentences and carrying-out of executions without a previous judgment pronounced by a regularly-constituted court, affording all guarantees which are recognized as indispensable by civilized peoples. 2. The wounded and sick shall be collected and cared for. 3. No adverse discrimination shall be practised on the basis of differences of race, colour, religion or faith, sex, birth or wealth. An impartial humanitarian body, such as the International Committee of the Red Cross, may offer its services to the Parties to the conflict. The Parties to the conflict should further endeavour to bring into force, by means of special agreements, all or part of the other provisions of the present Convention. The application of the preceding provisions shall not affect the legal status of the Parties to the conflict.	Second Working Party text (reworked French proposal).

TABLE 3.2. (continued)

MEETING	WORKING TEXT ON INTERNAL CONFLICTS	NOTES
	A. Wounded and Sick Conventions: "In the case of armed conflict not of an international character occurring in the territory of one of the States, Parties to the present Convention, each Party to the conflict shall apply all the provisions of the present Convention guaranteeing: Humane treatment for the wounded and sick; prohibition of all discriminatory treatment of wounded and sick practised on the basis of differences of race, colour, religion, sex, birth or fortune."	Soviet proposal (similar text for the POW and Civilians Conventions).
	B. POW Convention: "In the case of armed conflict not of an international character occurring in the territory of one of the States, Parties to the present Convention, each Party to the conflict shall apply all the provisions of the present Convention guaranteeing: Humane treatment for prisoners of war; compliance with all established rules connected with the prisoners of war regime; prohibition of all discriminatory treatment of prisoners of war practised on the basis of differences of race, colour, religion, sex, birth or fortune."	
	C. Civilians Convention: "In the case of armed conflict not of an international character occurring in the territory of one of the States, Parties to the Convention, each Party to the conflict shall apply all the provisions of the present Convention guaranteeing: Humane treatment for the civilian population; prohibition on the territory occupied by the armed forces of either of the parties, of reprisals against the civilian population, the taking of hostages, the destruction and damaging of property which are not justified by the necessities of war, prohibition of any discriminatory treatment of the civilian population practised on the basis of differences of race, colour, religion, sex, birth or fortune."	

Sources: ICRC, Report on the Work of the Preliminary Conference of National Red Cross Societies for the Study of the Conventions and of Various Problems Relative to the Red Cross, Geneva, July 26–August 3, 1946 (Geneva: ICRC, 1946). ICRC, Report on the Work of the Conference of Government Experts for the Study of the Conventions for the Protection of War Victims, Geneva, April 14–26, 1947 (Geneva: ICRC, 1947); ICRC, XVII Conférence de la Croix-Rouge, Stockholm, Août 1948, Commission juridique, Sténogramme des séances (Geneva: ICRC, 1848); Federal Political Department of Switzerland, Final Record of the Diplomatic Conference of Geneva of 1949, vol. 2-B (Bern: Federal Political Department of Switzerland, 1963).

catalog and resolve, particularly in relation to POW treatment.[29] France, for its part, having borne the brunt of Nazi occupation, enthusiastically embraced the idea of a revamp, especially in the project of a new convention to protect civilians. Yet some British officials were unsure about the timing, while others felt that drafting a civilian convention might involve undesirable commitments and distract from what should be the central task: updating the Wounded and Sick Conventions and the POW Convention. Nevertheless, the United Kingdom eventually accepted the ICRC's invitation, as did China. For their part, the Soviets remained silent and kept everyone guessing until almost a week before the Diplomatic Conference started in 1949, when they finally announced their participation.[30]

France, the United Kingdom, and the United States all formed interdepartmental committees (ICs) to manage revisions. The United States had laid important groundwork through a U.S. War Department study of "gaps" in the POW Convention.[31] Relying on this work and the ICRC prompt, the U.S. Department of State called for the appointment of a formal U.S. IC devoted specifically to this subject, comprising representatives of the Interior, Justice, Navy, State, and War Departments, the U.S. Postal Service, and the American Red Cross. The French created a similar IC months later with a similar mix of military, civilian, and technical ministries, including the French Red Cross, the National Council of the Resistance, the National Federation of Imprisoned Resistance Fighters and Patriots, and the Prisoner of War Federation, among others.[32] The fact that many former members of the resistance were now sitting in the government shaped French vision and priorities and explains their interest in the protection of civilians and of "internal combatants."

The United Kingdom had prepared for the revisions since early 1946, chiefly through the work of its War Office (WO) and Foreign Office (FO), in occasional consultation with the Home, Colonial, and Dominions Offices.[33] Two UK ICs were eventually formed in July 1947, with the War Office (WO) and Foreign Office (FO) IC devoting its efforts to studying revisions to the Wounded and Sick Conventions and the POW Convention, and the Home Office (HO) IC to the new Civilians Convention.[34] This division responded to responsibility held over subject matter: while the WO and FO had direct experience dealing with local and foreign wounded, sick, shipwrecked, or captured soldiers, the treatment of civilians was considered a province of the HO (which also consulted the Colonial and Dominions Offices). Overall, however, the WO, FO, and HO maintained contact with one another through point persons, so decision making on the revisions to the conventions was known to all involved.

Reactions to the Idea of Regulating Internal Conflicts

Including internal conflicts in the conventions was not in the original plans of France, the United Kingdom, or the United States. Most states learned of the idea through the official ICRC preparatory documentation for the April 1947 Conference of Government Experts.[35] Sixteen governments sent delegates to Geneva.[36] Unsurprisingly, government representatives were less generous than national Red Cross societies; the formula on internal conflicts obtained a year earlier proved frail. The Dutch representative, for example, suggested this time that only the humanitarian principles of the conventions should apply. He reasoned that in internal conflicts it was often hard to know who was responsible for what, making an article-by-article application of the full treaties difficult.

From then on, the two options for "humanizing" internal conflicts became either extending the *entire text* of the conventions to internal violence without "translation," or finding a formula that included only (yet-to-be-defined) principles underlying them. In the end, the latter would win out, in the form of one especially designed article common to all the conventions.

Other interesting changes to the working formula emerged in 1947. France fought to insert the disclaimer that any civil war regulations should not impact the legal status of the combatants and or involve the recognition of the rebels' belligerence, highlighting the persistence of this concern.[37] Government experts also opted for a more precise definition of the conflicts to be covered, changing the previously vague text from 1946, "armed conflict within the borders of a state," to read "civil wars on any part of the metropolitan or colonial territory of the contracting parties."[38] They failed, however, to define "civil war" or to set a clear threshold of violence, undercutting the precision advocated earlier. Further, they reversed the changes that the national Red Cross societies had made in 1946, going back to the formula of conditional reciprocity that allowed states to only apply the rules *if* the opposite party did so in practice.[39]

The resulting text was disquieting to the ICRC. It now believed that the clause of conditional reciprocity threatened to annul the rule's application, since governments could easily use it to avoid the law. Yet it also knew that the 1947 meeting was preliminary and the language provisional.

Once the conference ended, the French, UK, and U.S. delegations reported back to their superiors and noted extensive support for the idea of including civil war in the conventions. Delegate Albert Lamarle of France noted that "the prevalent trend is to extend the scope of application as far as possible. This poses, however, a delicate issue for its juridical aspects and the foreseeable discussions on the legality or illegality of this or that authority."[40] Various members of the UK delegation listed treatment of civil war in the conventions among the "bigger points of policy to be settled" by the British team.[41] And the U.S. meeting reports, like those of the French, noted the "unanimity of opinion" regarding the proposed extension to internal conflicts.[42]

States continued to work out their views in preparation for the next meeting in 1948. Concerns over the inclusion of internal conflicts, however, did not seem to be central to the preparatory work of France and the United States. This was puzzling in the case of France given its reported distaste for the clause, but it may be partly explained by the fact that the French had other issues to worry about, including securing protections for partisans.[43] The U.S. IC did not reject the inclusion of internal conflicts on principle but opted instead to tighten the terms of its application; rather than accepting the Red Cross–proposed expression ("armed conflict not of an international character") it suggested going back to "civil war" (presumably implying a high level of violence) and inserting conditional reciprocity in the POW and Civilians Conventions, though not in the Wounded and Sick Conventions. The U.S. IC's logic was that since the latter dealt with wounded and sick combatants on land and at sea, humanitarian concerns should prevail over military ones.[44] These modifications were included in the draft conventions that the U.S. team would later bring to the following gathering of governments and Red Cross Societies in 1948.

Civil war, however, figured centrally on the long list of UK concerns. Given the important role the British assumed later on, I examine their internal revisions process more deeply.

Initial UK Attitudes

The initial reaction of the British WO/FO team after the 1947 meeting was to *accept* the civil war extension for the Wounded and Sick Conventions and the POW Convention under the condition that "the adverse party accept the obligations."[45] William Gardner, a military officer and chair of the UK WO/FO team, reasoned that the ICRC's desire to cover civil war "probably . . . springs . . . from the experiences of the IRCC [*sic*] in the Spanish Civil War reinforced by the treatment of the Resistance Forces in the European countries occupied by the Germans."[46] This supports my assertion about the importance of the Spanish Civil War on states' reception of the ICRC proposal. Despite this, Gardner worried about the application of protections to "such situations as the present difficulties in Palestine or the 'resistance' movement in Germany."[47]

Others, including the legal adviser of the FO, Joyce Gutteridge, shared this concern about the lack of a precise definition of civil war to avoid protections amid such "undesirable" situations. In addition, Gutteridge disliked the expression "adverse party" (presumably because of its potentially legitimating effect), and worried about who would be responsible for establishing whether the insurgents actually respected the conventions.[48] So difficult was the idea of internal conflicts for this UK team that it was one of the last issues to be worked out in preparation for the upcoming Stockholm meeting.[49]

By 1948 the working position of the WO/FO team was that some of the humanitarian principles of the Wounded and Sick Conventions and the POW Convention could apply to civil war (per the text adopted in 1947), with one crucial condition: it should be up to the sovereign power to decide *when* the law should become operative.[50] That decision, moreover, could only be granted after states discretionarily accepted that the rebels had met other objective conditions: they controlled territory; they had issued a formal declaration of independence and a renunciation of allegiance to the government; and/or they had formed an organized rebel army and were engaged in ongoing hostilities against their "former sovereign."[51]

Although the WO/FO IC felt that with all these safeguards the application of humanitarian principles would not prove a great burden, it decided to include conditional reciprocity as an additional guarantee that British soldiers in rebel hands would receive good treatment. These tall requirements simultaneously worked to reduce the likelihood that the law would apply, but made it more probable that *if it did*, rebels would have a clear incentive to show good conduct. The WO/FO IC recommended that any tightening of this language was undesirable.[52] Finally, for this UK team, it was important to avoid the recognition the formal belligerency of rebels even if a state decided to apply the conventions. The reason for this was twofold. First, granting belligerence would mean recognizing (and hence constituting) the opposing party as a "state," attributing an internal conflict the character and status of international war. Second, belligerence recognition allowed the insurgent party to trade and forge alliances with third states, something that obviously threatened to escalate the war and strengthen the insurgents.

The HO team's position on including civil war in the Civilians Convention was slowly shaping and would not be finalized until later.

The Seventeenth International Conference of the Red Cross in Stockholm, 1948

The working text that had emerged from the 1947 Conference of Government Experts, which included conditional reciprocity, limited humanitarian protection to "principles" (i.e., not the full conventions), and the use of the term "civil war" to imply a high level of violence, displeased the ICRC.

The organization used its position as drafter to selectively reconcile and incorporate states' suggestions and decided to eliminate conditional reciprocity from the version it presented the following year at the Seventeenth International Conference of the Red Cross in Stockholm.[53] (States were well aware of and very annoyed by this ICRC practice.) The ICRC's "tinkered" draft also expanded the scope of application to internal conflicts by making civil war one among other types of violent situations ("armed conflicts not of an international character, especially cases of civil war, colonial conflicts, or wars of religion"). Finally, the ICRC embraced states' suggestion to clarify that acceding to this rule would not have legal consequences in regard to the status of insurgents, without which it probably knew it had no chance of moving forward.

Delegations from fifty-six countries (national Red Cross societies and government representatives) came to what would be the final preparatory meeting (see table 3.1). The political context, in terms of active and latent internal conflicts, was particularly tense as the Cold War started to take shape, the Israel-Palestine conflict intensified, civil war raged in China and Greece, and colonial tensions in British Malaya (later Malaysia) and French Indochina festered. Emotions ran high, but the ICRC, with the help of its highly esteemed Swedish hosts, steered the conference successfully.

The 1948 debates on internal conflict varied slightly across three subcommissions discussing the draft conventions, but general patterns emerged. This time many delegations, including those from France, Greece, and the United States, acquiesced to the idea of an imprecise definition of conflict so as to avoid the inevitable definitional quarrels, accepting a return to the language of "armed conflict not of an international character."[54] The reference to specific types of internal conflicts (civil war, or religious and colonial conflicts) was, however, dropped after the ICRC, with American and French support, argued that adding this level of precision might weaken or narrow the scope of application. The majority of delegations also agreed that *all* the provisions of the conventions should apply instead of only their humanitarian principles.[55]

Conditional reciprocity, however, remained a bone of contention. The American delegates tried to persuade others that unless that requirement was explicit, states would only be binding themselves, not their opponents. Rebels, after all, could not sign on to international conventions and become "contracting parties"; this was a privilege of states. Hence, if a mechanism for securing rebel commitment (such as conditional reciprocity) did not figure into the rule, only governments would be responsible for complying with the law, a situation that rebels might exploit to their benefit.

By 1948 the ICRC worriedly warned against conditional reciprocity, arguing that instead of giving rebels a free pass it was more likely to give cynical governments an escape clause. Despite U.S. insistence, most participants were unconvinced of the risk of deleting conditional reciprocity, at least from the Wounded and Sick Conventions, which were by then the oldest and least controversial agreements. Accordingly, conditional reciprocity was dropped for the conventions.[56]

Faced with this loss, the United States rejected the idea that this formula should be extended to all four treaties. Its concern related specifically to the POW Convention, which would grant both parties to internal conflict the right to having a foreign "Protecting Power" care for them. This idea, tantamount to legitimating outside intervention by a state in another's internal conflict, seemed plainly unacceptable to the American and Greek delegates. Although some states worried about approving different terms for each convention, U.S. warnings about opening the door to the intervention of foreign states resonated with other participants and the majority accepted conditional reciprocity for the POW and Civilians Conventions.[57]

What emerged from the 1948 conference was not entirely discouraging to the ICRC; this compromise seemed to strike a balance between humanitarian and sovereign concerns. In addition, these drafts did not formally commit anyone. The resulting texts still awaited the final test: the Diplomatic Conference, with full treaty-making capacity.

The Final Stretch: States Prepare for the 1949 Diplomatic Conference

In 1948, France and the United States had scored some victories with regard to the rule on internal armed conflicts, and their representatives were not greatly disturbed by the ensuing formula upon their return home. However, and probably at the behest of the United Kingdom, the United States decided to push for supplementing the definition of "armed conflict not of an international character" with additional requirements for application similar to those entertained by the British.[58]

The United Kingdom's Gardner had attended the 1948 Stockholm conference mostly with the intention of "observing" other states' attitudes rather than revealing his country's cards. Once the meeting ended, he returned to London and wrote up a confidential report. Revealed in private soon after the conference to the U.S. head of delegation, his opinion was that "the draft Conventions as they now stand were not such as any government could sign if it was concerned with their workability." Despite this, Gardner thought that "with the exception of two or three major issues, the Prisoners of War, Wounded and Sick . . . Conventions would probably not present serious obstacles to our acceptance; but there may be very hard battles to get those two or three major issues settled in a form which we could accept."[59] One of those hard battles was the application of the conventions to internal conflicts.

The months prior to the Diplomatic Conference were intense for the UK teams as they produced three documents: a brief for the UK delegation to the conference; an internal paper for approval by the cabinet, with a detailed description of their preparations with suggested instructions for the delegation; and a public memorandum for circulation to participants in the Diplomatic Conference. The WO/FO team devoted to the Wounded and Sick Conventions and the POW Convention was particularly anxious to have its views authorized at the highest level possible.[60] The WO/FO IC eventually submitted a long report to the cabinet on its work, while the HO IC, responsible for the Civilians

Convention, wrote smaller documents on issues where the teams diverged, especially on internal conflicts.

"A Step in the Dark": The UK Attitude toward Internal Conflicts

Broadly speaking, there was no major disagreement of principle with the treatment of internal conflicts between the teams studying the different conventions; both disliked it and found it dangerous.[61] The WO/FO IC's option was to propose a formula including precise conditions for application. And, as has been noted, the WO/FO IC saw some potential (if marginal) humanitarian advantage from securing reciprocal humane conduct in a full-scale civil war.

To this end, the WO/FO team proposed that the application of the Wounded and Sick Conventions and the POW Convention to internal conflicts could only become possible if a violent situation occurring within states' boundaries resembled a war between states (with both sides controlling territory, acting with organized armies), if rebels respected the laws of war, and if they were willing and able to respect the Geneva Conventions.[62] The last requirement was the British team's way of including conditional reciprocity without stating it explicitly; the team knew the majority of states opposed it.[63]

The HO IC team, on the other hand, fiercely rejected any possibility of applying the protections of the Civilians Convention to internal conflicts. The issue was one "bristling with difficulties"; the risks it posed were so high, and its implications so "fantastic," that it should not "become obscured by theorizing."[64] In particular, the team worried that the conventions might protect and even give special treatment to a civilian population supportive of a rebel group; this would have all sorts of dangerous military and political implications and would hamper states' ability to apply the domestic law of treason. In short, for the HO IC the civil war idea was "at best *a step in the dark* . . . and at worst an encouragement to rebellion."[65] The team stressed the risk of legitimating rebels and considered the formal clause inserted to avoid this as mere "lip service" which in practice would do nothing to safeguard the position of a UK government.[66] For these reasons, and despite their expectation to find great pressure against their view in Geneva, the HO IC essentially recommended that the United Kingdom should risk pushing for the rejection of the clause by convincing other states of the perils involved.[67]

Cabinet approval for these positions remained uncertain until less than a month before the 1949 conference opened. On March 28 a high-level meeting took place to make final decisions; in attendance were the prime minister, Clement Attlee; the lord chancellor, William Jowitt; the secretary of state for the Home

Department, James Chuter Ede; the secretary of state for war, Emmanuel Shinwell; the attorney general, Sir Hartley Shawcross; the parliamentary undersecretary of state for foreign affairs, Christopher Mayhew; UK head of delegation, Robert Craigie, and the War Office's William Gardner. In a nutshell, attendees sided with the HO team and scolded the WO/FO team for being dangerously flexible. The summary of the confidential discussion is worth quoting at length:

> It would be a matter of great practical difficulty to say at what point a riot or rebellion reached the stage at which it should be regarded as a civil war for the purposes of the Convention. In law, it was by no means clear that, as the proposal stood, the decision would lie within the discretion of the Sovereign Power. . . . This country could not rule out the possibility of insurrection by anti-partition elements in Northern Ireland and there was always the danger of Communist uprisings in various European countries. . . . The only practicable course was to apply civil war at the instigation of the Sovereign Power. . . . [T]he British Government should decline to sign the Convention, or sign it subject to reservation, if its views were not met on this matter.[68]

If the UK delegation (through the WO) had internally shown a modicum of ambivalence, these instructions made no bones about how to proceed: kill the provision, and failing that, in the words of Attorney General Hartley Shawcross, "resist it to the 'the bitter end' for the Civilians Convention."[69]

Status Politics in 1949

Before analyzing what transpired at the 1949 Diplomatic Conference and, given their importance to my theoretical argument, let me address the international politics of status and hierarchy at the time.

Historians broadly agree that World War II and the early Cold War brought about intense material and ideological struggle internationally.[70] The war and its outcome radically upset preexisting social hierarchies. The United States emerged as *the* Western superpower, while European empires saw their great-power status threatened. The Soviet Union demanded superpower recognition and treatment, and European colonies in Africa and Asia were quickly swept over by the impetus to acquire self-determination. America's superpower status went largely unquestioned, yet the European empires and the Soviet Union faced deep status anxiety as they reconciled their postwar capabilities with their self-identity and their aspirations.[71] Britain and France were caught in a special bind: they were war victors, but both had been materially weakened (particularly France), were overshadowed by U.S.-Soviet superpower rivalry, and—most importantly—their imperialism clashed with an increasingly strong postwar movement toward human rights and self-determination.

Historical accounts extensively document British and French status anxiety at this time. As Ernest Bevin, the influential foreign secretary, opined, "His Majesty's Government do [*sic*] not accept the view . . . that we have ceased to be a Great Power, or the contention that we have to play that role. . . . The very fact that we have fought so hard for liberty, and paid such a price, warrants our retaining this position; and indeed it places a duty upon us to continue to retain it."[72] Charles de Gaulle harbored deep concerns with preserving French prestige after the war. He cited "the two-thousand years' pact between the grandeur of France and the liberty of the world" to persuade war victors to accord his country a seat at the Great Power table.[73] And despite its clear postwar material weakness, "De Gaulle and his foreign minister attempted to 'sell' the idea that France's unique vocation and role in the world rest on its glorious past, and that the world needed the leadership of France no less than France wished to continue leading it."[74] Regarding the Soviet Union, Eric Ringmar notes, "Instead of being secure in the great power status granted his country, Stalin became the leader of an insecure superpower wanna-be. Sensitive to the slightest humiliation, Stalin sought to avoid any occasion that would emphasize the relative inferiority of his country and the supremacy of the capitalist enemy."[75]

In the unstable postwar environment the emerging East-West conflict was, David C. Engerman notes, a positional "battle for influence," precisely in the sense of socially competitive status politics. He adds, "What made this conflict an ideological one . . . was the nature of the ideologies themselves. Soviet and American ideologies were both universalistic; they both held that their concepts of society applied to all nations and peoples." Therefore, "each side feared the advance of the other as a step backward."[76] Robert Jervis goes further and classifies the Cold War as an *identity* competition, since "what was at stake was nothing less than each side's view of the rightness of the cause, the universalism of its values, and the answer to the question of whose side history was on."[77]

Status competition likewise pervaded British-Soviet relations. Anne Deighton explains that "leading British decision-makers assessed early on that they would have to base postwar foreign policy both on the threat from Communist ideology and on the consequences of the arrival of the Soviet Union as the new great power on the world stage." Prominent figures believed that the Soviets had chosen the United Kingdom "for a political and diplomatic onslaught" from which it had to defend itself in all manners. Therefore, at the postwar moment, "the defining trait of foreign policy was to maintain Britain's place as a major global and imperial power in a rapidly changing period of fresh ideological and power-political challenges. . . . The quest to sustain the image and the reality of great powerdom through leadership, influence, and 'punching above our weight' was part of the *mentalité* of British planners, the military, and the politicians." In short, since 1946 a Cold War mind-set dominated Whitehall, identifying Soviet communism as the crucial external menace of the British Commonwealth and the democratic West. It was a "war of ideas, of loyalty to beliefs, and of all political mischief short of war."[78]

The postwar push for decolonization added to the explosive Cold War social contest. Although American administrations initially showed distaste for continued European imperialism,[79] Cold War containment altered such thinking in short order. Deighton notes that "by the turn of the decade both the British and the Americans had come to see Britain's imperial possessions as having strategic utility for a global balance that was favorable to the West."[80] And even before the decolonized world gained sufficient strength of its own (around 1955), the USSR used anticolonial rhetoric to chastise European powers and with them the broader liberal democratic West in an international propaganda war for "hearts and minds." By late 1947, key officials within the USSR had explicitly outlined a strongly anti-Western foreign policy strategy which "divided the world into two camps: the non-democratic, imperialists led by the US, and the democratic, anti-imperialist, led by the Soviet Union."[81] International forums and diplomatic conferences quickly became a key battleground of Cold War / decolonization politics.[82] In 1962, Harold Jacobson asserted that "the USSR and the Soviet Bloc have been the most outspoken critics of colonialism in the United Nations . . . [they] have granted the colonial powers no quarter."[83]

In short, status concerns and struggles were characteristic of the postwar period, and postwar normative politics specifically challenged Britain and France's deeply held status, self-identity, and interests as liberal-democratic, imperial Great Powers.[84] Previously they were the stewards of international order; now they risked becoming retrograde declining middle powers.[85]

The Diplomatic Conference of 1949

Convened by the Swiss government, the Diplomatic Conference that revised the Geneva Conventions opened on April 21, 1949, and lasted four months. Delegations from nearly every state in the world attended (a total of sixty-four, five as observers without the vote; see tables 3.1 and 3.3.) Although several nongovernmental organizations sent representatives and written suggestions, the ICRC remained the central nongovernmental protagonist. The press in Geneva and elsewhere in Switzerland actively followed negotiations; the international press covered them occasionally.

The conference agreed on a one state, one vote procedure, with decisions in committee and plenary taken by simple majority via a public show of hands and a recorded roll-call vote upon request. To its conduct proceedings, the conference created four substantive committees: three devoted to the main texts of the conventions, and a fourth Joint Committee focusing on the Articles common to all conventions, including CA3. All governments entitled to a vote sat within the Joint Committee.

The issue that most marked the political dynamics before the conference was the question of Soviet attendance, announced to everyone's surprise only two weeks prior to the start of proceedings. The news that the Soviets were coming in the company of seven "satellites" sent Western channels abuzz with uncertainty. Very quickly the Soviets revealed to behave in exactly the opposite way most expected them to: instead of sabotaging the conference, they appeared thoughtful, well prepared, and more rhetorically humanitarian than any Western liberal state present. This would prove to have important effects on the process and outcomes.[86]

The first debate on the application of the conventions to internal conflicts happened over two meetings held late April in the Joint Committee. The ICRC introduced the text approved in Stockholm with a reminder that states had decided in 1948 to delete conditional reciprocity in two of the conventions (the POW Convention and the Civilians Convention) and to include it in the other two (the Wounded and Sick Conventions). "The two texts should be brought into conformity,"[87] noted the ICRC's representative, wisely framing the debate to be about the *how* and not the *whether*. At this stage, the idea was still to *extend the full conventions* to internal conflicts, not to create a tailored article.

France and the United Kingdom reacted swiftly. Setting the tone right from the start, French delegate Lamarle stated that it was "impossible to carry the protection of individuals to the point of sacrificing the rights of States. In order to protect the rights of the State the French delegation would propose an amendment making it impossible for forms of disorder, anarchy or brigandage to claim the protection of the Convention under a mask of politics or on any other pretext."[88] Lamarle suggested that only well-organized military forces with a responsible authority capable of enforcing and respecting a convention in a given territory should become eligible for any protections.

The UK head delegate, Robert Craigie, plainly declared that the conventions could only apply to wars as defined in international law—that is, wars between sovereign states. Covering other forms of conflict, he said, was a source of "great difficulties" because it "would appear to give the status of belligerents to insurgents, whose right to wage war could not be recognized." This, as Craigie put it, "would strike at the root of national sovereignty and endanger national security."[89] This was a thinly veiled public admission of the private British desire to kill the extension.

Australia, Canada, China, Greece, Spain, and the United States sided with the French and vouched for having clearer, stricter terms to avoid overinclusion. The conditions cited in 1949 were basically the same as those raised in previous meetings: a high level of violence; clearly establishing *who* would decide if a civil war was taking place; excluding protective powers from internal conflicts; requiring that rebels have an organizational structure, control of territory and population, and that they are willing and able to respect the conventions; and decoupling the application of the conventions from the legal recognition of belligerence.

Not all other states agreed, however. Denmark, Hungary, Mexico, Monaco, Norway, and Romania voiced their discontent with such heavy requirements. Mexico noted that "in civil wars there might also be movements for emancipation of a morally creditable character," praising the "courage" states had shown in Stockholm to subject the rights of states to humanitarian considerations. Even if certain precautions were valid, "the Conference should not be deaf to the voice of those who are suffering."[90] Hungary and Romania reminded others that the point of the conference should be to extend humanitarian protections as widely as possible without undercutting them through conditional reciprocity.[91]

However, the most forceful rebuttal of the position shown by Western states came from the Soviets. Soviet representative General Nikolai Vassilievitch Slavin took the Americans, British, French, and Greeks to task, noting that their proposals all tended to undermine the humanitarianism of the conventions. His arguments are worth quoting at some length:

> The United Kingdom Delegation had alluded to the fact that colonial and civil wars were not regulated by international law, and that decisions in this respect would be out of place in the text of the Conventions. This theory was not convincing. . . . Since the creation of the Organization of the United Nations, this question seemed settled. Article 2 of the [United Nations] Charter provided that Member States must ensure peace and world security. They could not be indifferent to the cessation of hostilities, no matter the character or localization of the conflict. Colonial and civil wars came within the purview of international law.

Slavin also chastised the French for pushing the idea of conditional reciprocity, arguing that that "if [it] were followed, there would be a danger of one party declaring, without proof, that the other party was not in a position to ensure order, and of justifying any violation of the basic humanitarian principles of the Conventions." This reasoning was exactly identical to that of the ICRC.[92]

About a Greek proposal to subject the application of humanitarian principles to formal recognition of belligerence in civil war, Slavin said that it was "unacceptable. . . . This amendment restricted the scope of the text of the Draft which was approved at Stockholm and sapped its humanitarian bases." Similarly, "the proposal of the United States Delegation, by subordinating the application of the Convention to the decision of one Party, was no longer in harmony with the humanitarian principles governing these Conventions." In conclusion, Slavin "pointed out that civil and colonial wars were often accompanied by violations of international law and were characterized by cruelty of all kinds. The suffering of the population in the instance of civil and colonial wars was as distressing as that which led Henry Dunant to realize the need for regulating the laws of warfare."[93]

This spirited Soviet stance surprised everyone. Although there are reasons to explain genuine Soviet sympathy for the prevention of civil war atrocities—the USSR having itself emerged from a bloody revolution—it seems naive to accept that the Soviets were simply acting out of humanitarianism.[94] Rather, their position at the conference, as in other international forums and rule-making processes occurring at the time, seemed strategically crafted to embarrass Western countries, highlighting the inconsistency of their concrete legal proposals with their professed liberal-democratic worldview and seeking to gain the international moral high ground.

Moreover, it is imaginable that by pushing for broad protections in internal conflicts, the USSR wished not only to "facilitate" communist uprisings in various parts of the world but also to influence the political direction of the postcolonial world. These claims will require careful weighing at Russian archives, yet primary evidence confirms that the British and the French did perceive the Soviet prodding as a hypocritical attempt to undermine them politically.

Soviet intentions aside, in light of all these stark discrepancies, the Swiss representative suggested forming a subcommittee to work out a compromise formula. The British acquiesced, and asked for a few days' postponement "to enable delegations to consider this problem in informal talks before the Committee suggested by the Swiss representative was set up."[95]

London and Paris: We Have a Problem

The confidential correspondence exchanged between the British and French delegates sitting in Geneva and their governments back home shows that alarms went off after these initial debates. Lamarle wrote various memoranda to Paris in late

April and early May describing the diversity of arguments, and particularly the polarization of the British and the Soviets. His reports confirmed that while France supported some kind of formula extending some of the protections of the conventions to civil war, it also found the 1948 Stockholm text dangerous. In response, he introduced an initial French draft that more closely resembled his country's preferences, especially looking to avoid granting protections to "any violent movement or even mere banditry."[96]

British correspondence, however, revealed extreme anxiety. Three members of the UK delegation wrote to London depicting the tensions and requesting more flexible instructions. One wrote:

> As . . . anticipated the Delegation has run into very heavy weather already on the subject of civil war. . . . The whole of the fire of this subject is being concentrated on our attitude to civilians and the Soviet Union is allying itself very strongly with the humanitarian school in pressing for the widest possible application of the Conventions to civil and colonial wars. Those who have ventured to suggest that the application to civil war should be restricted are being labeled legalistic. . . . The whole delegation is, I think, now convinced that if we maintain our attitude we shall probably find ourselves in a minority of one.[97]

British delegates fretted nervously over the negative impression their conservative position was creating in the eyes of domestic and foreign public opinion and among a majority of delegations. They worried over a recent article in the *Times* encouraging "every civilized Government" to embrace the rule on internal conflicts, as well as about the negative attention British skepticism was receiving in the local press in Geneva.[98] One British delegate wrote, "There have been some very critical articles in the Swiss papers. One of them even goes as far as to suggest, in effect, that the disintegration of the British Empire is proceeding at so fast a pace that we are determined to keep every possible power we can in order to preserve some of the empire. We here are quite satisfied that we shall never get what our instructions require." Not even the support of friendly New Zealand was assured: "The international background here is against us. Our authority and influence as reasonable people will be seriously undermined if we acquire a reputation for intransigence on an issue in which the overwhelming body of opinion is against us."[99]

Inside the negotiating room, British delegates were aware of the fact that most delegations had "picked out this as one of the necessary extensions to the Convention which recent hostile events had demonstrated as essential." They worried that "nearly every nation of any importance, (including those who are in, or have recently experienced civil war,) have gone to the rostrum to adhere to this principle, the United Kingdom *being the solitary voice* raised in favour of not applying the Conventions to civil war."[100]

The delegates were notably shaken by the bad publicity and isolation among "nearly every nation of any importance," including close Western friends, and sensitive to Soviet rhetorical lashing. While other states had suggested limits on the internal conflicts proposal, none publicly wanted it dead. Further exchanges with colleagues in London clarified these concerns. A delegation telegram noted, "There is no doubt *we shall be alone* in adopting a purely negative attitude. . . . The political situation is that . . . the United Kingdom Delegation is being described in the Conference as 'obstructive' by the followers of the U.S.S.R. line and 'restrictive' by, for example, the Australians."[101]

Clearly the UK delegation felt anxious in its isolation. Other states had suggested limiting the inclusion of internal conflicts in the Civilians Convention, but none wanted it nixed. This evidence, I argue, strongly supports the operation of the opprobrium through the forum isolation of the minority in Geneva.

Yet these and subsequent communications also revealed that the British were not prepared to support just any text that emerged. Rightly noting the divergences of opinion and concerns about how "broad" the Stockholm proposal was, they reasoned, "if we adopt an intransigent attitude we will lose everything. If we are accommodating and prepared to compromise, we may well be able to get not all what we want but very much that we want [*sic*]."[102] This was the logic according to which they would act from then on, one that can be characterized as "rational" but under heavy social constraints.

Devising an "Acceptable Compromise"

The situation in Geneva did not improve for the detractors of the idea of humanizing internal conflicts. After three weeks of debate, the Joint Committee voted on the general question of whether the topic should be included in the conventions, with an overwhelming positive vote of 10–1 (with one abstention).[103] The verdict on the *whether* had at last come; the struggle now turned to the *how*.

And indeed, the *how* continued to stir much controversy. Some options already existed: the 1948 Stockholm text; an initial French proposal that allowed for the application of the conventions given formal conditions had been met; and a proposal by the American delegation including conditional reciprocity, as well as a mix of subjective and objective requirements for application.

Disagreement prevailed between those supporting conditions and those against. In search for a solution, the chairman of the Special Committee of the Joint Committee suggested forming a smaller Working Party to hash out a compromise text between the different proposals (see table 3.2). The resulting text, however, retained several of the requirements aired previously (state recognition, rebel control of territory, high level of internal organization, conditional reciprocity), again drawing strong critiques from the ICRC, Italy, Switzerland, and the USSR.[104] The ICRC was emphatic in noting that "the text drawn up by the Working Party could never have been applied in any recent case of civil war. It did not represent a progress with regard to the present situation."[105] Given these reactions, the Working Party went back to the drawing board.

Although they were frustrating for the participating delegates, these debates were useful for states in collectively shaping the parameters of acceptability of the eventual rule—that is, they progressively clarified which elements might be too controversial to make it into the final text (namely, the requirements of conditional reciprocity, state discretion, and the conditions of territorial control and organization by rebels). This attests undoubtedly to the rhetorical power of the ICRC, Latin American countries like Mexico and Uruguay, Switzerland, and, most crucially (though for different reasons), the nations of the Soviet bloc. Without their sustained pressure and persistent refrain that inserting formal conditions would work to invalidate the application of humanitarian law in internal conflicts by providing unscrupulous states with excuses not to apply it, any legal outcome of these negotiations would have probably included at least some of them. In the end, further confirming the persistent and widely shared concern among states of avoiding the legitimation of rebels, the only explicit condition that remained in the adopted text of CA3 was that the application of the conventions to internal conflict would not change the rebels' legal status.

Covert Pushback: The "Not Dotting the I's" Strategy

The British delegates in Geneva had cried for help, but had they been heard? The response from London showed sympathy with their compatriots' anxiety. One official wryly noted, "Our Delegations worst forebodings . . . have come true. . . . Other countries will oppose us for the sake of opposition or of showing us up in a bad light in the eyes of all the humanitarians; the Commonwealth delegates have been told to take a less restrictive stance than ours and the Americans, I gather, are sitting on the fence. I think it is important to consider the use the Communist and 'fellow-traveler' press will make of our legalistic attitude."[106] He later concluded, "If we stick to our guns, we shall not change the views held by the majority of other delegations and we shall earn more unpopularity than if we had refused the invitation of the Swiss to attend the Conference."[107]

Another London-based official shared this sentiment: "Now, surely there is something very surprising if you find the UK taking up a negative attitude to this proposal when it is supported by lots of other countries which have recently experienced civil wars and are likely to do so frequently. . . . [I]s not there probably some modicum of truth in what Sir R. Craigie describes as the 'reaction of the conference to our attitude' that the UK is influenced by conservative legalism and is indifferent to, and indeed opposing, the efforts of others to effect amendments and extensions to international law?"[108] He concluded, "It is quite clear, I think, that the Attorney General and Lord Chancellor will have to agree in the change of instructions."[109]

Showing recalcitrance before an audience that included allies, neutrals, and rivals alike was for the British quite embarrassing. But did such embarrassment translate into a change of heart? What follows confirms that it did not. Instead of being rationally convinced or morally persuaded, the British seem to have been socially pressured into recalibrating their tactics with a view to the humanitarian pressures in the room.

Alongside his plea for flexibility, UK head delegate Craigie drafted the terms of a possible accommodation and shared them with London. He reasoned that the original cabinet concerns "can be overcome. We all feel that it will be necessary to abandon any formula *specifically* leaving the decision in this matter to the Sovereign Power, and to seek rather some formula which, *while not dotting the i's,* would in fact leave the last word to the Sovereign Power."[110] This entailed decoupling the application of humanitarian law in civil war, from the recognition of belligerency or the legal status of the rebels and restricting the idea of extending the full conventions to internal armed conflicts, to a more limited and "tailored" formula featuring selected humanitarian provisions. Craigie mused, "If we make the relevant provisions relatively innocuous, would there really be an objection to this? On the contrary, might it not have the effect of side-tracking outside pressure for recognition of belligerency if it could be shown that these humanitarian provisions were being applied in a satisfactory way?" Tellingly, the British delegate explained that by achieving this,

> we would thereby have some room for manoeuvre and *it would go far to remove from us the stigma which was hampering us throughout the conference of being anti-progressive and humanitarian.* "The UK seeking international authority to use brutal methods for the suppression of revolt in the remnants of crumbling empire"—quotation in one Swiss paper. At the same time we could, with care, ensure that only the most harmless provisions would be made applicable and these would not in any way endanger the rights or power of a legitimate Government to re-establish, by all proper means, its control over its own territory against insurgents.[111]

Craigie also intimated that the French were "tracking along the same lines as we are, though we had not disclosed this particular point with them and we had arrived at our conclusions independently."[112] Indeed, it was only a matter of time before the British and the French joined forces.

In closing his note, Craigie commented on the status cost the United Kingdom might pay if instructions were not loosened:

> I should be glad to know whether, if the United Kingdom, alone [among the] nations represented here, were to make a reservation on civil war, this would be likely to have unfortunate repercussions on our foreign relations. Must we not expect, in such a case, to be strongly criticized in the United States, where the humanitarian tide seems to be running strong? And can we . . . afford to lose any friends there just at present? . . . I am afraid the question is rather urgent because our position here is becoming increasingly embarrassing. A member of the very friendly New Zealand Delegation privately expressed the hope that some change in our attitude on civil war would soon be possible because we were tending to lose much of our influence by ploughing this lonely furrow. I know this view is shared by other Commonwealth Delegations.[113]

The delegation was heard. A group of representatives from the FO, the HO, and the WO, as well as the Attorney General's Office, the Colonial Office, the Lord Chancellor's Office, and the Treasury Solicitor's Office met in London to discuss the civil war issue and decided that the United Kingdom should no longer press for the article's deletion.[114] In a subsequent high-level meeting, the cabinet of ministers essentially approved this recommendation.[115]

Pressured Empires Strike Back

French delegate Lamarle received orders from Paris to continue pressing for a restrictive text with formal requirements for application and conditional reciprocity. He knew this flew in the face of what most states in Geneva wanted. In effect, days later he wrote back confirming that despite his efforts, a great number of delegations were feeling more charitable. His strategy—he clarified—had been to continue participating in the debates to ensure that the terms of the civil war inclusion were "as attenuated as possible."[116] Adopting a wholly negative attitude, Lamarle warned, would risk tipping the balance in favor of the most humanitarian versions of the text and very far from their own preferences. This was essentially equivalent to the British position and strategy.

By mid-May the French and British delegates (separately) realized the similarity of their intentions and, in their words, the *petite minorité* they made up.[117] They devised a joint goal: to propose a text that guaranteed the application of some (selected) humanitarian principles that were not overtly threatening to an undefined class of internal conflicts ("armed conflicts not of an international character") without explicitly calling for conditional reciprocity but with the implicit understanding that lower-intensity rebellions were excluded.[118] Their goal from then on would be to craft a formula acceptable to them but with the potential of gaining others' support while keeping the more extremist humanitarian versions at bay. It is this deceptive, reactive attitude of the British and French that I label *covert pushback*.

Hammering out the desired magic formula would no doubt be difficult given the range of critiques. Lamarle went back to Paris seeking new instructions to see how far he could really go. In the meantime, the Working Party had circulated a revised draft. The UK delegate Craigie expressed his satisfaction with it, since it resembled his initial idea to craft different language for the Wounded and Sick, POW, and Civilians Conventions without conditional reciprocity but with several other requirements. Yet Craigie also recognized the importance of supporting France "not only because their position is closest to ours, but because the problem of civil war is, at the moment, a more serious one for France than for any other of our Allies."[119]

The French delegation returned with fresh instructions in early June. Paris was now in support of an article that would figure in all four conventions but that only included the "general humanitarian principles" originally listed in an eventually deleted draft preamble to the Civilians Convention and which contained neither explicit requirements for application nor conditional reciprocity. French instructions, surprisingly, claimed that the debates in Geneva had "convinced" the French government "that, on a matter such as civil war, which by its nature gives rise to such deeply divergent opinions, one thing is important: to apply as broadly as possible the humanitarian principles which lay at the basis of the Universal Declaration of Human Rights and the Genocide Convention recently approved by the UN. These principles are precisely the same as those that appear on the Preamble of the Convention on Civilians and which, it is desired, should be extended to the other Conventions." Surprisingly, the French no longer worried about formal conditions of application.[120]

It is hard to know exactly whether the "convincing" that had taken place in Paris was the result of persuasion. The instructions to Lamarle justified this change in part by saying that "in taking this position, the French government is consciously staying faithful to the ideal of humanity that has constantly inspired its policy." The rest of Lamarle's letter, however, revealed that the changed French attitude was not selfless: "At the same time, this position presents the advantage for states which like France, the UK, Belgium, the Netherlands, etc. have overseas possessions and which, in these dominions, can face conflicts bearing traits of a civil war, to avoid having to apply the precise text of the Conventions."[121] The letter also confirmed that the French were ready to file a formal reservation if their views as depicted were not met. It can be said with certainty, then, that the French had accommodated through the social pressures evinced in debates.

The next step was to see how the Special Committee debating the issue of internal conflicts reacted to the new options, including a redraft of the (still very restrictive) first Working Party text and the new French proposal. This debate took place on June 15. With the support of Burma, Monaco, the United Kingdom, Uruguay, and the ICRC, the French text gained some momentum. Still, Australia, Norway, and the United States continued to support the Working Party text, which offered greater humanitarian protection while stipulating stringent conditions for application. In response, the Greek, Norwegian, and Soviet delegates (who were allegedly sitting on the fence) encouraged forming a second Working Party to redraft the French text.

The French delegation seized the opportunity and took the drafting lead within this new Working Party. In the meantime, the British sought and received clearance from London about the French formula.[122] Having finally found a palatable text, the UK delegation set out to lobby other diplomats for support, particularly the British Commonwealth states and the United States, even using the implausible argument that supporting proposals from Western allies was militarily beneficial without clarifying exactly what these might be.[123] (Indeed, the military argument, however, was neither clear nor convincing because when Craigie pitched it privately to U.S. delegate Leland Harrison, the latter admitted he did not see where the benefit lay. Still, Harrison agreed not to oppose the French text.)[124]

The reworked French proposal—which when modified became the final CA3—was debated in the Special Committee on June 24. As Lamarle said while introducing it, "the text . . . contained no clause of a political character which could possibly lead to contestation."[125] During discussions, the United States admitted that while it preferred the binding application of a wider set of protections, it would accept the French text with improvements, including language allowing the ICRC to offer its services and a clarification on judicial guarantees.[126] Norway also proposed the constructive addition of considering humanitarian safeguards for captured combatants. At this stage the only two states that did not support the French text were Australia, which supported a stricter alternative, and the USSR, which had remained silent and reportedly awaited instructions from Moscow.

After this debate, the French-tailored text from the Second Working Party clearly stood out as the likeliest acceptable compromise. It still faced hurdles, however. On July 8, the Soviets finally received orders from Moscow and presented for the first time their own text on internal conflicts to the committee. As the British and French had anticipated, an "extremely humanitarian" Soviet proposal had emerged which essentially supported the application of the conventions as a whole to conflicts not of an international character. The French and British joint action to work out an acceptable text and lobby for support had been proved prescient and stood to ward off the Soviet formula. Would it?

A Missed Opportunity

On July 8 and July 11, after over a dozen meetings on the subject, the Special Committee put the options to a vote. Shockingly, all the formulas were rejected, with the French proposal failing narrowly.[127] Two contingencies led to this outcome. First, the Burmese delegate, General Tun Hla Oung, received instructions from his government to completely oppose inclusion of internal conflicts in the conventions, probably responding to an aggravating insurrection at home.[128] Second, the Uruguayan representative, who was acting as chair of the Second Working Party and who reportedly supported the French text, did not vote because he was unsure that as chair he could still cast a ballot. Regardless, the Swiss chairman wondered whether the idea of internal conflicts clause should be eliminated altogether.

After the long struggle to negotiate a formula, these results left most diplomats apparently deflated. Only Burma's Oung celebrated the outcome openly, noting that the "Eastern countries he represented" could not at all agree on the coverage of civil war through the conventions.

This turn of events offered the original detractors a precious opportunity to support the exclusion of internal conflicts from the humanitarian treaties. But they did not. Instead, Australia, the United Kingdom, and the USSR took issue with the vote and urged the chairman to submit the various options to the larger Joint Committee, where the issue could finally be settled.[129]

Why did this occur? The United Kingdom could have predictably recalibrated back to its initial preference for excluding internal conflicts from the conventions. This was the perfect moment for it, yet Britain did not seize it. Were British diplomats ultimately convinced of the morality or legal soundness of humanizing internal conflict? Did they suddenly see some real instrumental benefit from the redrafted rule? Neither answer comports with the evidence. Instead, alert to the social dynamics of the negotiating environment, the British strategically reasoned that they stood to gain more from supporting the French text, acceptable to the majority of the participants, than from supporting alternatives they knew were unpopular and unlikely to win out: total deletion, a very restrictive text, or an extremely humanitarian (Soviet) one.

After the French text was rejected, the UK delegation in Geneva reconvened to strategize, deciding against throwing its weight behind the other proposals. UK delegate John Alexander suggested they should accept the momentary failure "with good grace," and that the best tactic would be to try to reopen the debate in the Joint Committee "when it might be possible to gather Latin American support for the French proposal."[130]

Craigie, for his part, reported back to London admitting that they had "reached a strange position on our negotiations and votes." Craigie recalled "that our original hope had been to exclude the application of the Conventions to any form of civil war" and described the process by which they had come to support the French text. Yet given recent developments, Craigie wrote, "we are now faced with the possibility of being landed with one of the three texts or of having no reference to Civil War in the Conventions at all, i.e.: (i) No text at all; (ii) Stockholm text; (iii) First Working Party Text; (iv) Second Working Party text."[131]

He then spelled out a strategy which, though intricate, boiled down to the United Kingdom lending its support to the alternative most likely to win acceptance—that is, the French-tailored (Second Working Party) text. Although the UK delegation continued to prefer the complete rejection of internal conflicts in the conventions, it recognized that this outcome was, under the circumstances, improbable. The best option was to try to block the "undesirable" (overtly humanitarian) texts or "unlikely" (overtly conditional) drafts by throwing their weight behind their own text, which had, after all, emerged as a sort of compromise.[132]

In addition to strategy, Craigie expressed regard for the work his and the French delegations had put into designing a workable solution. In a private conversation Lamarle had told Alexander that "after all their efforts on the subject, the French delegation could not accept any proposal to omit entirely any reference to Civil War in the conventions. The French were anxious that the second Working Party's text should be adopted." The UK delegates also felt that they should support the French out of loyalty, a social motive.[133] Further proof of this is that when the Burmese delegate approached Craigie to rally support for total deletion, Craigie responded that "this was far more acceptable to the United Kingdom but that we could not break with the French, who had said that they would not now go back on the decision to have a reference to Civil War in the Convention." The Burmese then prodded the UK diplomats, saying that the French did not want a reference to internal conflicts either. Ultimately, Craigie clarified that "if he could support the Burmese amendment without breaking faith with the French, that would be the best line to take."[134] Yet he knew that the current state of the debate might make that impossible.

The behind-the-scenes alliance between the French and the United Kingdom seems to have worked, because once presented again to the Joint Committee, all the versions of the text were rejected except for the French draft, approved by a vote of 21–6 (with fourteen abstentions).[135]

The Moment of Decision

The decisive moment came at the final plenary voting when the approved draft faced off against the Soviet proposal and the Burmese motion to delete.

Spirited interventions preceded the final vote before the plenary. The words of the Soviet delegate were a testament of the road traveled: "No other issue has given rise to such a long discussion and to such a detailed and exhaustive study as the question of the extension of the Convention to war victims of conflicts not of an international character." Surely to the annoyance of the British, the Soviet diplomat further noted that from the debates it was clear that "the provision for the application of the four Convention to colonial and civil wars is supported by the overwhelming majority of the delegations at this Conference." The delegate's speech continued to vouch aggressively for the Soviet proposal, singling out a variety of provisions which would be left out if the French draft were approved, including the prohibition of reprisals against the civilian population and specific protections for women and children.[136]

Following the Soviets was Burma's General Oung, who had at this stage become the only public opponent. His speech, equally remarkable, systematically recounted the many options that had been considered throughout the preceding months and shrewdly highlighted the many different dangers they presented to national sovereignty. Taking other states to task for supporting amply humanitarian language, he noted, pointedly, that "some of you, especially the delegations of Colonial Powers, have really been remarkably broadminded to support the Article, though it is going to encourage Colonial wars. . . . So the only help that the Article will give, if you adopt it, will be to those who desire to loot, pillage, political power by undemocratic means, or those foreign ideologies seeking their own advancement by inciting the population of another country." The Burmese diplomat made a stellar case for not including internal conflicts in the conventions, pushing as many sovereignty buttons as he could.[137]

Yet the articulate alacrity and fearmongering of the Burmese fell on deaf ears. France and Britain did not move, and Burma remained the only delegation to publicly oppose the inclusion of internal conflicts in the convention. Others' reactions from other states varied in tone and content. Eastern European countries such as Czechoslovakia, Hungary, and Romania unsurprisingly preferred the Soviet draft, while others asked for clarifications on the meaning of the approved version or voiced support for the received Stockholm draft. Yet in the words of Swiss delegate Plinio Bolla, a stark defender of the French formula, "half a loaf is better than no bread."[138]

The weight of forum isolation proved heavy for the Burmese delegate, who publicly complained of suddenly being threatened with "losing the respect of other countries" and being "placed outside the laws of humanity" for voicing his considered views. His distress was such that he requested the final vote be made secret so he would not be placing his (closeted) "friends" in an embarrassing position.[139]

The final (public but unrecorded) votes in the Joint Committee and later in plenary confirmed the predictions of the colonial powers; in the Joint Committee, the Soviet proposal lost with a vote of 20–11 (with seven abstaining), while the French draft was overwhelmingly accepted with a 34–0 vote (with ten abstaining). Finally, the plenary of the conference adopted the French draft as Common Article 3 to all four conventions with a vote of 34–12 (with only one abstention).

The international regulation of internal armed conflicts through CA3 was not a preordained outcome. This chapter illustrates what a complex configuration of political circumstance, actors, forces, and contingency had to occur to produce it.

Despite the complexity, however, I identified the importance of a specific combination of historical conditions and agency. With regard to questions of where the impetus for regulation originated, the first section depicted how the shock brought on by additional conflict situations was compounded by the "underperformance" of the initial Red Cross resolutions from 1921 and soon prompted the ICRC to believe that international binding regulation was necessary. The International Committee's difficult experience during the Spanish Civil War operated as a crucial driver. The traumas that conflict brought on embedded within the broader revulsion toward the atrocities of World War II motivated a majority of states to welcome the revision of the existing body of humanitarian law, including the introduction of regulations for internal conflicts.

Beyond explaining regulatory impetus, this chapter demonstrated that CA3 was the product of social pressures, and specifically of forum isolation, between diplomatic delegations forcefully debating in Geneva. By the mid-1940s most states admitted that an international humanitarian rule for internal conflicts was desirable. Yet, attitudes toward its specific design varied, and a handful of powerful states showed no enthusiasm whatsoever for the idea.

While moral concerns colored the position of most states, national security interests retained their pull. Many states wanted to insert high requirements for the application of the law to internal conflicts while colonial empires, especially the British, acted as the most skeptical in the room. Remarkably, various very persistent voices effectively blocked the formal insertion of conditional reciprocity and other requirements into the text. The pro-regulation majority also effectively cajoled the British into acquiescing to accepting that a rule would emerge out of status anxiety. Notably, the Soviets' fierce public prodding seems to have pushed the sociopolitical "buttons" of a British delegation that was especially sensitive being perceived as backward, decaying, and legalistic particularly vis-à-vis the premier Communist state in the world. The emerging Cold War ideological competition evidently served as a crucial contextual factor that heightened the urgency and political poignancy of Soviet-induced pressures. In addition to the Soviets, the unwillingness of fellow Commonwealth allies or the US to toe the British line had a discernible social-psychological effect on the UK delegation. Swiss newspapers' derision of their retrograde stance rounded the circle of social pressure.

Yet, as described, the process did not end there. Forum isolation did not persuade UK diplomats to change their position. Rather, the Brits bounced back by strategically planning to insert language that "without dotting the I's," might safeguard their sovereignty woes. Along the way they realized they were not trekking a lonely path and liaised with the French to craft a joint text that pleased them as well as the humanitarian voices in the room. The fact that the Soviets came forward with an "ultra-humanitarian" version of the article only reinforced the British and French beliefs that pushing for their "moderate" text was the best bet given the circumstances, a reaction I referred to as *covert pushback*. Even when given the opportunity to support the demise of the idea (as was their original intention), both preferred to see their chosen version through the end, fully aware that the conference would not accept the absence of a rule. Sustained British and French efforts translated into the eventual acceptance of a vague scope of application for CA3.

On balance, the analysis suggests that the process and outcomes seen here cannot be explained by simple assumptions of rationality, sociability, and morality working independently. The conduct shown by the British and French during negotiations studied here can only be considered rational action *under social pressure.*

Beyond this, my argument here illuminates one crucial reason why CA3 soon proved to "underperform" in practice; while IHL promoters celebrated the rule's "openness" and argued for its application in X or Y case, states facing internal conflicts often interpreted the same openness as *vagueness* and refused to argue or accept that it should apply in their specific situation. The British case would continue to be crucial. Once the 1949 negotiations were over and delegates wrote up their reports, one of them indicated that "it would certainly embarrass us if the situation now existent in Malaya were to be regarded by anyone as covered by Article 3 (and it is certainly 'an armed conflict'.)"[140] The French initially refused the rule's application for years in Algeria and so did a few others in the decades that followed. Hence the analysis provided in this chapter can contribute not only to debates about where international rules come from and how they are produced but to whether and why they are observed on the ground.

A critical aspect also left ambivalent in the making of CA3 was whether and how its application by violent nonstate actors could be secured. The legal argument made in 1949 (by the delegates of Monaco and Greece) that rebels would be bound by virtue of being citizens of a signatory state's may have allayed fears among negotiating diplomats and satisfied the ICRC but would prove to have little traction with actual insurgents waging war, whose very reason for being is precisely to *oppose* their "home" state and its legal regimes. A provision in CA3 allowing for special direct ad hoc agreements between combatants—of which there have been various examples in practice—partially helped to make up for this weakness but did not fully resolve it. Those debates would continue to arise in the later history of IHL for internal conflicts.

Finally, it should be said that the fact that a text—any text—emerged at the end of such a deeply contested negotiation process was a clear testament to the power of the Red Cross Movement, particularly the ICRC, and of the pro-extension states involved. The International Committee's records in fact suggest that even its own representatives at the 1949 Conference privately doubted the extension to civil wars could survive the political turmoil.[141] Unfortunately for the ICRC and for the victims of internal conflicts, however, getting states to apply CA3 would, perhaps predictably, prove very difficult. This frustration partly set the wheels of further debate about legal development in motion, to which I now turn.

4

A WINDING ROAD TO THE ADDITIONAL PROTOCOLS (1950–1968)

The revised Geneva Conventions, Common Article 3 (CA3) included, were no doubt a collective achievement by the International Committee of the Red Cross (ICRC) and the negotiating states. The path to ratification began swiftly in December 1949, and while the major governmental players who contributed to its design found certain articles disagreeable, CA3 was not among them. Upon ratification, no state entered a formal reservation or interpretation of the negotiated article.[1]

Yet some within the ICRC suspected that CA3's strengths, particularly its broad but vague threshold of application, might prove a weakness in practice. Claude Pilloud, ICRC subdirector for general affairs at the time, noted that "Article 3 will almost always give rise to discussions between the interested parties and an organization that, like the ICRC, will come and demand its application in an armed conflict."[2] Indeed, ICRC experience prior to 1949 offered enough evidence of states' readiness to argue that the violence they faced within their borders did not constitute an armed conflict but mere "troubles," "tensions," or simply common crime and terrorism. This suspicion with regard to CA3 would soon become a reality, as internal violence of diverse degrees was either ongoing or would soon erupt in parts of Africa, Latin America, and Southeast Asia. (For a partial list of internal conflicts with ICRC involvement, see Table 4.1.) The rising tide of decolonization at the turn of the decade arguably posed the greatest challenge for the ICRC, occurring in areas that had remained largely unknown to it.[3]

To make matters graver, violence amid decolonization conflict was compounded by repression within the Eastern bloc and a perceived threat of commu-

TABLE 4.1. Partial List of Internal Conflicts with ICRC Involvement, 1949–1980s

COUNTRY	YEAR
French Indochina	1945–54
India (Kashmir)	1947
Paraguay	1947
India (Hyderabad)	1948
Israel-Palestine	1948
India (Bengal)	1950
Indonesia	1950
Indonesia (Moluques du Sud)	1950
Korea	1950
Venezuela	1952
Tunisia	1952–54
Kenya	1952–55; 1956–58
Guatemala	1954
Argentina	1955
Costa Rica	1955
Morocco	1955
Malaysia	1955–56
Goa	1955–57
Algeria	1955–62
Cyprus	1955–65
Hungary	1956
East Germany	1957–58
Vietnam	1957–75
Indonesia	1957–61; 1965–81
Laos	1958
Lebanon	1958
Nicaragua	1958
Goa	1958–62
Iraq	1959
Lebanon	1959
Ireland and Northern Ireland	1959–64
Cuba	1960–62
Rhodesia and Nyasaland	1960–65
Congo	1960–66
Tunisia (Bizerte Base)	1961
Rwanda and Burundi	1961–65
Ireland	1962–70
South Africa	1963–86
Dominican Republic	1965
Guinea (Portugal)	1965

(continued)

TABLE 4.1. (continued)

COUNTRY	YEAR
Yemen	1965
Mozambique	1966, 1968
Angola	1966, 1970
Nigeria	1967–70
Greece	1967–71
Cape Verde	1969
Bolivia	1971
Guinea Bissau	1971–74
Mozambique	1971–74
Northern Ireland	1971–83
Burundi	1972
Philippines	1972
Uruguay	1972–75
Thailand	1973–75
Angola	1973–76
Chile	1973–78
Ethiopia	1974
Iraq	1974–75
Lebanon	1975
Iran	1977–81
Philippines	1977–86

Note: This table is not exhaustive through the present, and may not account for prolonged (or posterior) ICRC involvement in any of these conflicts.

Sources: Jacques Moreillon, Le Comité International de La Croix-Rouge et la Protection des Détenus Politiques (Geneva: Institut Henry Dunant, 1973); Catherine Rey-Schyrr, De Yalta à Dien Bien Phu: Histoire Du Comité International de La Croix-Rouge, 1945–1955 (Geneva: Georg Éditeur, 2007); Françoise Perret and François Bugnion, De Budapest a Saigon: Histoire Du Comité International de La Croix-Rouge 1956–1965 (Geneva: Georg Éditeur, 2009); David P. Forsythe, "Legal Regulation of Internal Conflicts: The 1977 Protocol on Non-international Armed Conflicts," American Journal of International Law 72, no. 2 (1978): 272–95; Hans Haug, Humanity for All: The International Red Cross and Red Crescent Movement (Geneva: Institut Henry Dunant, 1993); ICRC, Conference of Government Experts on the Reaffirmation and Development of International Humanitarian Law Applicable in Armed Conflicts (Geneva, 24 May–12 June 1971), vol. 5, Protection of Victims of Non-international Conflicts (Geneva: ICRC, 1971).

nist revolutions elsewhere. Since most of these internal and decolonization struggles in the 1950s did not at first reach an indisputably "high" level of violence, the ICRC faced tremendous obstacles in effectively persuading states to abide by international humanitarian standards they had just signed.[4] Its hopes were dashed, at least initially, in places like Algeria, Cyprus, Kenya, Morocco, and Tunisia, where the British and French colonial authorities fought off the operation of the Committee or the application of CA3 during much or all the hostilities.[5]

This chapter traces the events that followed the adoption of CA3 in 1949 until 1968, when formal debates resurfaced in the United Nations (UN) about revising and developing the international legal rules for armed conflict, both between and within states, eventually leading to the negotiation of the two Additional Protocols (APs) complementing the 1949 Geneva Conventions.

At first glance, this eighteen-year gap might suggest that the ICRC rested on its laurels vis-à-vis the extension of CA3 where it seemed inapplicable, especially situations of internal violence that could not be plausibly characterized as "armed conflict not of an international character." Yet a detailed look at ICRC activities between 1950 and the mid-1960s reveals otherwise, evincing persistent efforts to make up for the operation of CA3 in the gray zones euphemistically referred to as troubles or tensions. In this period, as before, ICRC reflection is shown to have been punctuated by episodes of frustration and abuse on the ground—notably, involving concerns about detained persons in diverse internal violent contexts.

To understand the seeming gap in the process of legal emergence between 1950 and 1968 and the subsidiary role the ICRC seemed to play initially once discussions were reignited among states within the UN, I discuss a second (unsuccessful) legal initiative led by the ICRC during this time.

Although the Diplomatic Conference of 1949 had given birth to the brand-new the Convention Relative to the Protection of Civilian Persons in Time of War (hereafter the Civilians Convention), it in fact said little about the precautions and limits belligerents had to observe toward noncombatants while planning and deploying armed attacks or using certain weapons with "uncontrollable effects."[6] This was true regarding both international and internal war. The ICRC attempted to address the gap through a set of draft humanitarian rules that it hoped states would embrace, first as soft guidance and later as treaty law, to apply across conflict types. Yet the tense politics of the early Cold War, and especially a growing belief that recourse to nuclear weapons helped to keep global peace, compounded by the fact that many powerful Western states perceived the Red Cross to be the wrong forum for addressing weaponry issues, made this humanitarian initiative founder.

Given that the Draft Rules for the Limitation of Dangers Incurred by the Civilian Population in Time of War sought to cover both armed conflict *between* and *within* states at once, using their failure as a "negative" case to draw firm conclusions on legal emergence specific to internal conflicts becomes difficult.[7] Yet its consideration in this chapter is crucial for understanding the historical process of norm entrepreneurship by the ICRC leading up to the next "stage" of legal construction in the 1970s.

Concretely, the Draft Rules episode will be shown to have caused a momentary recoiling within the ICRC vis-à-vis pushing for formal legal revisions in general. Although the ICRC did not stay put in terms of conducting internal policy discussions and consultations with experts, having been burned publicly on the issue of civilian protection, its approach to pressing states to change the rules became more cautious and circumspect.

In addition, analyzing the case of the Draft Rules has a theoretical payoff, that of highlighting an important third condition for initiating new phases of humanitarian legal emergence: breaking past the recalcitrance of powerful state gatekeepers. This condition seems equally applicable to humanitarian treaty-making initiatives dealing with either international or internal conflict, at least during this period.

By 1971, however, states were again engaged in formal debate about revisions to the Geneva Conventions. If not the ICRC, what and who sparked the process of updating the law? What actors and circumstances operated to mobilize the idea that new and better law was necessary? The second part of this chapter describes and theorizes the role of new norm entrepreneurs and the changing (actor-specific, as well as world-structural) historical conditions that by the mid- to late 1960s had begun to facilitate a new stage of humanitarian legal development, particularly toward conflicts occurring within states' borders, including wars for self-determination and civil war. (Whether the former could and should be considered internal conflicts or not was a global battle in crescendo at the time, as discussed later.)

Specifically, the persistence of atrocity episodes motivated another actor, the International Commission of Jurists (ICJ), to advocate for the expansion of humanitarian protections across all types of conflicts. Thanks to the networking skills and political clout of its executive director, Seán MacBride, ICJ advocacy reinvigorated the path laid by the Red Cross. More importantly, it inserted the process within the UN General Assembly (UNGA) at a time when the UN's shifting membership had changed the internal balance of influence against the West, multiplying the number of supporters of legal revision and expansion. Indeed, the global politics of the epoch, marked by an emboldened process of decolonization and the growing legitimacy of freedom fighters, elicited an interest among the proliferating new states from Africa and Asia to alter the received body of international humanitarian law (IHL) to protect conflicts of self-determination. Coinciding with these developments but acting upon a distinct set of concerns, a previously skeptical actor—the United States—quickly and crucially developed a strong interest in extending protections for its own prisoners of war (POWs) suffering abuse in Vietnam.

Problems of Law and Practice in Situations of Internal Violence

CA3 enshrined the protection of "persons taking no active part in the hostilities" during "armed conflicts not of an international character." Most, however, found it difficult to figure exactly what this meant. The ICRC read it as saying that in addition to bona fide civil wars (fought in the image of the Spanish Civil War, for example, with clear territorial dividing lines and battlefronts), lower-scale conflicts—excluding riots, protests and short-lived insurrections—were also susceptible of coverage. Jean Pictet, director-delegate of the ICRC at the time and now amply recognized as the principal architect of the 1949 Conventions, claimed in 1952 that despite the various conditions or requirements states had insisted upon at the 1949 Diplomatic Conference during the making of CA3, "no Government can object to respecting, in its dealings with internal enemies, whatever the nature of the conflict between it and them, a few essential rules which it in fact respects daily, under its own laws, even when dealing with common criminals."[8] In Pictet's mind, CA3 represented a condensed version of those "essential rules."

Yet, unfortunately, states facing internal violence often rebuffed this optimistic reading by claiming such instability was nothing more than isolated "troubles" or terrorism. Notably, France and the United Kingdom, the two colonial powers that were socially pressured to accept CA3 but fashioned its scope so as to muddy its application, lived up to their duplicitous intent. The British had faced the armed rebellion of the Mau Mau rebels in Kenya since 1952, yet for years turned down ICRC requests to visit detained persons.[9] When the ICRC was finally granted access in 1957, the British government still declared that CA3 was not legally applicable to the situation, despite the fact that the violence and means of repression against rebels rose to the level of noninternational armed conflict.[10] Similar instances of British "conflict status" denial were seen in the cases of violence in Cyprus (1955–58), Aden (or South Yemen, 1966–67), and Northern Ireland (for its entire duration, 1969–98).[11] France, for its part, admitted ICRC visits to prisons in Algeria on the basis of CA3 only in 1956, after three years of escalating violence and much ICRC insistence on humanitarian access.[12]

But colonial powers were not the only ones at fault for fending off the full application of CA3. During the Korean War (1950–53) the U.S. Department of Defense and the UN Command operating there allowed ICRC visits on the basis of CA3 and the Convention Relative to the Treatment of Prisoners of War only to combatant detention camps, refusing similar access to refugees and other affected civilians, despite being cognizant of the deep humanitarian crisis and of forceful protestations from both the ICRC and the U.S. State Department.[13] During the Hungarian Revolution of 1956, the Hungarian government and the Soviet Union also refused ICRC requests for visits to detained persons, as foreseen in CA3.[14]

A systematic assessment of patterns and causes of CA3's implementation and influence across areas or recipients of protection does not exist.[15] To maintain focus on the process of legal emergence, this book does not address that important issue. Yet it seems fair to say, provisionally, that despite some interesting examples of acceptance (whether complete, partial, explicit, or implicit), in practice CA3 disappointed the expectations of the ICRC and other enthusiastic audiences.[16] Doubtless the biggest blocking factor was state refusal to admit its application for fear that it might increase the legal and political standing of the rebels.

Beyond the situations of internal violence that could plausibly have led to the application of CA3, in contexts euphemistically referred to as troubles or tensions states proved even less willing to grant the ICRC legal authorization to access prisons and camps, at best saying that any visits were only allowed on humanitarian grounds, at worst completely refusing or ignoring the committee's requests. For example, in French North African territories experiencing lower but still considerable violence during the early 1950s, colonial authorities largely refused ICRC action, arguing essentially that the situation was not the business of international actors. Importantly, during this time even the ICRC itself hesitated to request access on some occasions, unsure of the appropriateness of acting in contexts of political tension and low-intensity violence.[17] The problematic threshold and applicability of CA3 was compounded by the question of whether the ICRC could and should rely on it to justify its requests to governments for access in times of internal troubles or tensions. Although by the 1950s the committee had amassed practical (if mixed) experience in these murky contexts, this issue would continue to elicit much doctrinal reflection in the 1950s and 1960s.

An additional major worry hovered on the agenda of the ICRC—namely, whether the Geneva Conventions sufficiently protected the civilian population in both international and internal conflicts.[18] The new Civilians Convention, designed largely with the recent experience of World War II in mind, set out safeguards for civilians who had fallen into the hands of the enemy. Although it professed their general immunity as noncombatants and the procurement of their safety (for example, through the establishment of neutralized zones or humane treatment while interned), it did not touch on matters related to the precautions that warring parties should follow while attacking one another so as to spare civilians. In particular, the Civilians Convention lacked precise guidelines for the "appropriate" use of weaponry and deployment of attacks during conflict.

There are at least two reasons why the 1949 Diplomatic Conference had failed to touch upon this subject. First, historically (as was explained in chapter 2), rules placing limits on the conduct of hostilities had belonged to the "Hague branch" of the laws of war, not to the Geneva lineage of conventions focusing on the humane treatment of war victims.[19] Although the dividing line between the Geneva and Hague Conventions was eventually blurred in the 1970s and now seems like a curious historical artifact, in the 1950s it was still firmly ingrained in the minds of military lawyers the world over. States respected the role of the ICRC as the guardian of the Geneva Conventions, yet the Hague Conventions lacked such a patron. (The Dutch government nominally bore this responsibility but in practice seemingly exerted little if any leadership on the matter.) For this reason, since the early twentieth century, the law of the Hague had seen few additions to its canon or updates.[20]

A second, more powerful reason existed to explain why governmental circles might later show aversion to the idea of new restrictions on their war practices. The principal forms of "indiscriminate warfare," aerial bombing and nuclear weapons, were two tools of war that World War II victors had put to effective if grossly inhumane use. Most importantly, the member states of the North Atlantic Treaty Organization (NATO), with the United States at the helm, believed that nuclear weapons were essential for keeping world peace by deterring the Soviet Union and containing communism. This belief was compounded, much to the chagrin of the humanitarians, by the fact that the Soviet Union and its satellites had adopted calls for an all-out ban on such weapons as a fighting cry of their own since the 1949 Diplomatic Conference, which Western nuclear nations like the United Kingdom and United States perceived as nothing more than hypocritical propaganda. An issue of legitimate humanitarian concern had already, in the early to mid-1950s, become entangled with power politics and the East-West ideological struggle.

The ICRC was aware of these complications but was not deterred from at least trying to address this serious regulative gap. While proposing a complete prohibition on nuclear warfare was outside its purview, at this time the ICRC considered essential the setting of limits on means and methods causing unnecessary harm to combatants and noncombatants across all forms of conflict. Yet it could not foresee how elusive and contentious that would prove.

Political Detainees in Situations of Internal Violence

Although the lackluster application of CA3 to internal conflicts certainly worried the ICRC, at a minimum that article constituted a hard-law instrument enabling it to "knock on the door" of states ridden by higher levels of internal violence. In addition to procuring aid for civilians, the ICRC usually drew on CA3 to request visits to captured persons, who were often at peril in the hands of governmental authorities. Red Cross resolutions aside, however, no such authoritative tool existed for internal violent situations of lower intensity, leaving detainees in such contexts at a special risk of abuse or "disappearance." For this reason, in the years immediately following the Diplomatic Conference of 1949, the ICRC became especially concerned with addressing situations of internal troubles and tensions.[21]

Internal reflection began in July 1951 when the commission charged with reviewing the ICRC's statuses debated whether the committee should intervene in cases of flagrant violation of human rights. This proposal was considered too risky and impracticable, as some thought it might enlarge the "vulnerable surface" of the committee while potentially endangering its more traditional, limited role.[22] But others felt it was equally grave to ignore the fate of political detainees in internal violence, hence potentially tarnishing the ICRC's moral stature.[23]

The matter did not end there. According to Catherine Rey-Schyrr, the refusal of the French government to allow the ICRC to visit detainees in Tunisia in 1952, compounded by the inaction (if not hostility) of the French National Red Cross toward them, triggered efforts within the ICRC to set a policy for operations in internal troubles.[24] A report presented in January 1953 to the ICRC's Legal Commission proposed that while the national societies had the primary right to act in situations of internal troubles or tensions, the ICRC should also act if the situation met one or more specific conditions: (1) a certain degree of intensity or seriousness of violence; (2) a certain duration; (3) a certain level of organization on the part of the warring parties; and/or (4) a level of violence having produced victims.[25] The Legal Commission accepted these rough guidelines but suggested more study was necessary. Difficult questions remained: Would the ICRC actually be able to help political detainees in an unforeseen number of states around the world, or might it spread itself thin? What exactly was a "political detainee"—a person in administrative detention, or one (dubiously) deemed guilty of treason after trial?

The organization understood that these puzzles were difficult to resolve. Hence, at this time the ICRC seemed to oscillate between two positions: waiting for the revised Geneva Conventions to take root while attempting to create practical precedents in new areas or moving forward to address novel concerns formally.[26] This dilemma, as was seen in Chapter 2, had pervaded the activities of the ICRC since its inception.

The idea of attaching a protocol on political detainees to the Fourth Geneva Convention was entertained but dismissed as too rash given the novelty of the treaties, in addition to the growing politicization of the International Red Cross Conferences along Cold War ideological lines.[27] Yet despite being skeptical about the pursuit of a new legal instrument right away, ICRC jurists believed the committee should seek to create practical precedents to foreground later action, which in turn might buttress future treaty-law initiatives.[28] ICRC directives also recognized the importance of protecting political detainees for the humanitarian mission of the committee. Beyond an awareness of the gravity of the issue beyond the Iron Curtain and North Africa, ICRC president Paul Ruegger visited Central and South America and privately admitted being struck by the proliferation of political detainees there, citing the cases of Argentina, Bolivia, Colombia, and Venezuela.[29]

Taking a cautious path forward, the ICRC hosted a series of private meetings of international legal experts from various regions acting in their individual capacities. The first of these meetings took place June 9–11, 1953.[30] The specific focus of this commission was to discuss the treatment and assistance to be given to political detainees in internal conflicts and to help formulate some doctrinal basis as guide for ICRC action.[31]

In a nutshell, the experts opined that the ICRC should strive to trespass the legal limits set by CA3 and seek to protect "all categories of political detainees," a role that they considered appropriate for a neutral organization concerned not with the motivations behind prisoner arrest but rather with the conditions of their captivity. Like ICRC jurists months prior, these experts declined to recommend the drafting of a new protocol or convention, believing that CA3 was as much as was politically possible at that time, but considered nonetheless that the article, the general principles of the conventions, and the UN's Universal Declaration of Human Rights (UDHR) offered enough basis for attempted ICRC action in internal troubles.[32]

It appears that although lacking in binding legal force, the conclusions of this first expert consultation facilitated the work of the ICRC during the escalating situation of violence lived in Guatemala in 1954.[33] Exactly around this time, however, the ICRC experienced frustration as British and French authorities denied them access to Algeria, Kenya, Morocco, and Tunisia.

The ICRC wondered whether it should make public its internal reflections so as to cajole reluctant governments. But before doing so the committee decided that further consultation with influential experts was warranted to strengthen its emergent doctrine. To this end, a second meeting convened October 3–8, 1955, seeking to clarify more precisely the application of humanitarian principles to internal troubles, and particularly CA3.[34] The experts' conclusion was that in the absence of two "parties to conflict" with some degree of organization, CA3 did *not* apply.

Yet they added that, even absent a legal basis, all actors engaged in violence should still observe the principles of the Geneva Conventions. As a result, while the ICRC should not seek to rely on a legal argument or directly object to a government's response in internal troubles, it could nonetheless insist on states' respect for the humanitarian guarantees of the conventions—in particular, the provisions of the Civilians Convention relating to a fair trial, care for the wounded and sick, and the prohibition of mistreatment, torture, reprisals, and collective punishment.[35] These experts also considered that the ICRC had by then a well-earned and justified "right of initiative" which enabled it to at least try to act in times of troubles and tensions. Finally, they clarified that ICRC operations in internal troubles did not affect the legal status of detainees.

The general message was clear: minimum humanitarian principles should apply in situations short of high-level civil wars, and the ICRC stood ready to offer its help to the captured, wounded, and sick, as well as victims of all sides.

Protecting Civilians in All Forms of Conflict

As with the issue of internal troubles, the ICRC resumed its plans to work on limiting the effects of warfare on civilians. In 1950 it issued a circular to all states urging states to consider the grave consequences of nuclear and "blind" weapons on civilian populations; their use, it justifiably thought, threatened the very essence of the Geneva Conventions and of the Red Cross itself.[36]

ICRC preparation for the postwar development of such rules began in 1952 through private conversations with American, British, and Swiss legal and military experts, including preeminent names in international law such as Hersch Lauterpacht. These conversations were far from encouraging, however. Lauterpacht, for instance, admitted that recent belligerent practice had tended to eliminate the distinction between combatants and noncombatants and that states were unlikely to agree on limits to nuclear weapons and aerial bombardment.[37]

ICRC lawyers were not discouraged by initial skepticism, believing that the committee was indisputably responsible for setting the normative wheels in motion on this issue while greater consensus among states was obtained. A first meeting of experts to treat this subject was convened for April 6–13, 1954.[38] Like the meetings on internal troubles and political detainees, the experts in attendance were invited in their personal capacity, but this time clearly with a view both to wider regional variation and to their home states' political importance.[39] According to the ICRC, at this initial meeting the experts reached a consensus on a few important law-of-war principles, including the prohibition of attacking noncombatants directly and of causing superfluous harm. They also seemed to agree that aerial warfare should be regulated, and that military exigencies should not always prevail over the precepts of humanity. (Later events suggest that the ICRC overestimated experts' level of agreement.) At the same time, however, experts seemed to acknowledge the difficulty in translating these aspirations into prescriptions regarding aerial bombardment and considered the risks of proposing inefficacious rules on nuclear warfare, especially if governments were not willing to completely rule out their use.[40]

On the basis of the 1954 debates in Geneva, the ICRC decided to formulate a draft set of guidelines that it hoped would eventually become an international convention.[41] This initiative, the Draft Rules, quickly became the subject of one of the most acrimonious yet simultaneously obscure disputes in the history of IHL. It is important to delve into the history of the Draft Rules here in some detail not only because they purported to apply to *all* types of conflicts but also because their fate helps explain the attitude of the ICRC in subsequent years and foregrounds changes and continuities in certain states' attitudes toward the development of IHL.

The Draft Rules consisted of twenty articles regulating the conduct of combatants during hostilities in both international and internal conflicts. Article 1 provided their essential bedrock and summarized their intent: the right of parties to conflict to adopt means of injuring the enemy was not unlimited, and parties should confine their operations to the destruction of the enemy's military resources, sparing civilians.[42]

The rest of the document fleshed out in greater detail this principle by, among other things, prohibiting attacks expressly directed at the civilian population, setting out a list of objects that could be legitimately considered as military objects susceptible of attack, or insisting that attacks be proportional to the target they intended to neutralize. Most controversial would prove to be Article 14, prohibiting weapons whose harmful effects "could spread to an unforeseen degree or escape, either in space or in time, from the control of those who employ them, endangering the civilian population."[43]

The ICRC's hopes for state support of the Draft Rules were high. It circulated them in 1955 to national Red Cross societies and to the experts who had attended the first meeting with the purpose of gathering comments in preparation for submission to the upcoming International Conference of the Red Cross, to take place in New Delhi sometime in 1956–57.

The initial feedback from certain powerful states arrived like a bad omen. The United States, in a detailed legal analysis addressed to Claude Pilloud, then the deputy director of the ICRC, and written by U.S. State Department legal advisers Raymond Yingling and Richard Baxter, quickly took issue with the Draft Rules' underlying principles.[44] Their memorandum noted the "general unwisdom" of the Draft Rules and offered two main critiques. First, in attempting to regulate the conduct of warfare, the ICRC was overstretching its traditional role: to alleviate the horrors of war through humanitarian protections.[45] Revising the laws of war (by which they meant the Hague Conventions) was not a matter for the ICRC or the Swiss government. Second, the U.S. response claimed that the Draft Rules rested on a fallacy—namely, the assumption that in times of total war it was possible to differentiate between the members of the armed forces and the civilian population. Rules of war needed to be realistic, the authors said, and at the time, the realities of war made such distinction impossible. Therefore, in their view, to presume that civilians could be rendered immune from the direct effects of modern warfare was "fanciful."

This did not mean, however, that governments were necessarily indifferent to the destruction of civilian life and property. Some efforts might perhaps be taken in that direction and certain counterproductive terror tactics avoided, but in Yingling and Baxter's opinion, moral principles could only be effective if they were militarily sound. Ominously, they declared that "it may be far more effective in winning the war to destroy a city like Pittsburgh or Essen than to destroy a battleship or a division, and in the destruction of such cities the civilian population cannot remain untouched. This is true, unfortunately, of cities in general." Further, they noted that a revision of the laws of war in the absence of inter-state agreement on the ban or restriction of use of nuclear weapons was premature and that "unless the nations principally concerned" reached an agreement "paper prohibitions emanating from any other source" would be unsuccessful.[46] The U.S. lawyers were doubtless referring to the sluggish efforts on arms control taking place bilaterally with the Soviet Union and within the UN at the time.

Such words, coming from key legal advisers to one of the two superpowers, effectively marked the fate of the Draft Rules. The USSR did not respond to the ICRC, and one can only guess what position it took. As the only other nuclear nation at the time, the United Kingdom similarly found substantive reason to dislike them.[47]

Despite the pushback, the ICRC was still not entirely discouraged. By March 1956 President Leopold Boissier privately counted thirty responses to the Draft Rules project from national Red Cross societies and states, noting that only three of them—those from Australia, the United Kingdom, and the United States—showed a marked opposition to the project. The ICRC hoped that a wider diffusion of the Draft Rules and more work of persuasion among the Anglo-Saxon Red Cross societies might get the humanitarian point across.[48] To this end, it convened a new meeting of experts in May 14–19, 1956.[49] Some critical voices aside, most of the participating experts supported the project and after incorporating their feedback the ICRC decided to submit the revised Draft Rules for discussion at the upcoming International Red Cross Conference in New Delhi, which was now scheduled to take place in October–November 1957. In the meantime, the committee worked to influence several national Red Cross societies and experts neutral or sympathetic to the project, believing that they could form a majority.[50]

American revulsion to the Draft Rules, however, intensified. While the ICRC carried out consultations in 1957 in preparation for the New Delhi conference, NATO nations, led by the United States, began to anxiously coordinate their position vis-à-vis the project. The U.S. government admitted in private correspondence with its allies that it was "most desirable if the rules did not exist or if they could be conveniently forgotten" and studied ways to pressure the ICRC to drop the Draft Rules from the agenda. Yet consultations with the United Kingdom and the ICRC itself alerted the United States to the fact that this was unlikely to happen not only because the project was near and dear to the ICRC but also because giving it up might put the ICRC in an awkward position in the eyes of socialist states, which could then reason that the committee had given into the wishes of "war-loving" Western countries.[51]

France and the United States debated not attending the New Delhi meeting at all, wondering whether their absence might take the air out of the initiative. Opinions between the U.S. Defense and State Departments on this issue were divided, and an initial decision to send an observer mission was made but soon upgraded to a full delegation with voting abilities.[52] France eventually followed suit.

The main concern for the United States was to secure a consensus position among its allies about the undesirability of the Draft Rules and to get other moderate countries to support it. Realizing that some discussion was unavoidable, NATO countries sought two outcomes. First, the conference should not give formal endorsement to the Draft Rules or summon a diplomatic conference to sanction them. Instead NATO should insist that effective decisions about nuclear limitations rested solely with the UN and *not* with the Red Cross. Second, it had to find ways to avoid a detailed article-by-article debate that would provide socialist countries with room for propaganda and opportunities to embarrass NATO members publicly. Overall, absent the possibility of a complete dismissal, the best tactic in their view was to press for a general resolution expressing vague support for the principles embodied by the Draft Rules, urging the ICRC to send them back to governments for their consideration. Such a resolution, the United States and its allies reasoned, would have the virtue of pleasing everyone at the meeting while at the same time kicking the ball to the states, where it could later be ignored and "buried" as desired.[53] After much bilateral and multilateral diplomatic coordination and various meetings prior to the International Red Cross Conference in New Delhi, the NATO states agreed on this common stance.

The Nineteenth International Red Cross Conference finally took place in October 1957. As colorfully portrayed by François Bugnion, this meeting featured political fireworks and ended in "psychodrama," though for reasons unrelated to the Draft Rules. The issue of whether to allow the "two Chinas," nationalist Taiwan or the delegates from the communist mainland, to sit as the legitimate representatives of "the Republic of China" wrought havoc and led the meeting to end with several delegations, including the Indian hosts, walking out abruptly.[54] More relevant to the present discussion, after extended debate during the conference and much political maneuvering behind the scenes, Western delegations succeeded in having their preferred resolution text on the Draft Rules passed, declaring that the next phase of the project should consist of governmental study and decision.

The ICRC abided by this mandate and circulated the Draft Rules to states in May 1958. NATO plans were then carried out faithfully; no great power replied, and the majority of the replies the ICRC received were merely ceremonial.[55] By 1961 only five replies (from India, Ireland, Japan, Pakistan, and Switzerland) out of approximately forty dealt with the substance of the Draft Rules. Given lackluster results, the ICRC discarded plans to summon a further meeting of government experts, and although it continued to consider the issue as one of the highest importance, it eventually decided against further promoting the Draft Rules in their original form.[56]

Effects of and Follow-Up to the Doctrinal Debates of the 1950s

The failure of the Draft Rules was a major blow to the ICRC. The project represented several years invested in research, reflection, and consultation. Existing histories claim that this loss pushed the ICRC into conservative mode with regard to the progressive development of IHL.[57] This appreciation is accurate to an extent; states' private dismissal of the project convinced the ICRC that the moment was not ripe for the swift introduction of a new international legal commitment, and especially one dealing with weapons. Yet archival evidence suggests that the impact was rather one of momentary delay: the ICRC recoiled and turned inward, resuming the tactic of internal reflection and discreet consultation with experts. This reaction can be explained in two ways. ICRC experts were frustrated by the politicization of the debate, but their belief in the need for better protections for the civilian population remained.[58] Simultaneously, the practical challenges the ICRC faced on the field continued to remind its members that normative discussion was necessary, however slowly and in low-key mode.[59]

Also toward the late 1950s and early 1960s, the committee revisited the topic of operating in contexts of internal violence. By then the ICRC felt its policy and practice during internal troubles was well founded. Clear ICRC policies, however, were not yet in place to deal with situations of political tensions or instability that led governments to engage in arbitrary arrests and detention without sufficient judicial guarantees. Some voices within the committee felt the humanitarian mission of the ICRC justified action to aid detainees in such scenarios, while others warned that this surpassed its mandate to act during armed conflict.[60]

Hoping to attain sharper direction on two issues of such importance, in the period 1960–65 the ICRC resorted again to private expert roundtables: one on the provision of aid to and protection of victims of noninternational conflicts broadly conceived, and another on the legal protection of war victims in all types of conflict against the dangers of warfare.[61]

The former, which took place October 25–30, 1962, reaffirmed the notion that CA3 was legally applicable to conflicts that gave rise to hostilities and where the opposing party had a minimum degree of organization.[62] Yet even absent these conditions, CA3 should also cover internal troubles on the basis of the ICRC's recognized humanitarian practice and right of initiative. Rebels were also believed to be obliged to observe CA3, but reciprocity was not a condition for states' own compliance. For their part, detained persons should be treated according to the standards set in CA3 and be likened to prisoners of war in international conflicts whenever possible.[63] And although experts did not fully examine the case of internal tensions, they nevertheless concluded that the ICRC could request to aid victims and detainees after armed hostilities had ceased, providing a humanitarian entry-point in unstable contexts lacking actual confrontation. Finally, beyond humanitarian norms, experts cited recourse to the UDHR and the UN Charter as a basis for aiding political detainees in all contexts.

The roundtable organized to follow up on the work on civilian protection from the dangers of warfare met April 11–14, 1962, gathering an interesting mix of public opinion leaders, military and legal experts, and prominent scholars on military strategy.[64] Participants agreed that the ICRC should continue to pursue its traditional work despite the threat of total war. They recommended, however, that the ICRC refrain from trying to bind states through international law at that time, considering instead that narrower arrangements might be more attainable, for example, on the evacuation of civilian populations. They reaffirmed in general the principle of distinguishing between combatants and noncombatants, the prohibition of attacking civilian populations as such, and the obligation to take every precaution not to harm the civilian population.[65] Finally, they argued that while a new treaty was inconvenient the ICRC or the Red Cross movement could draw up a resolution stating these basic principles and circulate it among states, which would then be free to make public announcements of their willingness to respect them despite their nonbinding character.[66]

Although in the eyes of the ICRC the conclusions from this roundtable had been useful to gauge the state of expert opinion on the matter, the overall conclusion was bleak. In 1965 the ICRC publicly recognized that "the problem of the respect of the civilian population in the event of armed conflict does not yet seem anywhere near a prompt solution." Moreover, it acknowledged that "in the field of humanitarian law, the Red Cross can but propose agreement and endeavor to persuade Governments to conclude them; it has no power over them to do so. The final responsibility remains solely with the Governments."[67]

An Assessment Midway

Let us briefly recapitulate. Despite the legal inroads made in 1949 through the adoption of CA3, clearly most states facing internal violence during the 1950s averred its implementation. Similarly, states deliberately resisted formal efforts at legal expansion during this time, as confirmed by the experience of the Draft Rules. Therefore, even if the major roadblock leading to the Draft Rules' demise was their relationship to nuclear weapons, it is evident that states—especially Western NATO powers—opposed meaningful dialogue about filling legal gaps in IHL. Securing the assent of the gatekeeping major Western powers was at this time a *necessary condition* for the initiation of new episodes of legal norm emergence or transformation, whether for international or internal conflicts.

Beyond states, some observations are warranted about the role of the ICRC as a norm entrepreneur on the issue of internal conflicts in 1950–1965. First, the ICRC clearly kept its concern alive and pursued modest doctrinal means to build and propagate expansive interpretations of CA3. Given that its expectation that formal extension of the law to cover internal troubles and political detainees was unlikely to prosper, it pursued the alternative tactic of fostering a legal "epistemic community" via the convocation of expert roundtables.[68] These consultations became a useful mechanism for legitimating expansive readings of CA3 validated by the authority of influential international legal experts with varied backgrounds, many of whom also operated in or hailed from governmental circles. And though the published proceedings concealed disagreements among experts to some extent, the legal epistemic community convoked by the ICRC was already an increasingly plural and contentious group bound by a shared sense of respect for the law.

Ultimately, however, these encounters and documents fell short of achieving broader state acceptance of CA3's expansive interpretation and failed to provoke interest in amending IHL to address evident humanitarian protection gaps.

Hitting a Wall

Let us now return to the historical process. On the basis of the new round of expert consultations, the ICRC drew up summary reports for consideration by national Red Cross societies and governments at the Twentieth International Red Cross Conference, to take place in 1965 in Vienna. Plenary debates on civilian protection from against the dangers of hostilities at this conference were not particularly acrimonious.[69] The ICRC report contained a suggestion for a "solemn declaration" (as suggested by experts) that national Red Cross societies and governments could make to reaffirm the following principles: (1) that the right of the parties to a conflict to adopt means of injuring the enemy was not unlimited; (2) that to launch attacks against the civilian populations as such was prohibited; and (3) that a distinction must be made at all times between persons taking part in the hostilities and members of the civilian population to the effect that the latter be spared as much as possible.[70] These ideas constituted the core of the Draft Rules, yet in this version they were merely declaratory, not binding.

Given this modest conclusion, the lack of controversy was unsurprising. However, evidence from other portions of the conference proceedings and confidential U.S. cables confirm sharp divisions between neutral and socialist countries, on the one hand, and Western (particularly NATO) states on the other. While the former supported further work on this issue, at least publicly, most NATO powers continued to dislike the idea that new rules could be introduced. In fact, during debates at the commission level in 1965, various (probably socialist) countries had managed to add a fourth principle to the ICRC draft on the application of the general principles of laws of war to nuclear and similarly "uncontrollable" weapons.

On the opposite side, and further confirming the link between the issue of warfare regulations and internal conflicts, the U.S. delegation had been instructed to oppose any further resolutions on the regulation of hostilities because "the nature of much modern warfare, as exemplified by guerilla tactics and wars of national liberation, has blurred the distinction—already difficult—between the 'military' and 'civilian.'" As a result, the U.S. position paper argued, "a declaration along the lines now suggested by the ICRC could easily become the propaganda vehicle for precisely those regimes and forces who themselves demonstrate utter contempt for civilized rules of warfare and humane treatment of civilian populations." As a last resort if the adoption of a resolution on this issue was imminent, U.S. delegates were instructed to try to make it "as innocuous as possible."[71]

At the same time, however, the U.S. team was told to "strongly support" a resolution calling on parties to the Geneva Conventions to strictly abide by CA3 and to accept ICRC offers of services.[72] In addition, the United States introduced a resolution of its own drafted in conjunction with the American Red Cross calling upon all authorities involved in an armed conflict to ensure that POWs were accorded the treatment prescribed by the Third Geneva Convention.[73] U.S. views of IHL were not uniformly conservative but rather strategically selective; while it considered certain topics essentially taboo (e.g., new rules on weapons), the United States saw a certain value in supporting other motions—particularly respect for *existing* law, such as the minimum humanitarian provisions for noninternational conflict contained in CA3, as well as the informal extension of guarantees to detained combatants in all armed conflicts. This was not surprising at a time when American soldiers were reportedly being badly mistreated by their captors in North Vietnam.

In general, correspondence between the United States and its NATO allies reveal that American reticence toward the regulation of warfare was still widely shared by its military allies in 1965. And although certain European countries such as Belgium, Denmark, and West Germany felt they could support a declaration of basic principles on the conduct of hostilities, they would only do so because it was "the lesser of two evils," an implicit reference to the 1957 Draft Rules which were meant to eventually becoming binding not simply declaratory.[74]

The United States was not the only force behind the scenes working to boycott the regulation of warfare. During the actual plenary debates in Vienna, UK delegate Gerald Draper attempted to shape the text of the draft resolution to refer to international conflicts *only*, arguing that the inclusion of noninternational conflicts worked only to confuse matters. This reaction was consistent with the British government's past (and future) worry about humanitarian meddling in internal conflicts. The ICRC rejected this reasoning, alongside delegates from East Germany, Iraq, Poland, Turkey, and Yugoslavia, and the British amendment was struck down.[75]

The British delegation also attempted to water down an ICRC draft resolution on the protection of victims in noninternational conflicts which, following recommendations of the 1962 expert commission, included language about protections being accorded during internal troubles. Draper argued (again) that to include this expression was to confuse the legal tenor of the text, but his amendment was once more rejected.[76] The resolution itself, which encouraged the ICRC to continue its work in strengthening the protection of victims of these types of conflicts and recommended that governments and National Red Crosses support it, was approved unanimously.[77]

As this shows, by the end of 1965 the ICRC had a mandate to "continue" facilitating work on the legal protection of civilians from the dangers of warfare across all forms of conflict but faced the clear opposition of Western powers. In contrast, the United Kingdom notwithstanding, it also appeared to have wide support to continue providing aid and working to protect the victims of noninternational conflicts including in internal troubles and to urge the application of CA3 by combatants in such conflicts.

Yet neither situation warranted a swift move toward new binding rules. The included resolution on the dangers of warfare mentioned the creation of (yet another) committee of experts "with a view to obtaining a rapid and practical solution of this problem."[78] Instead of a new roundtable, the ICRC conducted a new round of private consultations with a diverse set of experts from East, West, and Third World countries during 1966 and early 1967.[79]

According to the ICRC, on the basis of this "broad survey of opinions," in Spring 1967 it took two measures: (1) endeavoring in the short term to obtain rapid official confirmation by governments of the principles of protection against warfare contained in the 1965 resolution; and (2) as a longer-term measure, to extend the work of revising IHL.[80] The ICRC then circulated a memorandum to governments, requesting them to sanction the four basic principles of protection during armed conflict and "if need be develop these general rules in an adequate instrument of international law." In addition, the ICRC invited governments "to reaffirm . . . through any appropriate official manifestations, such as a Resolution of the United Nations General Assembly the value they attach" to the principles contained in the 1965 Vienna resolution.[81]

Much to the ICRC's disappointment, this memorandum met a rather timid response from only a dozen states. The organization blamed this outcome on the fact that a week after the note was sent to governments war had broken out in the Middle East between Israel and its neighbors Egypt (then the United Arab Republic), Jordan, and Syria—the Six Day War. Undeterred, a representative of the ICRC traveled to New York to promote the idea of a submitting a resolution during the UNGA in 1967. Yet, in the ICRC's own words, "there it became evident that the Middle East crisis and concentration of efforts on the nonproliferation treaty made it impossible to submit such a draft resolution."[82]

IHL development led by the ICRC hit a major roadblock. Beyond the war-related impasse of 1967, it was far from evident that a major revamping of existing rules would become possible any time soon. Major Western states were skeptical about this course of action, and without the acquiescence of a substantive number of states, and particularly the usual powerful gatekeepers (particularly France, the United Kingdom, and the United States) consulted formally and informally by the ICRC, the project had weak legs and slim hopes for success.

Yet, a short four years later, in 1971, governmental experts were convening to discuss just such a revision of the humanitarian rules for international and internal conflicts. What happened between 1967 and 1971 to trigger such a change?

In what remains of this chapter, I offer an explanation grounded on three major factors, some tied to the agency of specific actors and others to changes in international society: (1) the emergence of new political entrepreneurs which mobilized international concern for this issue, albeit outside the purview of the ICRC and under the alternative banner of human rights; (2) major conflict–related shocks of international proportions which directly or indirectly motivated previously unbelieving governmental gatekeepers to take up the issue or made it harder for others to publicly deny its urgency; and (3) the entry into the international scene of a great number of newly independent states, with their strong aspirations for political legitimacy and with the ability to find allies and wield decision-making majorities in international organizations, especially the UNGA. I argue that these factors, in addition to the ICRC's cumulative work, constituted once again the crucial mechanisms behind the renewed impetus toward the revision and development of IHL in the late 1960s and early 1970s.

Resetting the Scene

A New Norm Entrepreneur: The ICJ

Until the late 1960s, the majority of efforts to revise IHL had been made by the ICRC.[83] In the immediate postwar period and with a revamped architecture of international organization, this task could have logically been assigned to the UN International Law Commission. However, the combination of general war weariness and its outlawing through the UN Charter made discussion of the regulation of *jus in bello* within the UN unpalatable. Moreover, the UN quickly became seen as a deeply politicized forum for the prescription of international public policy—particularly for Western states that, over a short number of years, had lost the majorities they once held. In addition, after nearly a century of humanitarian work, the ICRC had secured pride of place as pioneer and guardian of IHL. Few governments dared question its prerogative.

As a result, two branches of global lawmaking that in practice are quite related—the laws protecting victims of conflict-related (particularly internal) violence, and those regulating governmental conduct toward its own citizens (human rights)—for years developed almost independently.[84] The historical separation of these two sibling bodies of law came to a momentary halt in the mid-1960s when a relatively new nongovernmental organization (NGO), the ICJ, began to campaign in the policy circles of Geneva and New York, among other places, to bring to fore the issue of "respect for human rights in armed conflict." The ICJ's role as norm entrepreneur in this area injected renewed impetus to the cause of revising the laws of war by sparking a formal political process within the UN that the ICRC itself had been unable to ignite.

The ICJ was founded in 1952 as "a small offshoot of a comprehensive US policy to contain Soviet expansion." According to Howard Tolley Jr., the initial purpose of the organization was to recruit intellectuals to oppose communist political influence, for which it relied on funds from the Central Intelligence Agency.[85] By the early 1960s, however, the ICJ had reportedly turned away from anticommunism, transformed itself internally by recruiting professional staff and notable jurists, established its home in Geneva, opened international offices, and gathered experience campaigning worldwide for the respect of the rule of law in countries on both sides of the Iron Curtain.[86]

In 1963 the Executive Committee of the ICJ appointed Seán MacBride as secretary-general of the organization. He was a multifaceted Irishman with a distinguished background. MacBride was, notes Keith Suter, "first a journalist. He then rose to become the Chief of Staff of the Irish Republican Army during the early 1930s, which was then in combat against the Irish government."[87] He later gave up violence and opted for a career as a lawyer, making a career defending Irish Republican Army members.[88] He went on to become a member of Ireland's Parliament and minister for external affairs, and in the latter capacity he worked as vice president of the Organisation for European Economic Co-operation, helped found the Council of Europe, served as president of its Council of Foreign Ministers, and jointly sponsored and signed the 1949 Geneva Conventions and the European Convention on Human Rights. After leaving the Irish government, MacBride helped found Amnesty International and chaired its International Executive Committee through 1975. In 1974 MacBride was awarded the Nobel Peace Prize, and the Soviet Union's Lenin Peace Prize in 1976. This was clearly a testament to his credibility in the Western and socialist worlds.[89]

The appointment of MacBride in 1963 reinvigorated the ICJ's work on international law and institutions.[90] Among many other activities in the international human rights realm, MacBride led an (unsuccessful) ad hoc coalition to establish the position of UN High Commissioner for Human Rights and founded a permanent human rights NGO committee in Geneva.[91] Substantively, around this time, MacBride became concerned with the allegations of conflict-related atrocity committed against civilians in places like the Congo, South Africa, and Vietnam and concluded that the Geneva and Hague Conventions did not provide enough protections for victims of internal conflicts. He saw an opportunity to campaign for change when in 1965 the UNGA decided to convene the very first International Conference on Human Rights, to take place in 1968 as part of the celebrations of the twentieth anniversary of the UDHR.[92] One of the stated goals of the conference was to formulate and prepare a "human rights programme to be taken subsequent to the celebrations of the International Years of Human Rights," so the occasion was ripe for inserting new ideas.[93]

Starting in 1965, MacBride spoke at various high-level international public events and worked to build coalitions of NGOs and sympathizers around the issue of increasing the legal protections for victims of violence in international *and* internal conflicts as well as improved international oversight over them. He decried not only how outdated existing law was, and particularly the Hague Conventions of 1907, but also the separate and disparate growth of international humanitarian, human rights, and criminal law (the Nuremberg principles, chiefly), a phenomenon that in his view led to lacunae, confusing overlaps, and a problematic lack of coordination between the three bodies of law. Although he was a lawyer, MacBride was not encumbered by the legal subtleties and doctrinal differences between them since in his view all three formed part of the broader law of nations and ought to operate together. Yet he also seemed aware of the difficulties for realizing this objective. In his interventions MacBride recognized the "marvelous work" of the Red Cross in trying to update existing regulations, quickly noting that the ICRC was "often powerless" in the face of governmental stubbornness.[94]

Through his capacity in the ICJ and his prominence among international NGOs, MacBride decided to help push the process forward. In January and March 1968, prior to the UN International Conference on Human Rights, hosted in Tehran, he cochaired a meeting of seventy-six NGO experts in Geneva and another of fifty experts in Montreal (the Montreal Assembly on Human Rights). The conclusions of the January NGO meeting included explicit references to the need to revise the 1907 Hague Conventions to address the dangers posed by weapons of mass destruction, particularly for civilian populations, as well as increasing efforts to ensure compliance with the 1949 Geneva Conventions "by all involved in a conflict, whether international or internal." With this NGO mandate, MacBride flew to Tehran with one of his ICJ associates and set out to lobby governments for support for these initiatives. There his ideas for improving implementation and compliance mechanisms of the conventions seem to have been quickly frustrated, however.[95]

In a private letter to another member of Amnesty International, MacBride explained he had instead "decided to concentrate on trying to get proposed a concrete resolution on the protection of human rights in armed conflict . . . which ultimately, with some minor amendments, was proposed by India and co-sponsored by Czechoslovakia, Jamaica, Uganda and the United Arab Republic." MacBride explained that

> it was essential in the prevailing atmosphere to secure an "uncommitted" sponsorship and one which was representative of the various geographical groupings. My task was greatly facilitated by reason of the fact that the leaders of the Indian, Czechoslovak, Jamaican and UAR [United Arab Republic, now Egypt] government delegations were old friends of mine. This sponsorship in the prevailing situation at Tehran was nearly ideal and probably the only political and geographical combination that could have secured a quasi-unanimous support for the resolution. The major powers—East and West—were far from happy about the resolution, but they could not afford to oppose.[96]

MacBride also confided that his work on the resolution had produced some friction with the Swiss delegation and, indirectly, with the ICRC. The Swiss, along with the South Vietnamese, were in fact the only ones to abstain on the resolution; it was a curious pairing, to be sure. Swiss ambassador August Lindt explained that his opposition was due to the alleged fact that the ICRC had not participated in the drafting of the resolution in Tehran, a claim MacBride rejected since he claimed to have personally met with the ICRC, raising awareness of his work prior to the conference and even suggesting joint action. MacBride had reportedly also facilitated meetings between UN secretary-general U Thant and the ICRC. In addition, while in Tehran, MacBride claimed to have cooperated with Lindt in the drafting of the resolution and that although Lindt "was most helpful in this respect . . . he was unhappy because he felt that the resolution was to a certain extent forcing the hand of the ICRC."[97]

The text of the adopted resolution explains why the ICRC (and with it, Switzerland) felt uncomfortable. It touched on several controversial topics from which the ICRC had recently learned to steer clear—particularly the denunciation of specific means of warfare such as chemical and biological weapons. It also mentioned "minority racist or colonial regimes" and their refusal to comply with UN decisions and to respect the UDHR, and it decried the inhumane treatment given to freedom fighters. Procedurally, the resolution assigned priority to the UNGA (through the office of the UN secretary-general) to work on the better application and development of IHL, relegating the ICRC to a consultative role.[98] Yet despite all this, the 1968 resolution went in a direction not inimical to ICRC aspirations, only perhaps too aggressively and without sufficient clarity about the all-important question of who would steer the process.

The resolution, Respect for Human Rights in Armed Conflict, was one of the few clear accomplishments of the UN International Conference on Human Rights, hosted in 1968 in Tehran. Standard commentary on this event is usually dour; the conference appeared to be high on aspirational and denunciatory rhetoric but low on concrete ideas regarding how to push the global human rights program forward.[99] Against this background, and considering that the topic of improving protections during armed conflict was not on the original Conference agenda, MacBride's efforts to have a resolution quasi-unanimously adopted are notorious. Most importantly for our discussion, the ICJ's work managed to trigger formal discussion about revisions to IHL, which the ICRC had failed to do.

A Shock: Vietnam and a Changed U.S. Attitude

The 1960s were a deeply violent decade in many corners of the world, with gruesome bloodshed amid decolonization and secessionist wars in Algeria, Burundi,

Congo, Laos, Morocco, Nigeria (Biafra), Rhodesia, Rwanda-Burundi, and Vietnam, among others. Unsurprisingly, by 1968 some states' reluctance to revising existing IHL had subsided as conflict-related brutality continued to produce victims in the thousands—mostly civilians. The growing recognition around this time of the right to be free from colonial and racist rule became a decisive force in propelling the legitimacy and means for protecting freedom fighters, particularly among newly independent nations that now populated the UN. In chapter 5 I explain these events and dynamics more fully as they relate to the process of transforming IHL.

Surprising changes also arose in the attitude of certain powerful Western states regarding revisions to the Geneva and Hague Conventions. Earlier I showed that the United States, alongside key European allies, had opposed the development of new humanitarian rules since the mid-1950s. Indeed, until 1965 the United States at best supported work on improving the *implementation* of existing IHL, not its reconstruction or extension.[100] Yet toward the end of the 1960s, U.S. skepticism over IHL revisions diminished. The United States did not vote against the Respect for Human Rights in Armed Conflict resolution in Tehran. According to U.S. telegrams, this was because the country had a "strong policy interest in humane treatment for all persons involved in armed conflict."[101] Moreover, as the U.S. representative at the Third UN Committee, Jean Picker, declared while discussing the Tehran resolution in December 1968,

> Mr. Chairman, my Government voted for Resolution XXIII at Tehran and we will vote in favor of the present draft resolution. . . . Perhaps it is not premature to give some preliminary consideration at this time to an important procedural question in the event there is a recommendation for new or revised international agreements in this field. The question is, of course, what body should undertake this most important work . . . we would like to call attention to the satisfactory procedure followed in 1949. The efforts of the ICRC and the Government of Switzerland contributed in large measure to the success of that last major effort to revise international law in this field. We would hope that whatever procedure is adopted would have at least a good chance to succeed in drafting sound instruments to which a great many, if not all, states will quickly adhere.[102]

What brought on this change in U.S. attitude? In one word: Vietnam. More precisely, U.S. involvement in the conflict between North and South Vietnam had markedly increased since the early 1960s. By 1965 American aerial bombing campaigns and land combat units were being deployed to weaken the National Liberation Front (NLF, or Vietcong) and their North Vietnamese supporters.[103]

Increased U.S. participation was followed by allegations of American atrocity against civilians, either through indiscriminate or imprecise bombing or through manhandling by army personnel on the ground. Allegations of abuse extended to the U.S.-backed South Vietnamese military. At the same time, the United States denounced cruel treatment and lack of humanitarian guarantees by the North Vietnamese with regard to American pilots fallen in captivity, and although other U.S. charges of communist atrocity would come later, I suggest that it was the concern for the fate of POWs, both those held by its enemies as well as by its own forces, that initially moved the United States to consider the need for updated humanitarian rules.[104]

Concerned with the escalation of hostilities, the ICRC wrote in June 1965 to the governments of North Vietnam, South Vietnam, and the United States, as well as to the NLF, to remind them of their responsibilities under the Geneva Conventions—particularly the Convention Relative to the Treatment of Prisoners of War.[105] The ICRC's vice president, Jacques Freymond, explicitly referred to Common Articles 1 and 2 to the Geneva Conventions as the formal legal basis for his appeal, implying that the Vietnamese conflict was an *international* war and not an internal conflict. This notion was reinforced by Freymond's insistence that the NLF was also "bound by the undertakings signed by Vietnam" without an explicit mention of CA3, suggesting that the ICRC was sufficiently convinced that the internationalization of the conflict triggered the application of all conventions and not only the humanitarian provisions of CA3.

U.S. secretary of state Dean Rusk replied to the ICRC in August 1965, declaring continued American respect for the Geneva Conventions and announcing plans to aid South Vietnam in expanding and improving facilities and procedures to process and care for captured combatants.[106] South Vietnamese minister of foreign affairs Tran Van Do also replied, reassuring the ICRC that South Vietnam was "fully prepared to respect the provisions" of the conventions, that "Vietcong prisoners have always received the most humane treatment from our civilian and military authorities," and vowing to "contribute actively to the efforts of the [ICRC] to ensure their application."[107] A few months later, North Vietnam announced it would regard any captured pilots as major war criminals for destroying property and massacring its civilian population, but would regardless treat them well. For its part, the NLF claimed it was not bound by the Geneva Conventions "to which others beside itself subscribed" but that, nevertheless, it would treat prisoners humanely and collect and care for the enemy wounded.[108]

These dissonant responses augured tough challenges that would pervade IHL revisions in the 1970s. From an American perspective, they highlighted the protective gaps that remained in the separation between international and noninternational conflicts toward captured combatants (recall that CA3 was far less comprehensive than the Third Geneva Convention), particularly in struggles whose status was disputed by its participants. Although for the United States the conflict in Vietnam was international, for the North Vietnamese it was both a civil war and a war of aggression, during which even the application of CA3 was in doubt. More alarmingly, from the standpoint of North Vietnam and the Vietcong wars of national liberation should be given special recognition, particularly those also fought against external "aggressors" whose behavior—they thought—was invariably criminal. Finally, there remained the difficult issue of whether non-state armed groups were bound by IHL which, as the Vietcong noted, were made and signed not by them but by their government opponents.

The violence of the Vietnam conflict has been amply documented and need not be rehearsed here.[109] I focus instead on showing how in the years 1965–68 the United States grew increasingly dissatisfied with the protections contained in IHL. A U.S. Department of Defense memorandum from March 1968 reveals the hurdles faced by the U.S. Army while trying to ascertain and improve the fate of American prisoners in the Vietnam conflict:

> As of February 1968, 959 American military personnel were either prisoners of war or missing in action. Of these, 167 are believed held captive by North Vietnam and 450 are listed as missing in action over the North. The Viet Cong hold 24 known PWs and 165 are carried as missing in action in South Vietnam. The Pathet Lao are believed to be holding 5 in Laos and there are 71 others missing in that country. Red China holds 2 men whom we refer to officially as "detainees" and there are 6 carried as missing in action in China. . . . Exact figures on PWs held by Communist forces in Vietnam and Laos are not available because neither Hanoi, the Viet Cong, nor the Pathet Lao has provided lists of names or numbers of prisoners.[110]

The same document claimed that the Interdepartmental Committee formed to deal with POW issues had "concentrated its efforts in attempting to make the enemy aware of its responsibilities as outlined in the Geneva Conventions Relative to the Treatment of PWs [*sic*]. This is our paramount interest. All avenues leading to this goal and to the eventual recovery of our captured servicemen are being explored."[111]

Similarly, a memorandum sent by the Office of the Deputy Chief of Staff for Personnel to the U.S. Army chief of staff in December 1967 reveals that the army had since July 1966 decided to assign "a select group of knowledgeable military and civilian personnel" to conduct a comprehensive review process of this issue. The study suffered delays but was finally completed in November 1968.[112] Among the areas selected for review was a section on international law and the related U.S. performance.[113] The army's in-house researchers had already identified critical problems with the Geneva Conventions: "1. The Geneva Conventions are applicable but not appropriate to modern warfare. 2. The Geneva Conventions are 'fuzzy' in ruling on the legality of certain policies. 3. The Geneva Conventions contain no enforcement mechanism."[114] More generally, the U.S. Army saw the conventions as "based in large measure on World War II experience and . . . in certain areas . . . no longer . . . appropriate in the present state of technology." The study would offer "recommendations for remedying deficiencies in international law," particularly on the treatment of POWs, warning that, absent revisions, the U.S. military risked the "continuation of operations under a body of law which does not recognize the realities of modern warfare."[115] Evidently, then, since at least 1965 a sense of urgency emerged within the U.S. military to diagnose perceived defects with the Geneva Conventions and to proceed with a revision of portions of the existing law.

I have so far only highlighted one aspect of these "deficiencies" for the United States: the treatment of POWs that primary evidence shows as the initial trigger of change in American attitudes. Yet as the Vietnam conflict dragged on and was accompanied by more allegations of abuse, several other concerns surfaced, not least the protection of the civilian population brought to the fore when the March 1968 My Lai Massacre became public in late 1969. I reference added concerns in chapter 5, as they pervaded the drafting and the negotiation of the APs during the 1970s.

A final and pivotal aspect of the question behind the move to the update IHL in the 1960s remains to be fleshed out: the swift arrival of newly decolonized states as a revolutionary political force and their ability to wield influence, particularly in the UN. It is to this issue that I turn before concluding.

A Global Structural Change: Decolonization

Between 1945 and 1965, international society was transformed through the massive attainment of independent statehood by formerly "non-self-governing" or colonial territories, mostly African and Asian, which had fought or negotiated their way out of dependent status from their (largely but not exclusively European) rulers.[116] This revolution in sovereignty was particularly consequential in international organizations where statehood came with a voice and a vote, the paramount example being the UN. A numerical summary succinctly captures the scope of change within the UN. In 1950 it had sixty member states, five of which had become independent since 1945; in 1960, out of ninety-nine states, thirty-three were newcomers; by 1967, membership had exploded to 123 states, fifty-six of them new. Put in percentage terms, in 1950, new states represented 8.33 percent of the UN's makeup; in 1960, 33.3 percent; and in 1967, 45.5 percent.[117]

Newly independent states brought their own common concerns to the international rostrum, foremost among which were decolonization, human rights, development, and permanent ownership of national resources.[118] Collectively they catalyzed a revolution in international law and diplomacy.[119] Their ability to wield voting majorities in the UNGA and other UN commissions, in coalition with socialist or Arab states, enabled them to get resolutions, declarations, and sometimes also binding treaties adopted with relative ease. This was the case of the Declaration on the Granting of Independence to Colonial Countries and Peoples in 1960 and the International Convention on the Elimination of All Forms of Racial Discrimination in 1965. As David Kay asserts, "One must view as an outstanding achievement of the new nations their successful forging between 1960 and 1964 of an international moral consensus against the continuation of Western colonialism. By 1964 the impropriety of any defense of the continued existence of colonialism was apparent to all except the retrograde regimes of southern Africa. Within the United Nations itself the new nations succeeded during this period in making their own uppermost concern, colonialism, the uppermost concern of the Organization."[120]

Debates about decolonization continue today, with scholars expounding conflicting views on whether the "international moral consensus" to which Kay refers can be considered causally responsible for the demise of colonialism.[121] What is indisputable, however, is that newly independent nations excelled at using the UN, and the UNGA in particular, as a site of *collective legitimization*.[122] Their concerns were sometimes conveyed in the language of human rights, in what some contemporary accounts consider an effective but controversial appropriation.[123] Reflecting critically in 1965 on the new states' alleged instrumentalization of human rights, Louis Henkin claimed that

> the struggle to end colonialism . . . swallowed up the original purpose of cooperation for promotion of human rights. The gradual elimination of dependent areas and their admission to the UN meant an ever-increasing Assembly majority with some agreed attitudes, particularly a determination to extirpate the remnants of white colonialism and white discrimination. These attitudes impinged on the human rights program as well. Of course, they assured the sharpest scrutiny of human rights in dependent areas. . . . But it was championship of anticolonialism, designed to accelerate "self-determination." It was not an assertion of general standards which other nations, including the champions, were prepared to accept in their own countries.[124]

The use of human rights language and law by new states expanded to IHL. That the Tehran resolution had been cosponsored by Jamaica and Uganda serves as evidence of this.[125]

We might ask, why was there no overt Western opposition to a resolution calling for improvements to IHL using rather incendiary language?

One possibility is that after years of seeing similar resolutions adopted by the UNGA, Western states had grown blasé about this practice. U.S. opposition to other resolutions at the Tehran conference, particularly those that appeared to legitimate the right to violent self-determination, nevertheless casts doubt on this hypothesis. An alternative is that, instead of indifference, U.S. acceptance of this resolution owed to diplomatic negligence. Other scholarship endorses this possibility. Roland Burke, for instance, decries the fact that at the 1968 Tehran conference "few states were willing to challenge the assault on traditional human rights from the confident, and numerically superior, Afro-Asian bloc. This was especially true for the US delegation, who did little to defend the legacy of Eleanor Roosevelt and the Universal Declaration. They chose instead to flatter the prejudices of their audience with prophylactic doses of self-criticism." This attitude leads Burke, in agreement with influential diplomatic figures like Daniel Patrick Moynihan, to denounce the 1968 Tehran conference as "a key moment in the collapse of US human rights diplomacy."[126]

This argument overlooks other plausible sources of U.S. conduct in this regard, however. Rather than negligence, it could be that sensitive American domestic and foreign policy considerations—namely, the nation's deep racial problems at home and a troubling experience in Vietnam—increasingly prompted rhetorical restraint on the part of the U.S. delegates. The nature of the speeches U.S. head delegate Roy Wilkins made in Tehran supports this view, as noted by Burke, insofar as Wilkins "emphasized the great progress made in racial equality, and the steps being taken to grant economic and social rights in the United States."[127] In Tehran the United States seemed more interested in deflecting criticism than in raising controversy, which explains the acclamation that Wilkins's "defensive posture" elicited in Washington, DC.[128] Moreover, archival evidence presented earlier on U.S. worries about Vietnam supports this view regarding the improvement of IHL protections for POWs.

U.S. rhetorical restraint raises the possibility that growing social opprobrium and forum isolation operated within the UNGA upon Western, and especially colonial, powers, particularly amid human rights discussions led by an assertive and majoritarian Third World. In the words of Burke,

> The sheer preponderance of Asian, Arab, and African states also made still further collapse in the Western position more likely. Comfortable

> majorities could now be assembled on questions of *apartheid* and colonialism without consulting the so-called Western and Others Group, let alone gaining assent. *Negative votes or abstentions became increasingly embarrassing in such a context*, even if the languages proposed bordered on that deemed unacceptable. As Ambassador Meyer noted on the Tehran Conference's *apartheid* text, the US was willing to capitulate on "extreme African demands" simply to avoid the humiliation of joining a friendless set of state absentees. The ambassador advised the secretary of state that he had in "mind the unfortunate impression which would be created if we were one of the few absentees."[129]

David Kay's systematic analysis of the negative votes cast by France, the United Kingdom, and the United States on issues of self-determination before and after the influx of the newly independent nations to the UN strongly supports the social opprobrium hypothesis. Kay's data shows "a steady, though somewhat irregular, decline in the percentage of negative vote cast by these three states commencing with the eleventh session in 1956," coinciding with the entry of new nations into the UN and their fierce campaigning for colonialism. He goes further to conclude that "the records are replete with . . . cases in which France, the United Kingdom, and the United States have since 1956 either acquiesced in or supported anti-colonial resolutions far stronger than these three states voted against in earlier years."[130]

This chapter has demonstrated once again the operation of a recurrent "impetus-creating" path to legal development in the area of IHL, consisting of atrocity effects and persistent norm entrepreneurship.

This was the case, first, of the ICRC and the issue of internal troubles in the 1950s and 1960s. Quickly after the adoption of CA3 in 1949, events on the ground in various situations of internal violence triggered renewed debates within the ICRC on how to address state reluctance to admitting the existence of "noninternational conflict" and also how to tackle situations that did not plausibly rise to that level (troubles and tensions.) Given an expectation that states were unlikely to take up new legal commitments on these issues so soon after the revision of the Geneva Conventions, the ICRC summoned various dialogues with influential international legal experts with a view to arriving at more expansive interpretations of CA3.

Generating progressive interpretations of existing law through meetings of legal experts seems to have had some policy and practical benefits for the ICRC, but ultimately it did not legitimize a move among states to create new IHL. However, the demise of the Draft Rules points to another necessary condition for triggering formal conversations about treaty revisions and development: piercing through the skepticism of important Western state gatekeepers.

Western states' (and especially NATO powers') desire for international humanitarian regulations regarding their conduct during hostilities and their use of certain "means and methods" of war (especially nuclear weapons and aerial bombardment) was low or nonexistent. The attitude of those powerful states effectively shut down the initiative in the late 1950s, confirming that states' risk aversion toward humanitarian normative expansion/emergence was not only perceived (as with internal troubles) but also real (as with the Draft Rules.) I have shown that the attitude of the ICRC toward the idea of formal legal developments in both international and internal conflicts became more circumspect as a result of this frustrating experience, although its interest and efforts did not subside.

I have also addressed the puzzle of why, despite the grim prospects for the emergence of new IHL around the mid-1960s, states were soon engaging in official meetings precisely to that end. In particular, three key conditions combined to change the fate of the story and led to this striking outcome. First, renewed atrocities motivated a new nonstate norm entrepreneur, the ICJ, to press for IHL revisions and to insert the issue within the UNGA. Second, the ICJ's actions occurred at an auspicious moment during which the international system transformed due to decolonization, creating scores of new states interested in promoting self-determination and protecting freedom fighters waging wars of national liberation. This transformation reduced the influence of the West within the UN and enabled the newly decolonized majorities to achieve and propagate an international moral consensus around self-determination as a central human right (and as corollary, colonialism as an international crime). The idea of revising IHL to incorporate these new concerns was soon folded into the UN's agenda, at once giving it the political impulse it had lacked in previous years and seemingly driving Western—especially colonial—powers to the international moral "wall." Third, the interests of another crucial actor shifted: the United States became mired in an abuse-riddled conflict in Vietnam and sought at all costs to protect its soldiers suffering abuse in the hands of their communist captors in North Vietnam. This change in American attitudes toward debates about the revision of IHL completed the set of conditions facilitating a new step of legal emergence for both internal and international conflicts.

5

A REVOLUTION IN LAWMAKING? (1968–1977)

> **The facts of life in the society of States are however not as sovereignty-bravado portrays them. Its rhetoric does not fit their reality. . . . Even Titans can find their range of options to be disagreeably restricted.**
>
> —Geoffrey Best, *War and Law since 1945*

International humanitarian law (IHL) was last revised in 1977, after a nearly ten-year-long process that started in Tehran. Each of the two resulting instruments, the Additional Protocols (APs) to the 1949 Geneva Conventions, dealt with internal conflict in rather particular ways. Additional Protocol I (API) regulates national liberation war on the same footing as it does interstate conflict, while Additional Protocol II (APII) applies only to (high-level) civil wars, in contrast to Common Article 3's (CA3) imprecise but broad scope of application.

The APs are complicated and fascinating instruments, encapsulating most major aspects of global politics at the time: the Third World's struggle to legitimize national liberation conflict through international law; Western efforts to manage the end of formal decolonization while containing damage to their security, image, and alliances; shifting Cold War politics and proxy warfare; and the correlated intensification of government repression and defense of the principle of nonintervention in Africa, Asia, eastern Europe, and Latin America.[1] This chapter explains how these tensions, interests, and demands all contentiously crystallized within the APs: two compromise agreements which despite being officially adopted by consensus thinly concealed deep discord and strategic deception among the negotiating states. I demonstrate, as I did in chapter 3 with regard to CA3, that the new rules for national liberation war and internal conflict contained within the APs constitute face-saving, contested international law.

When the four-year Diplomatic Conference on the Reaffirmation and Development of IHL Applicable in Armed Conflicts ended in 1977, it probably did so with a collective sigh of relief. Like other multilateral negotiations at the time, the making of the APs was filled with acrimony, uncertainty, and tension from start to end. Western states engaged not only in frustrating (and often surprisingly fruitless) efforts at coordination among themselves for years but also repeatedly fought and lost public battles against supermajority coalitions formed primarily by African, Arab, Asian, and socialist countries.

The chief controversy during the CDDH (the official abbreviation for the Diplomatic Conference, coming from its name in French, Conférence diplomatique sur la reaffirmation et le développement du droit international humanitaire applicable dans les conflits armés) was tied to an amendment to the most important article of API, which set out the treaty's scope of application. In addition to conflicts between states, the amended paragraph 4 of Article 1 proclaimed that API would cover "armed conflicts in which peoples are fighting against colonial domination and alien occupation and against racist régimes in the exercise of their right of self-determination."[2]

With this provision, states admitted in politically charged (and from the Western perspective, quite incendiary) terms that a binding multilateral humanitarian agreement would treat national liberation war in the same terms as interstate conflict. This "upgrading" of anticolonial, antiracist, and anti-alien-occupation conflicts was not merely nominal. In addition to Article 1, Article 44 of API established that even if combatants failed to meet the requirement of distinguishing themselves from the civilian population, they would nevertheless be given protections "equivalent in all respects to those accorded to prisoners of war" by the Third Geneva Convention of 1949 (the Convention Relative to the Treatment of Prisoners of War, hereafter the POW Convention) and by API itself.[3]

When first raised during negotiations, these two provisions sparked a veritable scandal. From the perspective of newly decolonized countries and Arab nations supporting Palestine against Israel, these were of course legitimate aspirations already enshrined in important United Nations (UN) instruments including the UN Charter, the Declaration on Principles of International Law concerning Friendly Relations and Co-operation among States (1970), and the International Covenant on Civil and Political Rights.

With few exceptions, however, Western states found the explicit inclusion of national liberation conflict to be dangerously regressive for IHL, a body of law long said to be agnostic to political motivation. Indeed, some Western delegations considered it as no less than a fatal affront to the purported objectivity and universality of IHL, reminiscent of outmoded "just war" doctrines.[4] Accordingly, when the committee discussing Article 1 in 1974 first took a vote on the controversial language, Western states voiced their horror and voted en masse against it. Unable to contain the majority, however, they lost.[5] Yet instead of walking out of the conference in disgust, Western states remained at the table and a few years later in 1977, when both Articles 1 and 44 were put to a vote in plenary for their final inclusion in API, only Israel voted against them. Western states either supported them or abstained. Why?

APII on noninternational conflicts also radically differed from initial aspirations and designs. While in 1971–72 the International Committee of the Red Cross (ICRC) proposed a draft treaty offering ample humanitarian treatment to combatants and noncombatants in internal conflicts, the final negotiated APII was limited only to conflicts fulfilling a more stringent set of conditions than those set out in CA3 (negotiated nearly three decades prior). What happened?

I argue that Western states' grudging acceptance of wars of national liberation in the scope of API was an effect of social pressure via *forum isolation*. Although materially powerful in the 1970s, Western states opposing the legal legitimation of national liberation war were in the voting minority. They tried and failed to persuade the opposing Third World–led supermajority which held self-determination and the fight against racism and occupation as legitimate trump cards. Numerically and politically disabled, Western states reasoned they should not walk out of a humanitarian negotiation, fearing opprobrium at home and abroad, related international status and reputational damage, and potentially irreparable harm to IHL itself.

Located between a rock and a hard place, during the CDDH Western states opted for accommodating to the opposing supermajority while also ensuring to "remedy" the situation in private. They did so by making the language of the API rules indeterminate in key places and by inserting additional articles that lowered the likelihood of API's application to liberation war. In other words, although pressured into acquiescing, Western states covertly pushed back in the 1970s, saving face and avoiding status damage while securing their interests through deception. With respect to the provision granting generous prisoner of war (POW) treatment to captured freedom fighters in national liberation wars, I argue that forum isolation was complemented by the American delegation's interest in establishing humane treatment for *all* POWs, a product of U.S. experience in Vietnam and facilitated by the ICRC (as explained in chapter 4).

Western states' anxiety with the idea of assigning rights and responsibilities to armed nonstate actors (especially national liberation movements) related to ominous expected political and material consequences, and particularly the risk of legitimation and humanitarian protections that strengthened their struggle. Compounding this political suspicion was the ingrained conviction that the will and capacity of most armed nonstate actors to respect IHL were weak or absent, making the attribution of responsibilities and entitlements to them foolish and self-defeating.

The story of APII is also one of compromise between clashing groups of entrepreneurs with asymmetric influence. In the 1970s, considering the frailty of postcolonial states in Africa and Asia, the proliferation of repressive military governments in Latin America, the remains of British, French, and Portuguese colonialism, as well as situations of political conflict and terrorism in parts of Eastern and Western Europe, the odds were strongly stacked against the emergence of enhanced regulation for "nonliberation" internal conflicts. While ideologically these states had little in common, their fragile domestic security situations led them to coalesce in opposition to APII, arguing for the protection of national sovereignty and the principle of nonintervention. Committed to salvaging at least *some* humanitarian safeguards for the most prevalent type of violence around the world (internal conflict), moderate delegates from both the Western and Third World coalitions, with support from the ICRC, quietly came together behind the scenes and struck a deal which, while less encompassing than originally envisioned, nevertheless added substantive protections to those included in CA3.

This chapter first resumes the historical process behind the reaffirmation and revision of IHL toward the late 1960s, priming readers for the complex issues that surfaced later during the official prenegotiation phase, the *travaux préparatoires*. The second section clarifies the core dilemmas states faced prior to the diplomatic negotiations, foregrounding the multiple discussions held by Western states as they attempted coordination. The final section continues this task but delves into the actual negotiation phase of the protocols over a period of four years. It is this section that demonstrates the operation of forum isolation and covert pushback.

Resuming the Road to the Protocols

In early 1968 the idea that IHL should be revised entered the UN under the banner of "respect for human rights in armed conflict." However, unless the UN General Assembly (UNGA) seized on the subject, the passing of a resolution at a special conference promised nothing. As Suter explains, "for much of 1968 [Séan] MacBride was at the centre of a network of frenetic correspondence, with him as the co-coordinator of the five governments as well as trying to get U Thant [the UN secretary-general] and Marc Schreiber [the director of the UN Commission on Human Rights] more actively involved in this subject, trying to win the support of other governments, and trying to get NGOs to pressure their governments to support the Tehran resolution when it came before the 1968 General Assembly."[6]

In April 1968, even before the UN International Conference on Human Rights ended in Tehran, U Thant replied positively to MacBride, noting that he had been in close touch with the ICRC on this issue and that he only wished governments would take an interest and support the work.[7] In October 1968 the ICRC's director, Claude Pilloud, traveled to New York to follow the UNGA debates and persuaded governments sponsoring the "respect for human rights in armed conflict" resolution to incorporate the principles proclaimed by the 1965 International Red Cross Conference. India introduced the draft resolution, again in cosponsorship with a mix of newly independent socialist and Scandinavian states, that gained unanimous adoption both in committee and plenary.[8]

Preparing the groundwork for formal revisions, the ICRC quickly convened a meeting of private experts February 24–28, 1969.[9] The meeting touched on every substantive aspect of the law needing revision.[10] Importantly, experts reviewed the types of armed conflicts to which any new rules should apply, including international and noninternational conflict but also "hostilities conducted by the United Nations, guerrilla, and finally, by extension, situations of internal disturbance and tensions."[11]

The outcome of the February 1969 experts meeting bears some importance because it formed the basis of conversations moving forward. The ICRC was straightforward about the need to pay special attention to internal conflicts both due to their prevalence in recent decades and the few humanitarian rules devoted to them.[12] Two crucial gaps were singled out in CA3: a lack of clear definitions and general normative (substantive) underdevelopment. The ICRC urged that it should not be up to states to decide when CA3 was triggered; rather, the article ought to apply whenever armed forces produced hostilities.[13] This definition echoed the interpretation that experts had honed through the various commissions and dialogues held during the 1950s and 1960s, as discussed in chapter 4. The experts at this meeting agreed, claiming that "the conditions to be fulfilled by a noninternational conflict to be considered as such should not be too restrictive."[14] They also concurred with the ICRC's idea that if a foreign party intervened to support any party to an internal conflict, the situation became international and the whole body of IHL was applicable.[15] They were less certain, however, about whether IHL could regulate situations of troubles or disturbances, where states might be particularly averse to external meddling.[16] Other solutions could perhaps be sought in those contexts via explicit agreements by governments allowing ICRC operations, through resorting to human rights law or via UN resolutions requesting the ICRC to act, which governments would accept.[17]

The ICRC also argued that nonstate groups should be bound by the text and seek to follow its considerations.[18] Controversy ensued on the issue of whether wars of national liberation constituted international conflicts or rather internal ones.[19] Tensions followed between those wishing to extend humanitarian protections to freedom fighters and about their ability to observe traditional IHL principles and limits.[20] These hurdles continued surfacing over the coming years.

The ICRC and the UN tightened their liaison in 1970.[21] In April 13–17 of that year, the UN Human Rights Division organized a small meeting of government experts and various international organizations to address for the first time prospects for revising IHL in its entirety.[22] The ICRC offered to collaborate further and announced that it would convene a conference of government experts in the spring of 1971, the first official intergovernmental encounter to consider the eventual development of the law. To pave the diplomatic road, high-ranking members of the ICRC also began to contact certain states informally (including Canada, the Netherlands, the United Kingdom, the United States, and the USSR), hoping to gauge their interests with relation to the emerging process, emulating the pathway followed in chapter 3 that led to the revision of the Geneva Conventions in the 1940s.

The *Travaux* Begin: An Analytic Frame

This section provides an analytical framing of the main positions and perceived stakes with regard to further expanding IHL to internal conflicts.[23] Stripped to the basics, in the 1970s the major dilemma once again facing states related to deep disagreements about the extension of *legal protection* to armed nonstate counterparts and its *symbolic* and *material* consequences in internal conflicts. A lot hinged upon a deceivingly simple question, who would be afforded what humanitarian protections, and in what contexts?

Unsurprisingly, most governments approached the question through the lens of their own interests, a variable category that once more combined security and moral aspects, as well as domestic and international dimensions. Different groups of states can be discerned, each with a constructive and a destructive agenda concerning various types of internal conflicts.[24]

Foremost was the newly decolonized world gathering most of Africa and Asia, keen on cementing the idea that national liberation, even if waged violently, was a legitimate international cause that ought to accrue special legal recognition and heightened humanitarian protection. The legal legitimation of national liberation war (and of freedom fighters) was the decolonized world's *constructive agenda* in the 1970s.

Characterizing national liberation conflicts as international wars had obviously crucial political dimensions, notably pressuring colonial powers and their allies by discrediting imperial rule and precipitating their retreat from their occupied territories and by legitimating liberation movements under international law. It also entailed more specific legal demands with symbolic and material consequences. Perhaps most importantly, decolonized states sought to proclaim the application of international POW protections for so-called freedom fighters that fell in the hands of their enemy.

It is important to understand what being considered a POW (compared to a captured rebel) entails.[25] Put simply, the category carries with it sophisticated privileges under IHL. In terms of *treatment*, it activates a plethora of substantive protections contained in the 143-article POW Convention of 1949, including detailed guidelines on proper questioning, conditions of internment, work, food, clothes, and even recreation and the right to canteens. The POW Convention also authorizes the verification by a third state (called a Protective Power, in IHL legalese) of the humane treatment of prisoners.

Symbolic benefits also extend to POWs. First, governments and the general public usually afford them honorific, if not heroic, status that is denied to other fighters (e.g., "terrorists"). Additionally, in the framework of IHL, the *legal* status of POW presupposes that, once detained, a combatant cannot be punished by an opponent solely for having participated in the conflict. The combatant must also be released at the end of the hostilities.

All these benefits were absent from the rules for internal conflicts in which governments had preferred to withhold rebels any legitimacy or entitlements beyond the important but basic guarantees of CA3. What is more, states had historically been extremely reluctant to even allow the use of the terms *combatant* and *prisoner of war* in the context of internal conflict, fearing that to utilize such words might give not only legitimize the rebels but suggest that the conflict they waged was international, hence triggering more expansive regulations. In sum, until the 1970s, POW treatment *and* status (two separate but related dimensions) only figured in the international law regulating conflicts between states.[26]

We can clearly see why legally transforming national liberation wars into international conflicts and giving detained freedom fighters the status and treatment of prisoners of war was met with opposition from stalwart Western quarters. Potential consequences to the existing framework of IHL were prominent. Most importantly, such transformation challenged three of IHL's bedrock principles. First, the notion of conflicts "against colonial domination," "alien domination," or "racist regimes" appeared to bring back political motivation into a body of law long understood as agnostic to ideas of "just" or "unjust" war and which had sought to decouple the question of *why* combatants go to war from that of *how* they fight once war erupts. The legitimation of national liberation appeared to single out a specific type of conflict and to attribute it privileged status alongside wars fought between states. This might seem like a rather legalistic concern, but it was one that carried enormous force among learned audiences of IHL (the bulk of whom were still Western at this time). It also brought other tough questions to the table: How might nonstate actors devoid of international legal personality accede to international treaties? Can they be expected to *actually* apply the law in the same way that states are? Later in this chapter I will demonstrate how these contentious puzzles were addressed during the official negotiation of the APs.

Additionally, in order to qualify as POWs, the Third Geneva Convention required combatants to fulfill four requirements: (1) they had to be commanded by a person responsible for his subordinates; (2) they had to bear a fixed distinctive recognizable at a distance; (3) they had to carry arms openly; and (4) they had to conduct their operations in accordance with the laws and customs of war. Of these, the second and third requirements were geared to compel combatants to distinguish themselves from the civilian population, which, per the customs of war, enjoyed general protection from attacks. (This is known as the principle of noncombatant or civilian immunity.)

However, given the fact that during liberation conflicts the colonial power held the conventional military advantage over freedom fighters, for the law to require the latter to distinguish themselves at all times by wearing distinctive signs or carrying their weapons openly became tantamount to facilitating their annihilation. Alleging military bias in the law, decolonized states wanted these requirements to be relativized or eliminated. Doing so, in their view, was both realistic and humane.[27] Yet from received legal humanitarian perspectives, removing these requirements threatened both to increase the risk of violence to noncombatants whom colonial armies might be more likely to find suspect—hence targetable—as freedom fighters in civilian guise (violating the principle of distinction). It might also put state militaries at a formal disadvantage, violating the idea that the law should apply to combatants equally regardless of their motivation (known as the principle of equality of belligerents).

The newly independent countries also had a *destructive agenda* relating to internal conflicts, however. Just as they supported national liberation wars outside their borders, many decolonized states were fragile internally and found themselves waging conflicts of their own against rebellious or secessionists groups. Most of them proved resistant to the idea of committing to more humanitarian rules applicable to any armed violence occurring within states' boundaries save for that seeking "liberation."[28]

The perspective of the decolonized group was one that found some sympathy. Socialist countries, for instance, supported it wholeheartedly. Amid their battle for global moral and political as well as military superiority, socialist states were bent on embarrassing the declining Western empires and their allies and wasted no occasion to cheer on the anticolonial agenda at international forums. On the other hand, since internal repression was a backbone of the political viability of most socialist regimes, they held great revulsion for efforts to expand IHL further into their domestic realm, whether for those that might be considered as falling under CA3 or those better characterized as internal troubles or disturbances. The same may be said for much of the Arab world that, with few exceptions, rejected colonialism and external occupation (Israel being the main target in their case) but also disliked interference into their internal violent affairs. These groups of states found themselves largely sharing the constructive and destructive agendas of the decolonized world vis-à-vis national liberation war and nonliberation internal conflict, respectively.

Partial support for the wishes of the decolonized world also surfaced from other geographic areas. Whether or not they saw themselves as strong anticolonialists, Latin American states were in the 1970s similarly repressive domestically (Argentina, Brazil, Chile, and Uruguay, among others) or conflict-ridden (Colombia), and in a period when authoritarianism was on the rise in the region, ideas for increasing humanitarian restraint in the fight against organized internal dissent were unwelcome. Latin Americans' approach to the revisions process, at least as regards internal conflict, were mostly negative or reactive.

At the other end of the spectrum lay the Western world, which was fractured in its attitudes toward legal developments for internal conflicts. On the one hand, with the exception of Norway,[29] most Western states and especially colonial powers like France, Portugal, and the United Kingdom opposed the classification of liberation wars as international conflicts. On the other hand, however, the old European empires accepted that stronger rules might be desirable for taming the atrocities committed against civilians in internal conflicts of a high level, illustrated most vividly at the time by the Biafran secessionist war in Nigeria. Respectively, these two positions represented the Western group's destructive and constructive agendas.

One Western-proposed solution was to continue considering liberation conflicts as internal and to create a protocol with stringent and precise conditions applicable simultaneously to Biafra-style wars *and* conflicts for self-determination. These conditions were similar to those during the 1940s and discussed in chapter 3; nonstate groups would need to have an organized army under responsible command and exert sufficient territorial control enabling them to conduct their operations and to respect the body of IHL. *Any other* internal conflicts failing to meet these requirements, according to Britain and France, should remain outside the scope of the new protocols and only be regulated by CA3 or, in the case of troubles and disturbances, by domestic law or other instruments of international law such as human rights. The United Kingdom, privately alarmed about any consequences for Northern Ireland, was especially hostile to the idea that the internal conflicts below a certain level (CA3) should be covered by a new legal instrument. Preventing the application of any new instruments of IHL to Northern Ireland was, in fact, Britain's foremost goal throughout the revisions process in the 1970s.

Interestingly, though, Canada and the United States favored creating a protocol for noninternational conflicts that expanded the principles of CA3 but that also would be more or less automatically applicable once a conflict broke out within a state, whether it was waged for self-determination or not. In this they squarely confronted the British and French.

The Canadian view remains to be explained in the future, yet, as was shown in chapter 4, by the late 1960s the U.S. military had developed an interest in expanding POW protections to all persons detained while carrying arms openly during a military engagement, echoing a measure previously taken in Vietnam in 1966.[30] It was also around this time that the U.S. Congress became increasingly vocal on human rights and humanitarian legal issues. The subcommittee hearings organized by Representative Donald Fraser (D-MN) constituted a landmark example of congressional pressure in this regard. Fraser's office was aware of the humanitarian negotiations in Geneva, requested the U.S. Department of State to inform him of the American views, and issued recommendations for them in the ensuing report.[31]

Despite some deep disparities of opinion, one belief did appear to be widely shared by all Western states (except for Norway): an ingrained conviction in the inability and the will of national liberation movements or other insurgencies / guerilla groups to *actually apply* humanitarian rules. Profound distrust regarding the ideological and institutional inadequacies of such groups supported this view. This was one additional reason why Western colonial powers were so reluctant to design a new protocol for international conflicts applicable to national liberation struggles. National liberation movements, they held, could also not become official "high-contracting" parties to the conventions. As such, in this perspective, to accept the inclusion of national liberation wars in the draft protocols for interstate conflicts and to find ways to allow them to accede to the treaties might only serve to legitimize and empower them without truly achieving the goal of binding them—a politically and militarily self-defeating unilateral commitment.

Caught in these political-legal crosshairs was the ICRC. From its perspective too, it was desirable to extend humanitarian protections to as many types of internal conflicts as possible, including troubles and disturbances. But regarding national liberation, and despite the fact that the ICRC publicly recognized the strong movement and moral force behind its international legitimation, it did not seem persuaded that the UN documents that enshrined these ideas provided a robust enough basis to revise IHL accordingly or that the legal extension might effectively improve combatants' conduct on the ground.

Politically, however, the ICRC knew that failing to take into account the strongly held beliefs of the non-Western states might jeopardize its relations with them and with national liberation movements, even possibly hampering its access to victims on the ground. It ultimately refrained from inserting language referring to liberation wars in its draft API, merely mentioning it as an option for states to sort among themselves.

The positions and stakes just outlined surfaced slowly in the late 1960s and early 1970s as a series of public and private encounters took place at the behest of the ICRC, the UN, and states themselves. It seems crucial to convey just how time- and energy-consuming the process of "dialogue about revisions" was between 1969 and the first months of 1974, lest one still believes that the Geneva Conventions ranked as a low priority for governments at the time. I count both intergovernmental debates in public forums and to the extent that archival resources have allowed, of private meetings hosted by the ICRC, or by the United Kingdom, the United States, and other Western-NATO states. Government experts and delegates participated in at least twelve official or semiofficial group meetings *prior to* the start of the Diplomatic Conference in 1974. (For a partial list of meetings, see table 5.1.)[32]

Domestically, it was in 1971 that states' bureaucratic machineries began to ruminate on their views regarding the plethora of issues on the table. The speed, mechanics, and intensity with which different states approached legal revisions varied depending upon their degree of capacity and the salience of IHL for them. Major Western powers ranked high on both counts as France, the United Kingdom, and the United States had assembled interdepartmental teams to prepare for and exert influence during the slew of exploratory meetings laying ahead.[33] The teams formed in 1971 resembled those working on the revisions in the 1940s, combining civilian and military staff from a variety of relevant ministries. In the United States the Defense Departments (along with various subdivisions) bore most of the work. The UK team included mainly officials of the Ministry of Defence (MOD), the Foreign and Commonwealth Office (FCO), and the Home Office. The French team included staff from the Ministries of Defense, Interior and Public Health, Justice, and Social Security, as well as from the French Red Cross.[34]

As noted earlier, the United Kingdom and the United States emerged as crucial brokers among their Western political and military allies around 1971 and 1972. They constituted the heart of the Western Group and jointly determined whom to invite or exclude. Since the views of some North Atlantic Treaty Organization (NATO) states proved so distant (particularly Norway, which held different

TABLE 5.1. Some State Encounters after the 1968 Tehran Conference

MEETING #	TYPE OF MEETING	WHERE (IF KNOWN)/WHEN
1	Expert roundtable	Geneva, February 28–29, 1969
2	Twenty-first International Red Cross Conference	Istanbul, September 6–13, 1969
3	UNGA	New York, November 1969
4	Expert roundtable	April 13–17, 1970
5	Bilateral UK and ICRC	London, July 1970
6	UNGA	New York, November 1970
7	National Red Cross and Red Crescent Societies	The Hague, March 1–6, 1971
8	ICRC Conference of Government Experts, First Session	Geneva, May 24–June 12, 1971
9	Bilateral UK and US	Washington, DC, September 9, 1971
10	Bilateral UK and ICRC	November 25, 1971
11	Bilateral UK and US	London, November 29, 1971
12	UNGA	New York, November–December 1971
13	NATO	Brussels, April 6–7, 1972
14	ICRC Conference of Government Experts, Second Session	Geneva, May 3–June 3, 1972
15	Bilateral UK and ICRC	August 1972
16	Bilateral UK and US	August 7, 1972
17	Western Group	London, September 11–14, 1972
18	ICRC Small Government Expert Consultation	Geneva, January 15–20, 1973
19	ICRC Small Government Expert Consultation	Geneva, March 5–9, 1973
20	Western Group	London, October 15–19, 1973
21	Twenty-second International Red Cross Conference	Tehran, 8–15, 1973
22	UNGA	New York, November–December 1973
23	Western Group	January 1974
24	Western Group	September 2–3, 1974
25	Western Group	September 18–20, 1974
26	Western Inner Core	January 13–14, 1975
27	Western Group	January 27–30, 1975
28	Western Inner Core	Washington, November 17–19, 1975
29	Western Group	London, March 15–17, 1976
30	Western Inner Core	Bonn, November 1976
31	Western Inner Core	Brussels, January 1977
32	Western Inner Core	Geneva, March 14, 1977
33	Western Group	Geneva, March 15–16, 1977

Note: Table created by the author, drawing on the archives of France, Switzerland, the United Kingdom, and the United States listed in Archival Sources.

views on national liberation wars and weapons regulations), their delegates earned colorful epithets privately and were only invited when politically convenient. By 1973 Western coordination efforts broke the NATO "mold" to form larger and smaller groups of fluctuating membership: a Western Group comprising more or less permanently Belgium, Canada, Denmark, France, Italy, the Netherlands, the United Kingdom, the United States, and West Germany,[35] and a smaller Inner Core (Canada, France, the United Kingdom, and the United States, later expanded to include West Germany). Participants in the smaller group were asked to be tight-lipped regarding their meeting plans and in-group views to avoid creating jealousy and embarrassment among the expanded circle of allies. These group dynamics of ranking and inclusion/exclusion comport with recent insights in international relations about the construction and maintenance of pecking orders in multilateral negotiation.[36]

Interestingly, not even the closest Inner Core of Western allies saw eye to eye on key issues. Although France usually held more stringent views than the United Kingdom and the United States, it often acquiesced to their ideas in public while throwing tantrums in private. A concern for social reputation and isolation shone through the interaction between states holding progressive views (either for moral or alleged self-interested reasons), prompting anxiety and sometimes policy change in skeptics. West Germany, for instance, shamed Britain for its restrictive view on certain topics, including on the protection of civilians. In view of these reactions, the United Kingdom reasoned that it might have to moderate its position "*to avoid a damaging isolation* on positions which many people, including some of our friends, find over-rigid and inhumane."[37]

Relations *among* groups of states were similarly tense and, crucially, rife with social competition. The United Kingdom (and the Western Group more broadly) balked at the Soviets and socialist states' posturing as "the champions of protection for the civilian population." The British had some reason for propagandizing motives, since "certain of the delegates, e.g. those of Hungary and Yugoslavia told us in private conversation that their aim was, quite simply, to make the rules so difficult that war would be virtually impossible."[38] This attitude in the 1970s resembles that taken by the Soviet delegation in the 1940s, as discussed in chapter 3.[39]

That said, intergroup dynamics varied across issues, and some within the Western Group, particularly the Americans, eventually found it convenient to coordinate with the Soviets.[40] The United States attempted to exert influence over the Latin American delegations, as the United Kingdom did with Australia and New Zealand. And the Western Group expanded to include countries such as Turkey and Japan when it was deemed convenient.

Yet it was the interaction (or lack thereof) between the Western Group and the delegations from the so-called Afro-Asian nations that was perhaps most curious. It should have been obvious to the Western Group from the dynamics at the UNGA, or at the ICRC-sponsored events, that Third World states would constitute a majority with positions radically different from theirs in key areas. Despite this, the Western Group made no discernable effort to influence or spark joint dialogue with the decolonized world prior to the start of negotiations. Once the first session of the Diplomatic Conference closed in the spring of 1974, the British delegates concluded that the Western Group had spent too much time talking to itself and not to Third World states, whose voice was decisive.

In the end, after almost three years of intense dialogue, little Western consensus emerged on the quagmire of how to revise or develop IHL. Except for a shared understanding that national liberation wars should not qualify as international conflicts, Western states disagreed on exactly how to deal with captured fighters or with the threshold and protections to include in APII to regulate (nonliberation) internal conflicts. Strategic coordination became frustrating, time-consuming, and ineffective, and political anxieties over security matters and international standing were quite alive. Unfortunately for Western allies, the situation during the actual Diplomatic Conference would only get more complicated.

Status Politics in the 1970s

Before analyzing the dynamics of the 1974–77 Diplomatic Conference, broader contextualization is essential to understand the global status politics of the time. Status struggle and competition among the major state groupings involved in the IHL revisions process were prevalent in the 1960s and 1970s, all of which had concrete aspirations or anxieties in the relatively fluid social hierarchies (international and regional) of the period.

Although by the early 1970s British and French decolonization had advanced apace through a combination of armed struggle and negotiation, both states still held colonial territories.[41] Incomplete decolonization continued to make them vulnerable to international criticism. Here the British seemed especially sensitive, having recently faced violence in Aden (South Yemen) and enduring ongoing troubles in Northern Ireland. France had made the creation of close ties with French Africa a key part of its foreign policy, carefully fostered the project of the Communauté Franco-Africaine.[42] This meant, in part, learning to cope with the diplomatic stridence of certain of its former territories (and particularly Algeria) in their quest for international prominence. Elsewhere, altering Charles De Gaulle's grandeur doctrine, Georges Pompidou strengthened French ties with the European Economic Community (EEC), regained an interest in multilateral diplomacy, and worked to promote good relations with the United States.[43] Britain, too, despite its troubled accession process to the EEC, increasingly looked to Western Europe as a means to enhance its regional influence and find its role as a middle power, all while maintaining its special relationship with the United States.[44]

Military Cold War rivalry between the United States and the Soviet Union subsided (and gave way to nuclear cooperation and the Helsinki Accords) during détente in the 1970s.[45] Yet the political struggle to gain Third World allegiance survived.[46] Vietnam provided Third World countries with plentiful ammunition to denounce U.S. interventionism and atrocity, outrage from which the Soviet Union reaped obvious political benefit. The Soviets and other socialist states also continued to support national liberation movements and postcolonial demands in international forums, denigrating Western states and relegating them to an increasingly smaller, regressive minority.[47] U.S. support for Israel further increased its vulnerability vis-à-vis the Third World. Most of all, as noted, the decolonized world embarked upon a remaking of world order.[48] The steady decline of formal colonialism did not silence its demands (for the victory of national liberation movements, for a revised body of IHL, disarmament, new human rights law, a new international economic order, etc.); instead, it multiplied them.[49]

In this mix of aspirations and concerns, the waning European empires and the United States were most vulnerable. Britain and France resented anticolonial rhetoric as they accommodated to second-rank middle-power status,[50] and looked to the EEC as their in-group and to the United States for support. The United States scrambled to contain Vietnam-related domestic and international pressure amid ongoing Cold War ideological competition. And although not immune to social pressure, the Soviet Union, socialist bloc states, and the Third World were at this stage (in 1974) still comparatively less sensitive to human rights criticism at home and from abroad.[51]

As the protocols' formal negotiation approached, the international political environment remained volatile, presenting some players with social resources and opportunities that others, increasingly fewer in number, were denied. The scene was set for an explosive clash, and events did not disappoint.

A Revolution Unleashed: The Diplomatic Conference of 1974–1977

Following two days of debate by the heads of delegations, the 1974 Session of the CDDH officially opened on February 20, gathering 125 state delegations and thirty international observer organizations.[52] Decisions would be made by consensus wherever possible; otherwise, by a simple majority vote in commission, and a supermajority vote (two-thirds of those present and voting) in plenary.

Political fireworks broke out immediately. The first plenary session featured the president of Mauritania promoting the recognition of just wars and claiming that "it was quite obvious that it was the Zionists who wanted to throw all Arabs into the sea."[53] (The Israeli delegation walked out in protest.) Distraught, the conference then spent two full weeks in procedural politics, especially sorting out participation matters: Should liberation movements allowed to participate? Should Guinea-Bissau, which had unilaterally declared independence from Portugal in 1973, be admitted into the conference? After painstaking efforts, however, the United States successfully blocked entry to the Provisional Revolutionary Government of the Republic of South Vietnam (PRG), and negotiations began.[54]

Due to the procedural drama, the 1974 session of the conference languished in terms of concrete results. Yet among the few adopted articles featured was perhaps the most crucial one of all: Article 1 of API, which defined the international armed conflicts to which the new instrument would apply.

The Western Group's fears were quickly realized: various groups of states introduced different amendments (see options 1–7 in table 5.2), all with a view to legitimating national liberation wars as international. These texts ranged from politicized ("colonial and alien domination against racist regimes") to more legal-technical ("armed struggles waged by peoples in the exercise of their right of self-determination"). The voices of the Afro-Asian leadership mattered here. Egyptian legal scholar and diplomat Georges Abi-Saab sharply reminded colleagues debating in committee that there was "abundant proof" providing juridical footing to notion that wars of national liberation should be considered international conflicts, which was a "social phenomenon affecting millions of human beings," not just an issue of semantics. "Participants were thus not being asked to accept anything new; it was merely proposed that they should affirm explicitly in the field of IHL what they had already accepted as binding law within the United Nations and within general international law."[55]

Differences of language and tone aside, all these amendments fell like cold water on most Western delegations.[56] To defend their position, they relied on legalistic and utilitarian arguments, claiming that it was entirely inappropriate to insert motivations into IHL and that since decolonization was on the wane, permanent consideration of these struggles in international law was unnecessary. Moreover, Western skeptics raised the inability of liberation movements to apply the law, something that the representative of the Mozambique Liberation Front sharply countered, noting that "cases were known where States had departed from the established rules far more grossly than the liberation movements," a sentiment echoed by the Palestine Liberation Organization.[57]

The Western Group was publicly and privately stunned. British delegate Gerald Draper asserted that these amendments amounted to "damaging the structure

TABLE 5.2. Proposed Amendments to Article 1, Additional Protocol I, 1974

OPTION	AMENDMENT COSPONSORS	PROPOSED LANGUAGE
1	Algeria, Bulgaria, Czechoslovakia, East Germany, Hungary, Morocco, Poland, Tanzania, USSR	"The international armed conflicts referred to in Article 2 common to the Conventions include also armed conflicts where peoples fight against colonial and alien domination and against racist regimes"
2	Algeria, Arab Republic of Egypt, Australia, Cuba, Democratic Yemen, Guinea Bissau, Ivory Coast, Kuwait, Libyan Arab Republic, Madagascar, Morocco, Nigeria, Norway, Pakistan, Senegal, Sudan, Syrian Arab Republic, Tunisia, United Arab Emirates, United Republic of Cameroon, Yugoslavia, Zaire	"The situations referred to in the preceding paragraph include armed struggles waged by peoples in the exercise of their right of self-determination, as enshrined in the Charter of the United Nations and defined by the Declaration on Principles of International Law concerning Friendly Relations and Co-operation among States in accordance with the Charter of the United Nations"
3	Argentina, Austria, Belgium, Federal Republic of Germany, Italy, Netherlands, Pakistan, United Kingdom	"In cases not included in this present Protocol or in other instruments of conventional law, civilians and combatants remain under the protection and the authority of the principles of international law, as they result from established custom, from the principles of humanity and the dictates of public conscience" (Martens Clause)
4	Romania	". . . and in armed conflicts in which the people of a colony, a Non-Self-Governing Territory or a territory under foreign occupation are engaged, in the exercise of the right to self-determination and the right to self-defence against aggression, with a view to ensuring more effective protection for the victims of aggression and oppression"
5	Turkey	"The present Protocol shall also apply to armed conflicts waged by the national liberation movements recognized by the regional intergovernmental organizations concerned against colonial and foreign domination and racist regimes in the exercise of the principle of the self-determination of peoples as set out in the Charter of the United Nations"
6	Algeria, Arab Republic of Egypt, Bangladesh, Bulgaria, Burundi, Byelorussian Soviet Socialist Republic, Chad, Congo, Cuba, Czechoslovakia, German Democratic Republic, Ghana, Guinea-Bissau, Hungary, India, Indonesia, Iraq, Ivory Coast, Jordan, Kuwait, Lebanon, Liberia, Libyan Arab Republic, Madagascar, Mali, Mauritania, Mongolia, Morocco, Nigeria, Pakistan, People's Democratic Republic of Korea, Poland, Qatar, Romania, Saudi Arabia, Senegal, Sri Lanka, Sudan, Sultanate of Oman, Syrian Arab Republic, Togo, Tunisia, Uganda, Ukrainian Soviet Socialist Republic, United Republic of Cameroon, United Republic of Tanzania, USSR, Yemen, Yugoslavia, Zaire, Zambia	"The situations referred to in the preceding paragraph include armed conflicts where peoples fight against colonial and alien domination and against racist regimes in the exercise of their right of self-determination, as enshrined in the Charter of the United Nations and defined by the Declaration on Principles of International Law concerning Friendly Relations and Co-operation among States in accordance with the Charter of the United Nations"

TABLE 5.2. (continued)

OPTION	AMENDMENT COSPONSORS	PROPOSED LANGUAGE
7	Argentina, Honduras, Mexico, Panama, Peru	"The situations referred to in the preceding paragraph include armed conflicts in which peoples are fighting against colonial and alien occupation and racist regimes in the exercise of their right of self-determination, as enshrined in the Charter of the United Nations and the Declaration on Principles of International Law concerning Friendly Relations and Co-operation among States in accordance with the Charter of the United Nations"
8 (Merger)	Adopted in Committee I (1974) and in plenary (1977)	"The situations referred to in the preceding paragraph include armed conflicts in which peoples are fighting against colonial domination and alien occupation and against racist régimes in the exercise of their right of self-determination, as enshrined in the Charter of the United Nations and the Declaration on Principles of International Law concerning Friendly Relations and Cooperation among States in accordance with the Charter of the United Nations"

Source: This is a modified, expanded version of a table published as an appendix in Giovanni Mantilla. "The Protagonism of the USSR and Socialist States in the Revision of International Humanitarian Law (IHL)." *Journal of the History of International Law* 21, no. 2 (2019): 181–211.

of The Hague and Geneva Conventions and would involve the need to reconstruct the whole of IHL."[58] Behind the scenes, the UK delegation cabled London, alerting the government to the dangerous legitimating effect the amendment might cause. There might be "nothing to prevent the IRA [Irish Republican Army] from addressing the requisite declaration to the depositary and the Northern Ireland situation would thereby become an international conflict."[59] The French representative agreed that "the goal of IHL was to alleviate suffering, not to make statements on conflict motivations" and that "his Government was not prepared, under any circumstances, to sacrifice that basic principle."[60]

The United States also found the move "disturbing," since "it would make the determination of the protections to be accorded to a combatant depend on a political judgment about the nature of the cause for which he was fighting. . . . The result is totally inconsistent with the basic premise of the Geneva Conventions." The Americans so disliked the amendment that they pressured the Australians, who were cosponsoring one of them (see table 5.2, option 2) to desist: "We believe that for [Australian government] and other governments which are concerned about effective application of IHL to participate in undermining of basic foundations of that law for short-term political gain would be highly irresponsible."[61] Belgium reacted swiftly and with the support of a few others proposed an alternative amendment that hoped to meet the concerns of the Third World coalition by reference to the older but well-accepted legal formula known as the Martens Clause, which had been used in the 1899 Hague Conventions to deal with issues where consensus was elusive (see table 5.2, option 3). Canada, Italy, Monaco, the Netherlands, Spain, Switzerland, and Uruguay endorsed this view, while Denmark preferred the original ICRC text.[62]

After much debate without resolution, the ICRC proposed setting up a working group to find a compromise that "would be accepted by the greatest possible number of parties." Although that working group's verbatim records are unavailable, private government correspondence suggests this effort did not succeed. UK cables revealed that after long discussions, the coalition of African and Asian countries were unwilling to compromise on their "extreme" amendments.[63]

The British considered three options worth detailing: (1) to hold their legalistic line that national liberation wars should not be included in API; (2) to accommodate and modify some of the less offensive versions of the amendment on the table; or (3) to wait to see if any better options emerged through the work of other states interested in including self-determination but in neutral terms.[64]

The British recognized the political/social risk in showing themselves intransigent: "If we refuse to budge on the point of principle *we shall be in a fairly small minority* and efforts will be made to blame us for any failure of the Conference, but to concede the point will be the thick end of a pretty long wedge since a number of consequential amendments will be put forward for the rest of [the APs] will probably disappear. *The consequences for international law in general and the Geneva Conventions in particular would clearly be very serious.*"[65]

Crucially for my argument, the British explicitly addressed the cost of forum isolation in private: "It is for consideration in each case when the political cost of isolation exceeds the benefit in the field of international law . . . the US, France, Germany, Switzerland, Denmark, Benelux, Canada and New Zealand [are] among the countries sharing our minority position in this case."[66] In case of Third World refusal to compromise, they recommended voting against the amendment "*provided at least one* EEC partner is prepared to do likewise."[67] The British were quite alive to the social politics of negotiations: they seemed prepared to compromise (by abstaining) if they found themselves alone in opposition to an overwhelming majority.

Although within the special working group the Canadian delegation introduced a motion to summon an intersessional group of thirty states from all regions of the world to consider a textual compromise, the Third World coalition instead wanted its proposal put to a vote,[68] leading to the adoption of the text (see Table 5.2, option 8) by a vote of 70–21 (with thirteen abstentions).[69] Except for Australia, Greece, Ireland, Sweden, and Turkey, the Western Group members voted against the Third World proposal and lost.

To Western relief, the majority coalition did not immediately bring the text to final, plenary vote. Counting its losses, the Western Group agreed to join in the consensus acceptance of a commission report, an outcome that though far from ideal was welcomed as the best temporary solution.

Living to Fight Another Day

Postconference attitudes were gloomy. The UK delegation's last cable from Geneva perfectly illustrated the Western mood at the end of the 1974 session, stating that this was "an untidy and not very satisfactory conclusion but it could have been much worse. We have shown ourselves to be conciliatory; we avoided further confrontation and we live to fight another day though the chances of our seriously altering the amended text are pretty slight."[70] The French delegation was "depressed," the Americans noted that "the record of accomplishment . . . was not one of which the participants could be proud," and the British quipped that the results, "as far as there were any, they were lamentable."[71] Even the Swiss, less prone to dramatic rhetoric, thought the session was "deplorable" and declared that they were ready "to do what they can to pick up the pieces."[72]

A few weeks later the British Interdepartmental Committee (IC) reconvened to consider the road ahead. Despite being greatly bothered by what had taken place, the United Kingdom was determined to take leadership within the Western Group since, as Gerald Draper noted, "the limits of Western resourcefulness may not yet have been reached."[73] The West, it was said, had been well prepared legally but not politically. The burning question now was, what next?

Why Stay? Assessing Interest and Motivation

Why did materially powerful Western states, feeling pressured to acquiesce to unpalatable rules, decide to continue negotiating in a hostile environment facing negative odds? The UK postconference report noted that "a number of smaller countries (but who have the votes) show signs of wanting to impose such restrictions on the conduct of warfare that no military authority could possibly accept them, or if they did would break them the first day of hostilities. The results would be either protocols not accepted by any serious military power and/or agreements of no value. Either way they would tend to destroy the force of the Conventions of 1949 and we would be worse off than before."[74]

Some International Relations (IR) rationalist arguments maintain that in the face of unfavorable outcomes, powerful states—who, Lloyd Gruber notes, enjoy "exit" and "go-it-alone" options—threaten or actually leave the negotiating table; they can, according to James Fearon, "bargain hard."[75] Given what emerged from first session of the CDDH, one could have reasonably expected the United States or the United Kingdom to adopt such an attitude.

Counter to these conjectures, the British had some revealing words on their motivation to remain involved: "No state except the small has a material interest in the emergence of new protocols—certainly no Great Power. . . . But the political value for the Third World and vague humanitarian desiderata will probably keep up the momentum. *The real danger is that the basic fabric and assumptions of the Geneva Conventions will be threatened . . . it is important that the Geneva Conventions, which do after all provide the main safeguards, should not be endangered.*"[76]

Notice the embedded status argument here. The British team understood both the material interest and the "political value" of the controversial IHL amendments for a Third World looking to simultaneously protect national liberation via international law while deploying newfound prominence in lawmaking. Moreover, in terms of the social cost to be borne by the West in maintaining (or exacerbating) stubborn opposition to the Third World aspiration, the British cited the "*great anxiety* on all sides not to want to seem unsympathetic to the Africans or to appear racialist [*sic*]."[77] This leaves little doubt regarding the role of opprobrium on British calculations; no Western state wished to be seen as racist (a social reputation argument) or to place itself willingly alongside Israel, Portugal, and South Africa—states holding pariah status at the time. Moreover, in the British view, not one Western state was willing to bear the social cost of bringing down the Diplomatic Conference or to leave the ground open to the Third World to modify IHL and "endanger" the basic fabric of the Geneva Conventions.

Although the fear of anticolonial opprobrium weighed less heavily on U.S. delegates, they shared some of the British concerns more or less verbatim: "It would be a tragedy if the divisiveness shown at the Conference should endanger the fragile fabric of the existing IHL," that is, if "the fragile community of roughly 135 states that are now parties to the Geneva Conventions of 1949" were "shattered by the interjection of political considerations that could lead a number of states, including some of the world's major military powers, not to become parties to the two Protocols."[78] A mixture of various legal and political concerns operated to keep the Americans involved in the process.

Before the second CDDH session opened in February 1975, it was clear that Western Group preparations were critical to securing a unity of position on all or most issues, as well as bilateral efforts to "educate" a number of Latin American and other developing countries.[79]

France, the United Kingdom, and the United States all recognized that there had been slight overtures to compromise by a few moderates in the Afro-Asian coalition, and particularly Egypt, indicating that the text adopted in commission was not set in stone and that there "may be a way of separating out the issue of wars of national liberation . . . without necessarily accepting that obligation." Regardless, the Western Group had to assess the impact of accepting wars of national liberation into API "to avoid any formulation which permits unequal application of the Protocols and the Convention to different parties to a conflict."[80] Finally, the United States retained an interest in APII, for which a majority of delegations had shown disdain during the first session. The Chinese delegation, for example, upon the adoption of the Afro-Asian amendment, stated plainly that APII was unnecessary and could now be considered an improper intrusion into internal affairs.[81]

Continuing to play the role of brokers among Western states, in mid-June 1974 the British drew up and circulated a memorandum with four options: (1) postponing the 1975 session of the Diplomatic Conference, slackening the momentum of the opposite coalition and allowing for some of the ongoing conflicts in Africa to end; (2) negotiating an amendment acceptable to the West and liaising with the Third World coalition to compromise; (3) discussing options for reshaping the protocols (and the Geneva Conventions) to make them applicable to national liberation wars; or (4) accepting the amended Article 1 as a fait accompli and agreeing collectively on what amendments to make.[82]

The British also floated the idea of holding informal talks at an upcoming meeting of the Sanremo, Italy, based International Institute of Humanitarian Law, planned for September 6–9, 1974. To British eyes, this forum provided an "ideal cover," since it was not highly monitored and allowed a semblance of informality as many of the same negotiators from all regional groups were likely to attend. An eventual negotiation at Sanremo, however, had to be preceded by a further meeting of the Western Group and by diplomatic exchange. Besides Sanremo, contacts could be established during a weapons conference in Lucerne or at the UNGA sessions in New York. They knew that if their tactic was to work, they needed a great degree of ingenuity and liaisons with friends.

From their list the British preferred the first option; however, realizing that postponement was implausible, they decided to support the second. The third and fourth options were allegedly only to be tried at last resort;[83] interestingly, however, the fourth option was eventually chosen.

A "Solution" Emerges

Western démarches to Third World delegates at Sanremo failed. The session revealed that the majority of the victorious coalition felt extremely sensitive about yielding the gains made during the first session of the conference, and despite a few isolated signs to compromise, it was firmly opposed to making concessions.[84]

At the September 1974 Western Group meetings, however, another possible tactic to deal with perceived Third World intransigence surfaced. The American head delegate, George Aldrich, suggested that if the text were not modified, a *cordon sanitaire* could be introduced in order to prevent its application to cases beyond the specific ones that interested the Afro-Asian coalition (i.e., African anticolonial struggles and Palestine.) This might come in the form of additional articles negating the application of API to just wars or via other juridical means that compensated for Article 1.

As I will discuss later in this chapter, these American proposals were the seeds of the Western Group's strategy of inserting "antidotes" into the text of the protocol to undo the damage allegedly done by the contentious amendment. Following these consultations, the Western Group agreed to continue exploring this solution and tasked the United Kingdom with a study on the consequences of the adopted Article 1 for the entire API. It also occurred to Western countries that demonstrating an accommodating attitude toward the Third World regarding API might increase the chances of APII, provided that its threshold of application was increased and its contents abbreviated to allay those states' fears. Canada was entrusted with drafting a new "minimalist" version of that instrument which, as we will see, resurfaced years later and played a critical role.[85]

The Swiss report summarizing both of the Western Group's September consultations closed with the telling conclusion that, although heavy fights laid ahead, most within the Western Group were willing to "swallow the Article 1 pill."[86] A new round of Western consultations, the first restricted to the Inner Core (Canada, France, the United Kingdom, and the United States) and another gathering the entire Western Group, were scheduled to take place in January in Washington, DC, prior to the second session of the Diplomatic Conference.

A Crucial Meeting

The four-state Western Inner Core consultations of January 13–14, 1975, evinced that the American strategy regarding the dreaded Article 1 had taken root.[87] Aldrich's position was that if the Western Group questioned the principle of the amendment to Article 1 it would have to take responsibility for the breakup of the conference. Instead, the group could "afford to be cynical about Article 1 which would never be applied in NLM [National Liberation Movement] conflicts."[88]

The contours of *covert pushback* were emerging. According to the American view, the Western Group should continue negotiating a militarily acceptable protocol applicable to conventional (i.e., interstate) international conflicts while also inserting a few crucial provisions that neutralized the just/unjust war distinction and that made API's application to wars of national liberation subject to de jure and de facto conditional reciprocity by the nonstate armed groups waging them. The Norwegians had recently circulated a proposal allowing liberation movements to commit themselves to the instrument, and although Norway likely suggested this text to *enable* such movements to become parties to API, the United States cleverly reasoned that Western states might use this opportunity to exactly the opposite end.

Other delegates reacted with some reservation to the American proposal. Canada and the United Kingdom, though wishing to be cooperative, were unsure about simply accepting Article 1 and acting as if it did not matter, "sweeping so many problems under the carpet" and perhaps complicating ratification later on. Privately, France displayed discomfort about what it perceived as a ruse leading to impracticable treaties, but, importantly for my argument, recognized that opposing the Americans would spell isolation from both the Third World and the Western Group. Indeed, in the end, the weight of American presence within the Western Group locked in the approach suggested by Aldrich. The French acquiesced while quietly trying to liaise with friendly Third World delegations to craft an improved text.

Yet the consequences of the Western Group's decision not to make efforts to adapt API to national liberation wars were serious in humanitarian, victim-protection terms. In a chilling private memo, West German delegates exposed their utilitarian calculation. On the one hand, attempting to modify API and the Geneva Conventions would produce such a large amount of work and elicit such resistance that it was unlikely to be achieved. On the other hand, an API adapted to wars of liberation would "only" benefit "about 25 million people of the total world population." And since by the negotiations' end most of the ongoing liberation conflicts might have finished (with fewer people standing to enjoy API's protections), West German delegates concluded it was "unjustifiable" to have delegations from more than 120 countries devote their energy to the task.[89] This reasoning uncovers the most sinister layer of the Western Group's position: meaningfully adapting IHL to liberation war seemed so burdensome that the humanity of "about 25 million people" in black Africa was not worth the hassle.

The Western Group reunited as planned in January 27–30, 1975, and despite some reticence from France and Japan approved the American tactic toward the amendment to API.[90] They also agreed, upon Canadian insistence, that the West should force the conference to at least consider APII, albeit in a "more attractive" version "to other groups . . . as well as to ourselves," with reduced content and conditions for application.[91]

A New Round

The Vietnam War had not yet ended when the second session of the CDDH opened on February 3, 1975, and the United States remained worried that the PRG would again attempt to participate. Luckily for the U.S. delegation and despite much maneuvering over two days, the PRG failed to secure the majority it needed to reopen debate on its admission.[92]

Despite initial alacrity, the second CDDH session proceeded unaffected. To Western relief, in 1975 the coalition of African and Asian states seemed uninterested in polemics. Instead "the second session [was] a simple continuation of the first . . . and the Conference avoided all but the most passing tactful references" to the issue.[93] The United Kingdom mused that this denoted not just Third World awareness of a changing Western attitude but also a marked loss of interest on the part of many countries that, having secured the political gain they sought, did not much wish to meddle into the more technical improvements of the law.

Although important provisions of API were long debated and adopted in 1975, for our purposes the relevant development concerned APII.[94] Negotiations of its scope of application attracted extensive presence by Third World states and were some of the most heated of the conference. A mixed coalition pushing for high barriers to application and few humanitarian protections came out in full force, including an African state (Nigeria); Arab states (Egypt and Iraq); Asian states (Indonesia, Pakistan, and the Philippines); Latin American states (Argentina, Honduras, Brazil, and Mexico); and socialist states (East Germany, Romania, the USSR, and Yugoslavia). France joined their ranks while the United Kingdom, secretly pleased by others' majoritarian opposition to APII, did not need to expose its intentions.

The most radical proposals came from India and Iraq, which questioned the entire raison d'être behind a protocol for (nonliberation) internal conflicts as an unhelpful attack on state sovereignty. Brazil seemed to be the only state to openly propose what a few others had in mind—that is, that "draft [APII] could not be applicable unless its applicability was recognized both by the High Contracting Party in whose territory the armed conflict was considered to exist, and by the adverse party."[95] In addition, socialist states proposing high conditions for application sought ways to undermine CA3, either by declaring that the scope of APII should supersede its threshold or by inserting clarifying language that prevented CA3 from applying to conflicts below a high civil war level.

Some Western states, including Australia, Austria, Belgium, the Netherlands, and New Zealand, tried to contain these adverse efforts, but to no avail. Taking a pragmatic line, Canada and the United States volunteered the idea that APII should only contain a few fundamental humanitarian provisions with low conditions for application so as to cover a broader range of internal conflicts. However, Finland, Norway, and Sweden opposed both of these perspectives, refusing to water down APII's contents or to give into the demands of the extreme sovereigntists.

A working group comprising twenty-eight delegations was set up to discuss the scope of APII, and after six meetings arrived at a compromise formula, as follows:

> The present Protocol, which develops and supplements article 3 common to the Geneva Conventions of 12 August 1949 without modifying its existing conditions of application, shall apply to all armed conflicts which are not covered by article 1 of API and **which take place in the territory of a High Contracting Party between its armed forces and dissident armed forces or other organized armed groups which under responsible command exercise such control over a part of its territory as to enable them to carry out sustained and concerted military operations and to implement the present Protocol.**
>
> 2. The present Protocol shall not apply to situations of internal disturbances and tensions, such as riots, isolated and sporadic acts of violence and other acts of a similar nature, as not being armed conflicts.[96]

The working group proposal was presented to Commission II, where it was adopted by consensus.[97] With this, debate on the scope of APII was nearly sealed, completely transforming the original wishes of the ICRC by including a series of stringent formal conditions for application that would—in the eyes of most conference participants—only apply to high-intensity civil wars. The open question now was what substantive provisions it might include.

American, British, and French delegates reacted variously to these outcomes. For the United States, the 1975 session had dealt APII a serious blow, since it would no longer apply to the conflicts where it was needed most.[98] Additionally, a steady Scandinavian-led overburdening of the text with obligations unacceptable to the opposing supermajority coalition threatened to sink the entire instrument. For their part, the British felt satisfied with a threshold high enough to meet their security concerns in Northern Ireland.[99] Yet they, too, decried Scandinavian gestures, seen as reducing the chances for APII's adoption. In the British view, it now fell on the West to generate sympathy for as minimal an APII as possible in order to salvage it. Less altruistically, securing this version of the scope of application was fundamental for Britain, fearing that its frustrated Western allies might prefer to negotiate a separate, more protective instrument elsewhere.

Again lamenting the cynical Western approach to the scope of API and the seemingly heavy-handed approach of the Americans to obtain compromises behind the scenes, the French offered a sharp analysis of the negotiations up to that point. In their view the conference was an awkward encounter between two very different groups of self-interested states, the Western and the non-Western, against the idealist humanitarianism of the Scandinavians. This clash of views had, for France, led to treaty texts riddled by safeguards, idealistic prohibitions, tautologies, and otherwise "surprisingly pious vows" whose complexity and ambiguity would not facilitate practical application. The frustrated French concluded their delegation report bitterly, stating that "it is up to the supporters of adapting the law of 1949 to new forms of conflict to define their concepts, and to its authors, most of whom are Western, to help them without looking to ambiguity and nonapplicability as a way-out, which would do a durable disservice to the whole of IHL."[100] What the French analysis missed was that the "glue" keeping the West at the conference was as much social as it was self-interested. Yet it was clear that all of the Third World's social pressure had not persuaded the West, instead eliciting a deceptive, covert reaction.

Following the 1975 CDDH session, conversations on the APs resumed at a meeting of the Inner Core (which now included West Germany) in Washington on November 17–18.[101] The United States began to wonder whether APII was becoming a "white elephant," demanding too much energy yet unlikely to be applied in the end given its high threshold.[102] Canada bemoaned the Scandinavian-induced overelaboration of the clauses but worried that further pressing for its simplification might be misconstrued as antihumanitarian in public. The idea to propose a separate instrument of like-minded states surfaced anew with U.S. support. Perturbed by this thought, the British replied that it was "too soon to totally give up hope." Rather, the Western line should remain to argue for a simplified text, waiting to see what emerged. The West Germans agreed, but American delegate Aldrich remained unpersuaded, suggesting that they might want to leave the negotiation of APII until after API had been adopted. The Canadians, who reportedly saw APII as tied to their prestige, stood their ground, noting that this would be the "kiss of death" for the instrument and shrewdly pointing out "how unfortunate it would be if the impression were created that the US had washed its hands of [APII]."[103] (Notice the social threat/argument here.) The Germans remarked that this unfortunate situation was due to a "bad" Article 1 for API, and the French, though sympathetic, decided to hold back comments "since it would have been in poor taste."[104]

The entire Western Group reunited again in London on March 15–17, 1976, to review the most contentious issues in preparation for the third CDDH session, and despite some French venting, it maintained its support for the Article 1 compromise.[105]

Resolving the POW Issue

The third CDDH session opened on April 21, 1976. The end of the Vietnam War in 1975 put clashes over PRG admission to rest, yet progress that year proved slow due to the complex nature of articles under consideration. One of these was the critical provision offering POW protection to "irregular" combatants in international conflicts (in API, draft Article 42, paragraph 3; see Annex), the so-called freedom fighters. American head delegate George Aldrich reportedly acted again as the essential Western broker, liaising behind the scenes with representatives of the opposing coalition (reportedly Algeria, Norway, North Vietnam, and the Palestine Liberation Organization.)

Continuing with its role as norm entrepreneur, the ICRC seemed to have helped these delegations to devise a solution. According to former ICRC director of principles and law Jacques Moreillon, sometime between the 1975 and 1976 session ICRC officials contacted Aldrich and provided him with the legal formulas the United States had used in Vietnam (and the French in Algeria before that) to allow for the application of POW *treatment* (and in the American case, *status*) to detained "irregulars" who had been carrying arms openly before and during military engagements. The U.S. delegate then used this template as basis for a compromise that set out the conditions under which combatants could receive POW status and offered "POW-like" treatment to anyone who was captured while carrying arms openly.[106]

Yet textual deception was applied here too. In American eyes, this proposed language contained various ambiguities that allowed the West to believe it could ultimately deny status to national liberation fighters, facilitating their prosecution as criminals for their wartime offenses. Such ambiguities were probably not evident to Algeria, Norway, North Vietnam,[107] or the Palestinians to whom the compromise text appeared satisfactory, but they would soon create controversy within the Western camp.

The study of APII was once again made difficult in 1976 by persistent criticisms coming from Latin American states alongside India, Indonesia, Iraq, Pakistan, and the Philippines. Each of the thirteen articles debated and adopted that year gave rise to contestation at the committee level. Certain states were so allergic to the consequences of APII for their sovereignty that even the legal ability of the ICRC to do its humanitarian work during internal conflict was imperiled. Two of the opposition's leaders (India and Iraq) believed that giving the ICRC a legal right of initiative (to engage in humanitarian action) might open the door to unacceptable outside meddling in their internal affairs and benefit the rebel side.[108]

The turmoil of the proceedings, the frail compromises, and in general the uncertain future of APII had not eluded the Swiss hosts. Just before the third session of the conference closed on June 11, 1976, the Swiss Foreign Office organized a series of private interviews between the president of the conference, Swiss foreign minister Pierre Graber, and select important delegations. Conversations with Algeria, Brazil, Egypt, France, India, Iraq, Mexico, North Vietnam, Pakistan, Sweden, Tanzania, the United Kingdom, the United States, the USSR, and Venezuela confirmed the fears of the West: the animosity toward APII was pervasive and only a simplified, nonthreatening text might survive negotiation; the compromise on Article 1 of API was seen as a precious gain for the Afro-Asian states, and attempts to alter it were said to have dire consequences; and the article on POWs would be among the most difficult up for debate in 1977.[109]

The Swiss also maintained contact with the ICRC on the future of the conference. Interestingly, a conversation between ICRC vice president Jean Pictet and Swiss diplomat Jean Humbert in mid-July 1976 revealed that the ICRC was aware there were efforts in motion to simplify APII, yet the delegations in charge (Canada and Pakistan, primarily) had reportedly not invited it to participate in such work. The ICRC was concerned about the substantive outcome but also knew that the current draft stood little chance of adoption during plenary. In general, the ICRC worried that the following year the Third World delegations would come en masse to the closing session of the Diplomatic Conference and "impose their will." As Pictet perhaps nervously remarked, many delegates had admitted that 1977 would become "the moment of truth" for APII.[110]

Military Fears Surface

In late 1976 and early 1977 the Western Group debated the military implications of the APs for NATO. West Germany increasingly worried about the restrictions and confusions that it thought were being introduced; recent German-commissioned studies had suggested that API's obligations might make the alliance vulnerable to attacks from the East.[111] At German instigation, new Inner Core meetings were held in Bonn in November 1976 and in Brussels in mid-January 1977 to discuss these matters.

These encounters showed that West German security concerns had spread to the United Kingdom. During the preparation of the official briefs for ministers, the British MOD staff expressed sharp disagreement with the American tactic of crafting indeterminate texts on liberation movements and POWs.[112] The risk existed that opposing parties to conflict would exploit the ambiguities and interpret the text to their convenience. Additional bilateral contacts confirmed that others in the Western camp shared British worries, encouraging them to challenge the American line shortly before the final Conference session opened.[113]

These attempts came to naught, however. At February and March 1977 Western Group meetings, George Aldrich made it clear that the United States would continue to support the current version of the article granting POW protection to irregular combatants. Suspecting that Aldrich's view might not be shared by the U.S. Department of State, UK officials privately inquired of Department of Defense staff in the American delegation "whether the Pentagon was really prepared" to endorse the text. These officials responded that though "they were unhappy" about it, there was high-level agreement to accept it on the condition that American interpretation of draft's two major ambiguities were inserted in the negotiating record.[114]

The ambiguities specifically related to the meaning of two words within the text: "deployment" and "protection" (see Annex). The working text recognized that although "that there are situations in armed conflicts where, owing to the nature of the hostilities an armed combatant cannot . . . distinguish himself" from the civilian population, a combatant could retain his status as long as he carried his arms openly "during each military engagement" and "during such time as he is visible to the adversary while he is engaged in a military deployment preceding the launching of an attack in which he is to participate." The United Kingdom feared that this required liberation fighters only to distinguish themselves *immediately prior* to executing an attack, hampering states' ability to neutralize them and leading to potential civilian deaths.[115] The American team insisted, however, that "deployment" should be given a broader meaning, covering "all the period of time (and distance in space)" elapsed between a guerrilla member or group leaving their posts until that attack took place, permitting a state wide latitude to target them. In addition, the Americans believed that the legal protection for these combatants did not imply immunity from criminal trial.[116] And though the United States felt that risk to civilians existed, it was "likely exaggerated."[117]

Complicating matters, at this February meeting Aldrich had announced that the Soviet Union would agree to support the draft text on POWs. This alarmed the British not only because they knew that U.S.-USSR consensus would be difficult to crack but because Soviet acceptance of the text fed into the British fear of an attack from the East. A recent secret military report confirmed these concerns and added to them threats from international extremist terrorists against targets in Europe and elsewhere.[118]

Frustrated, the British MOD staff believed Aldrich himself was responsible for this "incredibly naïve" line, stating that "Pentagon thinking seems to be in the same direction as our own, the main difference being that they have to operate within the constraints imposed by a draft proposal prepared by their own Head of Delegation." In their view, "the US has gone out on a limb and their military now wish to extricate themselves from an impossible position." They also found that the Pentagon's interpretation of deployment gave the word "a totally different, artificial and inappropriate" meaning, and that as a whole, even if amended, "the result would not be a good article. The whole framework appears to be designed to encourage guerrillas and this would seem to be against our national interest."[119]

The Americans' naïveté, according to the British MOD, lay in hoping that their draft would prevent Vietnam-style arbitrariness against POWs: "No matter how an Article of this sort is drafted, it is always open to States to twist the law, taking advantage of the drafting to reach a conclusion which is totally contrary to the intention behind the Treaty." FCO legal advisers agreed, claiming that although "Mr. Aldrich has sought to allay Western fears by saying that we can feel perfectly free to exploit the ambiguities against the guerrilla . . . two can play at this kind of game."[120]

Yet given that any amendments were unlikely and reopening discussion might make the text worse, the United Kingdom decided the best course in the short-term was to associate itself with the American interpretive statements, even if these were "quite contrary to the apparent meaning of the Article and thus unlikely to get any wide acceptance."[121] The long-term solution for Britain was to consider making a reservation prior to ratification.

Final Western Group coordination before the fourth session of the Diplomatic Conference took place with meetings of the Inner Core on March 14, 1977, and of the extended Western Group on March 15–16. The Inner Core meeting served to air recurrent grievances.[122] Americans led the meeting and expressed satisfaction by the fact that they knew of few (if any) countries opposed the text on POWs. The United Kingdom reacted immediately, voicing its many problems with exactly that text, saying, "Guerrilla activity was seen as an increasingly serious threat in Europe by NATO; it was very important the text of [draft] Article 42 did nothing to encourage this activity."[123]

Aldrich acknowledged the concerns about the exploitation of the wording's ambiguity but believed that a "clear, satisfactory and agreed" interpretive statement in the negotiating history would suffice to overcome the problem. It was foremost, in Aldrich's view, to find a compromise acceptable to the majority. The West Germans agreed that interpretive precisions were indeed necessary, but the French doubted their legal validity. Instead they should strive to uphold the principle of distinction through clear means, preferably by demanding the use of a distinctive sign. To this, the American delegate correctly replied that forcing distinction by such means would inhibit guerrilla activity completely and prove unacceptable to the Third World majority. In the end the British reminded the

Americans that no article would be able to fully ensure the protection of captured combatants. To this the Americans replied that, nevertheless, "it would be useful to have a statement of law in the books which would be helpful to our personnel."[124]

The Western line was confirmed in the enlarged Western Group consultation a day later. Yet, behind the scenes, UK delegates remained concerned. The British IC had met in early April with parliamentary undersecretary of state Evan Luard to receive final approval of its delegation brief.[125] At this meeting, the British delegation made two telling decisions. First, although still maintaining a reserved position on the controversial Article 1 of API, it vowed not to oppose it publicly, and if it were put to a vote "on balance, abstention, *at least in respectable Western company*, appears preferable; a negative vote by us might have prejudicial consequences for developments in southern Africa *as well as provide ammunition for the Third World and East European militants*, and there seems to be no prospect of securing a blocking third. . . . It is unlikely that a vote can be avoided. If it can be, *the Delegation should not oppose a consensus*."[126]

The conditions for Western socially pressured acquiescence were now present: fear of forum isolation, the threat of a public vote, and an awareness of the social status costs attached to negative public position taking. What occurred?

The Moment of Truth

The fourth session of the Diplomatic Conference opened formally on March 17, 1977. The plan was that, following article-by-article adoption in plenary, states would be presented with the finished protocols and decide to finally adopt them either by roll-call vote or consensus.

Draft Articles 1 of API and APII, setting out their general scope, had been respectively adopted in 1974 and 1975 and only awaited plenary consideration. Draft Article 42 (of API, on POW protections) still needed examination. On the morning of April 22 and without much ado, the Egyptian chairman of Committee III explained that the (American-brokered) compromise draft was the product of "two years of hard work, official and unofficial contacts and prolonged discussion and meditation" which should be adopted by consensus. However, the Israeli delegate disagreed and requested a roll-call vote.[127] With a vote of 66–2 (with eighteen abstentions), the controversial POW article of API passed its first test.

Interesting questions emerge from the vote, but two aspects stand out regarding the social politics of voting or abstaining. First, despite the intense behind-the-scenes turf war within the Western camp, none among them opted for publicly opposing draft Article 42. Second, standing next to Israel was deemed dishonorable, and Brazil was apparently not good enough company to motivate breaking the near-universal consensus.

French documents confirm these opprobrium dynamics. Surprisingly, given its consistent frustration with the legal muddle and military risk this article supposedly brought, France voted for it: "Bearing in mind the political importance of [draft] Article 42 and given the protection it affords to combatants of resistance movements, it is convenient . . . to support it in despite of the textual imperfections and to join the consensus or, as the case may be, to cast a positive vote."[128]

A flurry of explanations followed the committee vote, with most Western states—even those voting in favor—inserting the interpretation they had agreed to privately.[129]

On May 23, the plenary sessions resumed to consider the articles of API, followed by APII. The contentious Article 1 of API took center stage three years after its adoption in committee.[130] Algeria suggested proceeding with adoption by consensus, but Israel again demanded a roll-call vote.[131] An outcome similar to that of draft Article 42 emerged, and after a vote of 87–1 (with eleven abstentions), no Western state dared to publicly oppose the dreaded Article 1 and it passed. As we have seen, among the Western skeptics only the United States appeared to hold a firm line, and France and the United Kingdom felt particularly irritated to accept it. Regardless, a desire to avoid straying from the consensus led them to abstain. Britain clarified that although "we found . . . and still find this to be a regrettable innovation . . . our understanding of the reasoning behind the amendment and our determination [are] not to see the protocol founder on this difference of opinion."[132]

In private, a representative of France was even clearer about the country's motivation:

> Article 1 . . . is of capital importance for Third World countries since their essential goal during the conference is to make IHL applicable to national liberation wars. *It would be politically harmful for us to cast a negative vote on this subject which would be poorly received and would ruin the very favorable impression* produced by our positive vote on Article 42 relative to the new category of prisoners of war, *for which we were warmly thanked by Vietnam, the Arab states and several African states.* The representatives of the United States, UK, West Germany and Canada, with whom I consulted, indicated they would abstain on Article 1.[133]

For France it was again social reputational concerns that dictated the decision to abstain. Following the vote, most Western skeptics again proceeded to issue explanations that clarified in polite legal terms their disagreement with the Article's underlying principle.

Article 42 of API (on POWs) resurfaced in plenary on May 26.[134] With a vote of 73–1 (and twenty-one abstentions), the controversial POW article passed its final test.[135] There were no surprises this time, and voting patterns and explanations corresponded to what had been seen in committee. Upon receiving the news via telegram, an obviously pleased British MOD official handwrote "good company!" next to the list of Western states that abstained alongside the United Kingdom.[136]

The final decision on the entire API came in the afternoon of June 8, where it was swiftly adopted by consensus.[137] A day before, the UK delegation had requested instructions from London on how to proceed: "If a vote is requested, we recommend we should . . . vote in favour. We think it unlikely that any WEOG [Western European and Others Group] delegations other than France . . . might abstain on Protocol 1."[138]

But France did not request a vote or abstain, as the British expected. French cables show that this decision was not made until the last minute. Only a few weeks earlier, on May 20, the delegation in Geneva had in fact received explicit instructions to abstain given the "confusions" introduced in the text and the fact that several provisions were incompatible with French national security policy.[139] As the debate approached, however, the French head of delegation wrote back to Paris with a telling plea:

> Although the Department instructed the delegation to abstain . . . I feel I must call its attention about the fact that *we are risking to find ourselves distressingly isolated (eventually with Israel) if we adopt such an attitude.* Third World countries would give this vote a political meaning it does not have, that of a complete dismissal of the extension of IHL to national liberation wars . . . *Moreover, we would be lynchpins of the opposition against the humanitarian progress* [in other parts of API]. . . . Finally, how could we continue to manifest so much reticence to a text that we have ourselves contributed to improve. . . . Our positive vote—preceded by a general declaration expressing our reservations—would not at all prejudge the future attitude of the government as regards signature: In a comparable situation, I was authorized to vote for the International Covenants on Human Rights, which we have not yet signed. . . . Bearing in mind the previous considerations, I would be grateful if the Department authorized the delegation not to disassociate itself from an eventual consensus on API, and if a vote were requested, to cast a positive vote.[140]

The threat of forum isolation produced French acquiescence.

(Un)binding Liberation Groups

A final key provision of API remains to be considered here—namely, the article offering the possibility for liberation movements to "undertake to apply the

Conventions and this Protocol" by means of a unilateral declaration addressed to the Swiss depositaries. This was now branded Article 96. While the article stated that by depositing a unilateral declaration "the said [liberation movement] authority assumes the same rights and obligations as those which have been assumed by a High Contracting Party to the Conventions and this Protocol," it clarified that the "High Contracting Parties" (states) were "bound by this Protocol *if the latter accepts and applies the provisions thereof*."[141]

As was explained earlier in this chapter, the inclusion of the language providing for liberation movements' "participation" in API had been an initiative of a coalition of African, Arab, and socialist countries (plus Australia, Finland, and Norway) similar to that supporting the amended Article 1. And given Western opposition to the idea that such movements could accede to (become "High Contracting Parties" to) the protocol, Article 96 had become an attractive option to secure the goal of liberation movements' commitment without legitimation. But most importantly, the text had a subtler virtue: it ensured that states would *only* be legally bound *if* the liberation movements accepted *and* applied the provisions of API. De facto and de jure conditional reciprocity were requisite for the applicability of API to liberation conflicts. Western calculations here were clear: given their military methods, hardly any liberation movement could demonstrate compliance with API. As such, API was unlikely to ever apply to such wars.

Deceptively pleasing to most of the critical actors in the room, Article 96 was adopted by consensus in committee, and again due to an Israel-requested roll-call vote, it was overwhelmingly adopted in plenary by a vote of 93–1, with Israel dissenting and Spain and Thailand abstaining.[142]

What Fate for APII?

Let me finally turn to the closing negotiation of APII. A high threshold of application had been adopted in committee in 1975. Under discussion in 1977 were multiple matters of substance, many of which were debated by working groups and sub-groups whose verbatim conversations went unrecorded. According to the available evidence, however, it appears that these discussions evinced Scandinavian efforts (plus the Holy See) to produce an APII that was *as similar as possible* to API (for international conflict). That push, however, was unacceptable to most states, and APII appeared to stand little chance of adoption in plenary. A French telegram dated June 1 was straightforward on this point: "The outcome of this debate seems very uncertain. In effect, many Third World delegations are extremely reticent about draft [APII] which they resent, on the one hand, for placing governments and rebels on a level of juridical equality, considering both to be parties to conflict. This constitutes, in the eyes of many . . . an affront to state sovereignty . . . and involving overtly detailed provisions and too constraining, which can again constitute an affront to state sovereignty. African delegations confirmed to us . . . their concerns on this subject."[143]

Western states, too, were worried about the future of APII. Although the strict threshold had allayed the original fears of France and the United Kingdom such that they were no longer viscerally opposed to the project, they continued to believe that a demanding protocol, overburdening both to states and to rebels unable to respect them, would sink. Canada and the United States, until then consistent supporters of APII, agreed with this "realistic" argument (even if they preferred a lower threshold). The Canadian delegation had in particular worked for years on a simpler, more widely acceptable version of that instrument, which the conference had not embraced.

Such was the state of affairs on May 31, 1977, when APII was sent to plenary for review. A day later (and a week before the Diplomatic Conference was scheduled to close) the Pakistani delegate, Judge Mushtaq Hussain tabled an amendment consisting of an entirely different, much shorter APII. During his public presentation of the project, he recognized that there was "considerable dissatisfaction" among developed and "underprivileged" countries with the length of the working text as well as with the fact that "it ventured into domains which they considered sacrosanct and inappropriate for inclusion in an international instrument." In his view, the protocol entered into "unnecessary details, rendering it not only cumbersome to understand to apply in the peculiar circumstances of a noninternational armed conflict."[144]

Hussain noted that his project was "partly inspired" by previous Canadian drafts, and that it was based on the following theses:

> Its provisions must be acceptable to all and, thus, of obvious practical benefit; the provisions must be within the perceived capacity of those involved to apply them and, therefore, precise and simple; they should not appear to affect the sovereignty of any State Party or the responsibility of its Government to maintain law and order and defend national unity, nor be able to be invoked to justify any outside intervention; nothing in the Protocol should suggest that dissidents must be treated legally other than as rebels; and, lastly, there should be no automatic repetition of the more comprehensive provisions . . . found in [API].[145]

Although the simplified draft was well received by many states, including Canada, Egypt, Nigeria, and the Soviet Union, the president of the conference decided that the plenary would examine the two projects side-by-side. Subsequent debates secured the adopted high threshold of application (despite last-minute demands by Colombia, with Brazilian and Saudi support, to make it even more stringent).[146]

Following detailed discussions and much Indian, Iraqi, and Scandinavian frustration (all for different reasons), the APII that emerged roughly corresponded to the Pakistani proposal. Gone was the language referring to the "parties to conflict" (excluded to avoid legitimizing rebels), the assurance of quarter, the delay of the death penalty, the ability to sign special agreements, or the provisions allowing the ICRC and similar humanitarian organizations to offer their services.[147] After so many years of wrangling and final statements from a multitude of states, this version of APII was at last adopted by consensus on June 8, 1977.[148]

The Diplomatic Conference, in keeping with its contentious proceedings throughout, ended with drama when the liberation movements asked to be allowed to sign the Final Act of the CDDH. After much protest from a West anxious about the legitimation effects of such an allowance, it was decided that liberation movements would sign a different sheet of paper attached to the Final Act, to include the following disclaimer: "It is understood that the signature by these movements is without prejudice to the positions of participating States on the question of a precedent."[149]

Writing about other international negotiations that took place in the 1970s, American realist IR scholar Stephen Krasner sentenced summarily: "Decolonization eroded American influence."[150] This chapter paints a more complicated picture. Certainly, the tortured negotiation of the APs in the 1970s shows how the combination of anxieties over forum isolation, an expected social cost from potentially "wrecking" the Diplomatic Conference, and fears of legal damage done to the Geneva Conventions pressured powerful Western skeptics, including the United States, to abstain from blocking some of the principal demands of the opposing coalition, particularly those dealing with the legal legitimation of national liberation and the protection of freedom fighters.

This outcome, however, did not mean that the United States or the West more broadly lost or gave up their influence. Rather, as it had been the case in 1949, pressured compromise provoked a Western tactical shift toward the use of backstage deception to neutralize or tame the national liberation-related innovations. This method was surely defensive and covert, but it nevertheless relied on an important degree of American influence, both upon its allies to shape a common position (however reluctantly for Britain and France), but also vis-à-vis the opposing coalition to broker the language on POW protection for freedom fighters. Research should continue to uncover how else the West made up for its newfound minority status in international negotiations during this historical period. Textual ambiguity was clearly one method; the subtle use of procedure to gain informal advantage and secure less harmful outcomes was another.[151]

Social pressure with regard to national liberation was recognized and felt as formidable in Western ranks. Was the Third World in turn impermeable to humanitarian pressure? Despite the sustained Third World opposition toward APII traced in this chapter, the survival of APII at the end of the negotiation process also suggests a more nuanced assessment. On the one hand, clearly the coalition of Third World and socialist states defeated the early aspirations of the ICRC and some other states for codifying an expansive set of protections applicable to non-liberation internal conflict. On the other, even though they could have well sunk APII through the vote, the Third World-led coalition ultimately supported a compromise version of APII, itself a text partially negotiated through the brokerage of a Third World delegation (Pakistan).

In the end, was the legal legitimation of national liberation through API "really" revolutionary? Does the deceptive stance of the West deserve praise or condemnation? What about the Third World's skeptical attitude toward a stronger APII? Was such an attitude understandably prudent, or rather conservative and cynical? These questions have no easy answers. The practical applicability of the adopted rules, and in some cases their substantive protections, certainly suffered (API never applied to national liberation war or freedom fighters, for instance). At the same time, a decision to compromise—however hypocritically and grudgingly—allowed both Western, Third World, and socialist states to adopt important rules on other stubborn issues which were finally codified in both APs and which have proved influential over time, particularly for the protection of the civilian population.

However one appraises the impact of the changes to IHL studied in this chapter, my analysis clearly demonstrates that the process of lawmaking is a political battleground in which states' normative wagers and social anxieties variously interact, sometimes producing outcomes that run counter to dominant political forces, theoretical expectations, and received histories. International law is a contentiously-produced collective political achievement constructed partially through face-saving. What future lies ahead for the codified law is not always easy to predict, as the post-CDDH development of IHL through custom shows. I turn to this discussion in the concluding chapter.

Conclusion

CUSTOM AND SOCIALLY PRESSURED CODIFICATION

Scholars and practitioners of global politics commonly point to the "international community" as the maker and enforcer of international rules. Yet, as the development of international humanitarian law (IHL) for internal conflicts demonstrates, the processes and outcomes of multilateral lawmaking are better captured by histories, concepts, and theories that denote not so much agreement or consensus but political struggle and degrees of contestation, face saving, compromise, and contingency. As Monica Hakimi argues, understanding global governance and the operation of international law and society more generally demands accounting for "the combined integration and discord" that actually characterize most international associations and interactions.[1]

Today the international humanitarian regulation of internal conflict appears to have gone the distance. Legal scholars go so far as to refer to a "revolution" in this area of law.[2] Curiously, when they do so, they are not writing about the codified treaty rules whose origins I have explained in this book and which it took states well over a century to create: Common Article 3 (CA3) and the Additional Protocols (APs). Instead they allude to the legal expansion occurring in the period *following* the negotiation of the APs—that is, after 1977.

Indeed, the last four decades have witnessed a wide expansion of IHL for internal conflict, not through treaty law but via customary international law.[3] In this conclusion I reflect on this post-1977 legal "revolution" through the lens of this book's findings and insights. Many commentators celebrate this customary revolution as a normatively "good" thing, being perhaps implicitly informed by an understanding of IHL's difficult, drawn-out, and incomplete codification history, particularly as regards internal conflict. Multilateral negotiation of new humanitarian rules, one might reasonably argue, has not and could not achieve rapid progressive change. Some even wager that, if it did not already exist, CA3 could hardly be adopted these days.[4]

Others disagree. Michael Schmitt and Sean Watts have, for example, sounded alarms about the potential overexpansion of IHL, worrying that absent active governmental involvement and explicit state *opinion juris* or consent in the legal development process, ambitious rule extension may threaten the credibility and influence of the law.[5]

This debate is hard to settle, not least because both perspectives partially rely on different claims or expectations about the influence of (existing and new) IHL upon states. I cannot adjudicate that controversy here, as my focus has remained on tracing the origins and theorizing the making of codified IHL. An empirical assessment of the law's influence in internal conflict remains a pending task.[6] What I want to do instead, based on this book's insights, is to suggest that no matter whether through treaty and customary form, the construction of IHL was and remains a contested process underpinned by social pressure, face saving, and strategic compromise, perhaps especially as regards the rules for internal conflict.

Making IHL: Normative Impetus and Contested Codification

I have explained the origins and development of the treaty IHL for internal conflict in two stages. The first stage concerned the questions of *impetus* and *agenda setting*. Where did the idea come from that internal conflicts should be regulated through international law? What actors mobilized behind it, why, and how? Under what conditions, and through what factors, were formal debates and rule negotiations initiated?

Through historical process tracing I have identified three jointly necessary conditions: (1) a background of recent conflict atrocity motivating norm entrepreneurship and humanitarian concern; (2) one or more determined norm entrepreneurs with institutional leverage and diplomatic competence that could galvanize widespread support; and (3) the acquiescence (or at least lack of proactive aversion) by major powers to the idea of engaging in international humanitarian lawmaking.[7]

Most innovatively, this part of my argument has incorporated the structural (political and normative) context in which IHL entrepreneurs operated historically. In chapter 2, I considered the influence of antirevolutionary norms in the nineteenth century, militarized nationalism, and reinvigorated imperialism as constraining factors on decision making for the International Committee of the Red Cross (ICRC). Chapter 4 discussed the context of the early Cold War with its associated belief in "total war" and the strengthening of anticolonialism internationally, as well as, more subtly, normative shifts related to atrocity amid varied forms of "internal" violence.[8] I connected these structural factors to key norm entrepreneurs' organizational elements (e.g., the ICRC's internal culture and politics, institutional competition) that could also be either constraining or enabling at different times. Finally, I paid attention to bottom-up or "outsider" advocate pressure calling for change.

In a second stage, by analytically separating out the issues of impetus and agenda setting from that of rule *negotiation*, I theorized the contentious politics underlying the diplomatic codification of CA3 and the APs, arguing that social pressure between majority coalitions and minority state groupings mattered decisively in their design and adoption. I underscored the role of opprobrium-inducing *forum isolation* upon state diplomats that were in the negotiating minority, compelling them to save face through public acquiescence as they covertly pushed back backstage to insert ambiguity within the law. And I linked the negotiation politics of the diplomatic conferences in 1949 and the 1970s directly to the international social competition of the Cold War and decolonization, showing their productive imbrication.

The Customary Revolution of IHL

This history and politics of IHL treatymaking may shed some perspective on the expansion of IHL through custom.

Let me first briefly describe this expansion. Immediately after the closing of the Diplomatic Conference on the Reaffirmation and Development of IHL Applicable in Armed Conflicts in 1977 and the adoption of the APs, certain legal advocates began promoting the view that, given the tribulations of those negotiations, the APs' perceived shortcomings, and an uncertain prospect of treaty ratification, "forward-looking" IHL jurists should work to strengthen the new law through "progressive" interpretation.[9] Influentially, Antonio Cassese expressed this view already in 1979,[10] and soon turned to arguments about the customary status of certain rules of the APs, a position first critiqued and then eventually endorsed by Theodor Meron.[11] In 1987 U.S. officials, too, asserted that their government viewed certain rules of Additional Protocol I (API) as customary, signaling a commitment to specific (palatable) aspects of that treaty and assuaging pressures produced by American nonratification of the APs.[12] Shortly after, in the 1990s, the ad hoc international tribunals for Rwanda and the Former Yugoslavia, with Cassese and Meron now in leading positions as judges, deepened the turn toward customary IHL via key watershed legal opinions, particularly in the case of *The Prosecutor v. Dusko Tadic.*[13]

Crucial as these legal arguments and tactics were,[14] the decisive move toward expanding IHL through customary law claims emerged from a major research project coordinated by the ICRC since the mid-1990s. Following a conference convened in 1993 by Switzerland in response to the grave violations of humanitarian law experienced at the time (especially in the former Yugoslavia), participants called for the creation of an Intergovernmental Group of Experts which, among others, asked the ICRC to prepare a report on clarifying the entire body of customary norms applicable in armed conflicts.[15]

The results of the ten-year research process were published in 2005 as a four-thousand-page, three-volume set, to sweeping findings, particularly with regard to internal conflict. Of over 161 rules of humanitarian conduct in armed conflict considered by the experts, nearly all (146) were deemed to be applicable as customary to both international and internal conflicts.[16] And though a few rules merited the qualifier of "arguably applicable in noninternational armed conflict," the proposed lists were nearly identical.[17]

Upon its release, a majority of legal scholars praised the ICRC's *Customary International Humanitarian Law* study for its empirical depth and comprehensiveness.[18] In a relatively short time it came to be increasingly cited by international and domestic judicial bodies and national militaries, a trend which for some signals its growing status as an authoritative legal source.[19]

But how did states react? Given the ambitious findings of the study, and the reluctance with which states had historically approached the regulation of internal conflict, one might have anticipated major responses. Yet, with only Egypt, Finland, Germany, Israel, the United Kingdom, and the United States (so far) publicly reacting, by and large governments met the report with silence.[20]

How should we understand widespread state silence toward this alleged major transformation of IHL through custom? Why has, as Schmitt and Watts ponder, the practice of state *opinio juris* vis-à-vis IHL declined? Should we take state silence here to mean acquiescence, obliviousness, or rather as a strategic choice not to confirm but also not deny a rule's existence, maintaining freedom of action while protecting their reputation?

There is ample room for speculation, not least because widespread governmental silence on the report has come accompanied by isolated criticism as well as by examples of domestic uptake, which continue to proliferate. How do we think about these various possible explanations, politically and normatively?

This book's argument and findings may prove illuminating here. Among other things, I have shown that at least for some powerful states the formal adoption of treaty IHL rules for internal conflict has been a grudging, socially pressured move.

As George Aldrich phrased it with regards to the APs' negotiation, "a codification conference forces national decisions on limits on the use of force that would otherwise be deferred. A government does not make such difficult decisions *unless it is forced to do so*."[21]

Yet the result of such pressured compromising through law is complex. Formal adoption does not mean embrace. As the cases of CA3 and the APs showed, even as it paved their way to acceptance in conference, reluctant states' backstage reaction to social pressure—their use of textual ambiguity and "antidotes"—undermined the potential effectiveness of the codified rules (CA3 and API).

The observation that emerges here with regard to the customary law study is thus simple: state participation in IHL treaty lawmaking, and states' formal adoption through signature and ratification, does not guarantee a meaningful embrace and implementation of the codified law. In this sense, the turn to customary IHL may be a lot less problematic than feared. Customary IHL, much like treaty IHL, is probably sustained by a combination of pockets of consensus and agreement, tactical consent, as well as partial disagreement and contestation.[22]

On balance, given how prolonged, haphazard, and fragile the outcomes of treaty rule codification for internal conflict have been historically, and admitting that it is still early to tell, I am inclined to suggest that the customary expansion of IHL may prove a positive development, or at least a worthy wager from the humanitarian standpoint, normatively warranted and less politically fraught.[23] Moreover, in terms of its technical qualities, by most accounts the customary law study represents a systematic and professionally robust effort.

None of this minimizes or eliminates the concern rightly raised by Schmitt, Watts, and others. There are grounds to worry about the health and contemporary legitimacy of the law of armed conflict, whether or not one fully accepts arguments about its alleged state of "crisis."[24] Reinvigorated state participation (including that of members of the military) in the lawmaking process should continue to be stimulated, as should be nonstate armed actor engagement.[25]

To venture a conjecture, I suggest that the customary law study's mere existence, buttressed by the fact that it appears to be gaining increasingly broad acceptance among authoritative actors and institutions, offers a nonnegligible chance of positive influence upon states. At the very least, by placing the burden of justification upon them—should they disagree with this or that rule—states may perceive pressures to save face and avoid social opprobrium, keeping them from dissenting publicly or strongly. In time the states that do not already do so may come to incorporate the study's rules and accept them as binding.

This dynamic (face saving through silence) may in fact explain some portion of the states' reaction to the customary law study. As I have noted, negative reactions by states to the study remain isolated, and they seem unlikely to begin proliferating in the short term, at least in a sweeping or brusque manner.[26] That domestic uptake of the study has so far been *selective* in form, not wholesale, may also count as plausible evidence of face saving combined with deliberate strategic legal choice.

Additionally, we may wonder, should the ICRC and other advocates *demand* that states clarify their views regarding the study? Should they perhaps suggest holding a new codification conference that translate customary IHL into treaty law?

Given the contemporary political climate, one should be very cautious. Although it is not impossible that a new codification conference could produce treaties enshrining and clarifying the findings of the customary law study as treaty law, it also would open doors for states to push back and promote legal *regress*, as some wished to do in the 1970s regarding CA3. Indeed, the positive politicization of the lawmaking process that partly gave us CA3 and the APs will not be easily repeated. Certainly, if (failed) efforts by the ICRC and the Swiss government since 2011 to strengthen the machinery of IHL compliance mechanisms are any indication, we should be very wary of pushing for further IHL codification or revision in the short term.[27]

Research Frontiers

Legal Influence

Although throughout this book I have kept my focus on the question of the legal emergence and negotiation of the IHL for internal conflict, let me return to the unavoidable question of its influence. I begin by reiterating that, perhaps surprisingly given the attention that internal atrocity has garnered since the end of the Cold War, social science research on the question of IHL influence in internal conflict remains scarce. This is partly due to issues of data availability and reliability (the proverbial "fog of war," which is even thicker amid internal violence), but it also responds to a historical lack of interest and knowledge about IHL in political science.[28] And though comparative politics research on civilian targeting during civil war has proliferated over the last ten or so years, it has rarely engaged IHL (its nature, history, and contested contents) or explored its influence beyond the puzzle of compliance.[29]

Thus, although important inroads have been made,[30] a focused mapping and assessment of the formal and informal means of IHL influence and implementation in internal conflict remains largely to be done. Further research (using pluralist methodologies and sources, including archives) is necessary across a range of topics: from analyzing the effects of the ICRC's "quiet diplomacy" upon states and nonstate actors, to studying the practice and effects of visits to detainees,[31] the evolution and quality of legal and military training by armed groups of all stripes, domestic legal incorporation/accountability, or the work of national Red Cross societies or of nongovernmental actors drawing on humanitarian norms. These are all largely uncharted territories.

Have CA3 and the APs been influential in world politics? Normatively, I believe the answer should be a qualified yes. These instruments have certainly altered the way in which states and publics regard the commission of atrocity in internal armed conflicts. Such violence and carnage are no longer solely the legal and political concern of those directly fighting or of the population surviving in their midst. These rules of IHL identify and proscribe several forms of abhorrent behavior and define and compel positive, protective conduct. In practice, however, the extent to which every aspect of these instruments is respected likely varies widely across contexts, time, and types of actors. Yet we should not assume that they simply do not "work," particularly on the basis of worst-case examples (Syria comes to mind.)

This makes clear that I do not view the "pressured" negotiation, adoption, and ratification of IHL necessarily as a reason to despair or to wholly deny it of value. Empirically, scholars have found that even commitments made insincerely can have important effects in the medium and long term. In the field of conflict studies, scholars are reconsidering the dynamics of what they call "cheap talk," concluding that it may have some influence.[32] In our field of international relations (IR) and law, the conditional operation of top-down and bottom-up mechanisms of reputational and institutional pressures around international law has now been extensively demonstrated.[33] And, following sociological arguments about "decoupling," with the passage of time "socially pressured" international law can shed its troubled origins and become more robustly embraced.[34] In the memorable words of Philip Allott, "Treaty-law, *like all lawmaking*, is a by-product of politics. Treaty-law negates the politics which produces it. . . . A treaty is not the end of a process, but the beginning of another process. . . . The treaty and the law become another . . . datum with a life of [their] own. . . . The parties to a treaty . . . no doubt have different ideas about what has been fixed in the treaty . . . but their degree of control over their own social situation is limited by the social effectiveness of the treaty or the law."[35]

Doubtless, further research is necessary concerning how "socially pressured" states behave toward the rules they have reluctantly accepted at international forums, the range of attitudes and tactics they pursue, and whether and how initial reluctance wanes over time.[36]

Just as it is premature to conclude that socially pressured treaty commitments will not have influence, it does not follow that imprecise or indeterminate rules are doomed to fail.[37] As noted in chapter 3, although Britain and France were successful (the former more than the latter) in refusing the application of CA3 in Aden, Algeria, Cyprus, Kenya, or Northern Ireland, or arguing that the violence there did not rise to noninternational conflict,[38] CA3 nonetheless gave the ICRC a legal tool with which to request states to allow visits to detainees and to press for better treatment. This represents important influence.[39] Concerning situations that did not indisputably amount to armed conflict, scholars suggest that CA3's vague scope may in fact have facilitated ICRC operations, leading ICRC officials to sometimes refer to CA3's vagueness as a blessing in disguise.[40] Imprecision may thus have both damaging and salutary effects, and scholars should continue studying the conditions explaining such interesting variation.[41] The study of the design of international should no longer rely on general hypotheses and assumptions about states' rationality and "efficiency-oriented" design; it must pay close attention to sociohistorical context and process.[42]

To be sure, given the perverse incentives and the stakes involved during armed conflict, it is possible that the restraining function of the IHL of internal conflict breaks down routinely. However, restraint during active hostilities is not the law's only function; it coexists alongside pedagogical, accountability, and even mediation purposes. In its pedagogical role there are grounds to expect some positive evidence: an increasing number of militaries around the world have incorporated the rules of CA3 and the APs in their training manuals, as have a number of nonstate armed groups.[43] States and rebel groups engaged in armed conflict have also sometimes included in unilateral declarations or bilateral agreements a commitment to respect the rules of IHL (CA3 or Additional Protocol II [APII]).[44] Similarly, fighting parties have chosen to enshrine their peace accords as "special agreements" under CA3, as has been the case of government of Colombia and the Revolutionary Armed Forces of Colombia.[45]

Whether and to what extent these commitments have been kept remains unclear, but the fact that they have been made reconfirms the legitimacy of this branch of IHL on the ground, and offers a greater-than-zero chance that actors wielding violence have observed some humanitarian rules in their operations.

The IHL of internal conflict has transcended widely in the area of domestic and international criminal accountability. Its core provisions have been incorporated into domestic legislation and criminal codes around the world.[46] Article 8 of the Rome Statute, which created the International Criminal Court (ICC), similarly enshrines violations against CA3 (and parts of APII) as international war crimes; many state parties to the ICC have gone on to incorporate such a list of crimes into their own domestic legislation. In terms of practice, war crimes prosecutions for internal atrocities have increasingly taken place in domestic, foreign, and international courts. In a widely publicized case, the U.S. Supreme Court determined that the American military must provide humanitarian protection under the terms of CA3 to Afghan and Taliban detainees.[47]

Obviously, none of this means that the IHL for internal conflict prevents, curbs, or deters all atrocity. It does mean, however, that—despite its troubled political origins and its design deficiencies—it has mattered and is not irrelevant. The law's greatest virtue lies in delineating, however imperfectly, what counts as good and bad behavior in deeply fragile "noninternational" contexts, in providing victims with some measure of protection, and advocates with the tools to demand it. Both of these effects—the normative and political—animate the contentious, tortuous, yet hopeful work of international law in world politics.

Social Pressure in International Lawmaking

Beyond explaining the political origins and development of the IHL for internal conflict, does this book's theoretical argument have purchase on other cases? Is the operation of social pressure and forum isolation domain specific, or can these mechanisms resonate across issue areas? Are they historically bound, or do they "apply" beyond world-historical contexts?

In my view, the structural and institutional conditions I have laid out as facilitating forum isolation—social competition amid public, universal-membership lawmaking processes—allow the consideration that the mechanisms can operate beyond this particular case. Elsewhere I have begun to probe the relevance of this framework in the study of the broader negotiation of the Geneva Conventions and the APs.[48] This work reveals that the making of other critical aspects of the IHL for interstate conflict, including civilian protection rules, can be explained via dynamics of social pressure and backstage strategizing that I propose here. Excellent work by other scholars points to similar dynamics during the making of international human rights law between the 1950s and 1980s.[49]

Social pressure and forum isolation also seem to be applicable beyond the historical period on which I focus here—that is, after the Cold War and decolonization. David Scheffer, for instance, narrated his own diplomatic experience with (failed, but felt) forum isolation during the negotiations of the Rome Statute in 1998, while Richard Price, Jennifer Erickson, and Margarita Petrova have each documented social pressures between states during the negotiation and adoption of the Convention on the Prohibition of the Use, Stockpiling, Production and Transfer of Anti-Personnel Mines; the Arms Trade Treaty; and the Convention on Cluster Munitions, respectively.[50] Beyond human rights and IHL, scholars of international political economy and intellectual property have also alluded to the importance of majority pressure in multilateral standard setting.[51]

There is further evidence for the claim that the social pressure dynamics theorized in this book are not limited to the cases of CA3 and the APs but can recur in international lawmaking. Where could future research expand this agenda?

One obvious follow-up could come from projects that compare successful and failed cases of codification occurring under the same (or similar) political and institutional conditions, a research design that would help refine the theoretical argument and clarify the historical and political conditions that inhibit the operation of forum isolation during codification.

More deeply, returning to theme of insincerity raised earlier, my findings here have suggested that hypocrisy can serve as a *productive* engine of legalization. Recall how, for instance, Soviet rhetoric weighed heavily on the British and French decisions to compromise in 1949. In the 1970s, even though Western states were convinced that the opposing African, Asian and socialist states were deep down only interested in scoring political legitimacy "points" through their proposals to make liberation wars into international conflicts, they nevertheless acquiesced to their demands for social and strategic reasons, allowing the APs to emerge. These findings regarding the *productive power of hypocrisy* amid lawmaking are intriguing,[52] and moving forward scholars could investigate and try to establish the conditions under which this effect succeeds or fails.

Can social pressure, particularly forum isolation, operate on all types of states, or will it only tend influence a select kind? Although the negotiations studied in this book were not all simple or neat cases of "the West versus the rest," it is true that, on the whole, Western states, especially European imperial powers, were consistently on the defensive, due to the dissonance produced by the clash of their professed embrace of liberal democratic politics and values and the increasingly illegitimate political practice of holding colonies. Moreover, these Western states were particularly anxious because they *cared* about the consequences of public embarrassment to their self-image, status, and reputation—they were more "socially vulnerable" because they wished to be seen as "good" standing members of the "international community," particularly amid social competition.

Yet we know that this type of social identity concern and vulnerability varies across time and type of state. Authoritarian or "pariah" states, or states self-identifying as antisocial, maverick, or self-righteous on other grounds, may, for example, feel more comfortable in ignoring international social pressure.[53] The conditions under which this occurs remain unclear. Additional research on nondemocracies—for instance, concerning the attitude of the Soviet Union during the broader negotiation of IHL in the 1970s or China regarding human rights debates within the United Nations (UN) Human Rights Council—suggests that the effects of opprobrium upon such states is more complex than assumed.[54]

Lastly, the attitude of Western major powers since at least 2016 (but perhaps well before that) shows that the conditions under which liberal democracies become susceptible or impermeable to social opprobrium are more variable and fragile than we had suspected. Future work should certainly continue to unravel these important puzzles.

The connection between domestic politics and social pressure during codification similarly remains underexplored. Under what conditions will domestic political factors facilitate or enhance social pressure dynamics occurring in international conferences? When will domestic politics "short-circuit" such pressure? In the postcodification moment, will social pressure exert any weight in states' decisions to ratify instruments they were unable to sink, oppose, or amend satisfactorily in negotiation? Emerging research suggests that social pressure can outlast the codification setting, and yet this effect is probably conditional and interacts with other factors.[55] Fleshing out these conditions and interactions is another avenue worthy of further inquiry.

Finally, and moving partially beyond my theoretical curiosity regarding social pressure in international law, I hope that this book demonstrates that there are very productive opportunities for dialogue and collaboration between IR scholarship and international legal history (and the histories and theories of international law more broadly). Indeed, I wrote this book not only as a contribution to IR theory but as a piece of international legal history in its own right.[56]

Of course, the particular questions all these fields raise, and the methods they use to answer them, do not match perfectly, but all are doubtless enriched through meaningful interaction. In this sense, more new histories of the law of armed conflict (and cognate fields of international law and institutions) are essential—particularly those built upon multiarchival research.

Given that IR theory has historically lacked sufficient nuance to capture the messy and complex reality of international law, through their careful work legal historians and theorists can contribute to improving our concepts and arguments about how law, diplomacy, and politics work and intermingle. New histories written on the basis of archives located in the Global South seem especially necessary; this book takes seriously the importance of Third World (and socialist) states in making and remaking IHL, but generally documents their importance through the reactions of Western states. This was done here out of necessity (e.g., limited resources, time, and access to archives), but moving forward we should make greater efforts to write international law, history, and theory, through the eyes, voices, and acts of non-Western agents.[57] Until that is accomplished, all our work—including this book—remains partial.

Appendix

RESEARCH DESIGN

Periodization

This book covers almost 150 years of international political and legal history. Given the long span, I broke up the chronological process of legal emergence and development into "stages." I divided these stages according to variation in legal outcomes. That is, each stage captured a historical moment process in which international debates about creating rules either "produced" a rule or did not.

At each stage I posed key questions: How did rules emerge? Why and how did states agree to them? How can we explain lawmaking processes and their change over time? The first two relate to the concrete historical episodes of rule emergence, while the third is attentive to global historical change and the dynamics of lawmaking. Since international social structures have changed considerably over the past 150 years, and with them the nature of political and normative debates about international humanitarian law (IHL), studying them carefully was crucial.

Table A.1 presents a summary of the different stages studied in this project, some relevant contextual factors, whether or not they saw the emergence of a rule for internal conflicts, and the types of questions asked.

Note that some "stages" involve processes that failed to produce the regulation envisioned by their proponents. Studying positive as well as negative outcomes partially allows me to posit that some factors and mechanisms may be *necessary conditions* for successful legal norm emergence, and thus may be susceptible of being transposed from one specific historical moment to another. The

TABLE A.1. Stage Classification and Research Questions

TIMELINE	DOES A RULE EMERGE?	STAGE CLASSIFICATION	SPECIFIC RESEARCH QUESTIONS	CHAPTER IN THIS BOOK
Mid-nineteenth century onward	After mid-nineteenth century with the creation of the ICRC, initial ideas arise leading to practical concern but are not made into international law	Norm entrepreneurs do not promote international treaty regulation	How did humanitarian concern for internal conflicts surface? What explains the approach taken by states and by the ICRC and the international Red Cross movement?	Chapter 2
1912, but especially 1918–46	Resolutions are drafted and concerns are formally introduced at International Red Cross Conferences	Normative pressure begins. Nonbinding proposals are initially dismissed but later adopted at International Red Cross Conferences	Where did the impetus for discussing these resolutions come from? Why were they initially rejected but accepted later?	Chapters 2–3
1946–49 (postwar context)	Yes. Common Article 3 to the 1949 Geneva Conventions	Normative pressure begins and produces legal codification	Where did the push to extend the Geneva Conventions to internal conflicts come from? What were states' views on this extension? How was the rule made, and what explains its design?	Chapter 3
1954–65	No. The ICRC attempts to extend substantive protections of the Geneva Conventions but the Draft Rules and expert conclusions are never adopted	Failed attempt	Where did the impetus for new rules come from? How did experts and states view them? Why did the initiative fail?	Chapter 4
1965–70	Yes. Impetus for IHL revisions, including on internal conflicts, resurfaces and is enshrined in UNGA resolutions	Normative pressure ensues and leads to codification process	Where did the UNGA interest come from? What were states' positions with regard to internal conflicts?	Chapter 5
1971–77	Yes. API regulates international wars and struggles for self-determination; APII regulates high-intensity internal conflicts (civil wars)	Legal codification	How were the rules negotiated? What were states' positions? Why were national liberation wars separated from other internal conflicts? What explains the final design and adoption of the APs?	Chapter 5
1977–present	Yes. Customary IHL is extended to internal conflict	Legal extension, mostly on the basis of customary law arguments	What explains the turn to other bodies of law? What were the politics of the emergence or extension of these rules?	Conclusion

strategy also allows me to evaluate the operation of different plausible explanatory mechanisms (described in chapter 1) in each of the episodes, as well as my own framework.

I pursued a single-case, longitudinal, and configurational logic of inquiry, explaining how interdependent legal outcomes *within the same issue area* emerged over time from a patterned configuration of relevant factors, actor types, and mechanisms. The configuration I propose—normative pressure, forum isolation, and covert pushback—constituted a repeat pathway to legal emergence in the case of IHL for internal conflict, and it bears potential application to other issues of interest.[1]

Method

The appropriate method to identify and assess the operation of causal mechanisms is *process tracing*, "the analysis of evidence on processes, sequence, and conjunctures of events within a case" with the purpose of identifying and probing causal mechanisms "in action."[2] My detailed multiarchival research allowed me to formulate my explanation and to evaluate alternative arguments through private evidence. Archival evidence, while not without problems, constitutes the best we have to trace the origins and development of the IHL of internal armed conflict.

A Note on Sources

This book draws on primary and secondary sources. Primary sources included research in multiple governmental archives as well as rare published documents found only in the archives and library of the International Committee of the Red Cross (ICRC; e.g., historical conference proceedings) in Geneva. Secondary sources included a range of documents pertaining to the IHL of internal conflict, including existing legal histories and academic analyses.

The core primary sources were the archives of select states and of the ICRC. At the outset of the project I identified four major state protagonists of IHL negotiations: France, Switzerland, the United Kingdom, and the United States. I also conducted research in the archives of Colombia, Ireland, and Mexico, though I used few documents found at these sources.

I collected and analyzed the following types of primary material:

- Confidential correspondence between the ICRC and each of these states on the scope of the meetings and the contents of the agreements, as well as about scheduling/attendance by other states and actors.

- Confidential correspondence between the various relevant agencies within each state involved in the preparations for the negotiations.
- Confidential correspondence between these states and other states/actors to compare or coordinate positions and strategies prior to and during the negotiations.
- Confidential working drafts and final secret instructions / position papers for state delegations, not only for the main diplomatic conferences but also for several of the preparatory meetings (known as the *travaux préparatoires*).
- Most of the confidential telegraphic correspondence (cables) exchanged "in action" between the delegations in Geneva and their home governments *during* the negotiations and other relevant international conferences. These also include some "update memos" periodically sent back home by some delegations.
- The confidential final reports after each conference / negotiating session, with recommendations and discussions about whether/how to approach signing and ratification.
- Confidential memos and correspondence related to domestic interagency, as well as interstate, debates about reservations, signing, and ratification.
- Evidence about states' intent to apply (or their actual application of) these norms/laws in current or future internal conflicts.
- Considerable documentation (of all the types described above) about the ICRC's (failed) efforts during the 1950s to complement the 1949 Geneva Conventions and about parallel debates in the United Nations in the late 1960s and 1970s on the "respect for human rights in armed conflict," freedom fighters / decolonization, and international terrorism.

At the archives of the ICRC, I collected the following materials:

- Internal policy debates in the ICRC's early period, particularly between the creation of the organization and the death of its first president Gustave Moynier.
- The private correspondence between the ICRC and certain important interlocutors with regard to internal conflicts and civil wars between 1863 and 1923.
- The confidential minutes of various ICRC bodies, including its Council of the Presidency (the second highest-level body of the ICRC) and its Juridical Commission, focusing on any important discussion of internal conflicts/civil wars in 1937–66, particularly in relation to the behavior of combatants from both sides, and the use and application (or lack thereof) of Common Article 3.

Draft Article 42 of Additional Protocol I (later reorganized as Article 44)

Combatants and prisoners of war

1. Any combatant, as defined in Article 43, who falls into the power of an adverse Party shall be a prisoner of war.
2. While all combatants are obliged to comply with the rules of international law applicable in armed conflict, violations of these rules shall not deprive a combatant of his right to be a combatant or, if he falls into the power of an adverse Party, of his right to be a prisoner of war, except as provided in paragraphs 3 and 4.
3. In order to promote the protection of the civilian population from the effects of hostilities, combatants are obliged to distinguish themselves from the civilian population while they are engaged in an attack or in a military operation preparatory to an attack. Recognizing, however, that there are situations in armed conflicts where, owing to the nature of the hostilities an armed combatant cannot so distinguish himself, he shall retain his status as a combatant, provided that, in such situations, he carries his arms openly:
   (a) during each military engagement, and
   (b) during such time as he is visible to the adversary while he is engaged in a military deployment preceding the launching of an attack in which he is to participate.

   Acts which comply with the requirements of this paragraph shall not be considered as perfidious within the meaning of Article 37, paragraph 1 (c).

4. A combatant who falls into the power of an adverse Party while failing to meet the requirements set forth in the second sentence of paragraph 3 shall forfeit his right to be a prisoner of war, but he shall, nevertheless, be given protections equivalent in all respects to those accorded to prisoners of war by the Third Convention and by this Protocol. This protection includes protections equivalent to those accorded to prisoners of war by the Third Convention in the case where such a person is tried and punished for any offences he has committed.
5. Any combatant who falls into the power of an adverse Party while not engaged in an attack or in a military operation preparatory to an attack shall not forfeit his rights to be a combatant and a prisoner of war by virtue of his prior activities.

6. This Article is without prejudice to the right of any person to be a prisoner of war pursuant to Article 4 of the Third Convention.
7. This Article is not intended to change the generally accepted practice of States with respect to the wearing of the uniform by combatants assigned to the regular, uniformed armed units of a Party to the conflict.
8. In addition to the categories of persons mentioned in Article 13 of the First and Second Conventions, all members of the armed forces of a Party to the conflict, as defined in Article 43 of this Protocol, shall be entitled to protection under those Conventions if they are wounded or sick or, in the case of the Second Convention, shipwrecked at sea or in other waters.

Notes

INTRODUCTION

1. For a succinct discussion of the diplomatic debate around this failed human right, see Johannes Morsink, *The Universal Declaration of Human Rights: Origins, Drafting, and Intent* (Philadelphia: University of Pennsylvania Press, 1999), 307–12.

2. Third Committee of the UN General Assembly, Summary records of Meeting 164, Draft International Declaration of Human Rights, A/C.3/SR.164, November 29, 1948, https://undocs.org/A/C.3/SR.164. This Chilean amendment revived an earlier French text introduced by René Cassin crafted in response to Cuba's original (1946) proposal.

3. Morsink, *The Universal Declaration of Human Rights*, 309.

4. United Nations General Assembly, Resolution 217 (III), Universal Declaration of Human Rights, December 10, 1948, preamble, https://www.un.org/en/universal-declaration-human-rights/.

5. Although the legal terminology under IHL is "armed conflict not of an international character" or "noninternational armed conflict," for ease of reading in this book I will generally refer to *internal conflict*, and sometimes *civil war* or *civil conflict*, which are lay terms lacking international legal meaning. However, as I demonstrate in every chapter, it is precisely the characterization of internal violence and its perceived consequences which have historically instigated the core political controversies among states concerning this branch of IHL.

6. Platon D. Morosov, quoted in Federal Political Department of Switzerland, *Final Record of the Diplomatic Conference of Geneva of 1949*, vol. 2-B (Bern: Federal Political Department of Switzerland, 1963), 325.

7. G. I. A. D. Draper, *The Red Cross Conventions* (London: Stevens and Sons, 1958); Jean S. Pictet, ed., *Commentary on the First Geneva Convention for the Amelioration of the Condition of the Wounded and Sick Armed Forces in the Field, August 12, 1949* (Geneva: ICRC, 1952); Geoffrey Best, *War and Law since 1945* (Oxford: Oxford University Press, 1994).

8. Christopher J. Finlay, *Terrorism and the Right to Resist: A Theory of Just Revolutionary War* (New York: Cambridge University Press, 2015).

9. Ruti G. Teitel, *Humanity's Law* (New York: Oxford University Press, 2011), 136–38; Fionnuala Ní Aoláin, "*Hamdan* and Common Article 3: Did the Supreme Court Get It Right?," *Minnesota Law Review* 109 (2006): 1523–61.

10. Samuel Moyn, *The Last Utopia: Human Rights in History* (Cambridge, MA: Harvard University Press, 2010); Steffan-Ludwig Hoffmann, ed., *Human Rights in the Twentieth Century* (New York: Cambridge University Press, 2010); Roland Burke, *Decolonization and the Evolution of International Human Rights* (Philadelphia: University of Pennsylvania Press, 2010); Christian Reus-Smit, *Individual Rights and the Making of the International System* (New York: Cambridge University Press, 2013); Steven L. B. Jensen, *The Making of International Human Rights: The 1960s, Decolonization and the Reconstruction of Global Values* (New York: Cambridge University Press, 2016).

11. For ease of reading, I use the terms *international humanitarian law*, *law of war*, and *law of armed conflict* interchangeably, although I understand their charged history and diverse disciplinary/political usage. For work on the law of armed conflict in IR, see Jeffrey W. Legro, *Cooperation Under Fire: Anglo-German Restraint During World War II* (Ithaca:

Cornell University Press, 1995); Ward Thomas, *The Ethics of Destruction: Norms and Force in International Relations* (Ithaca: Cornell University Press, 2001); Tanisha M. Fazal, *Wars of Law: Unintended Consequences of the Regulation of Armed Conflict* (Ithaca: Cornell University Press, 2018); Matthew Evangelista and Nina Tannenwald, eds., *Do the Geneva Conventions Matter?* (New York: Oxford University Press, 2017); Helen M. Kinsella, *The Image Before the Weapon: A Critical History of the Distinction between Combatant and Civilian* (Ithaca, NY: Cornell University Press, 2011).

12. Boyd van Dijk, "Human Rights in War: On the Entangled Foundations of the 1949 Geneva Conventions," *American Journal of International Law* 112, no. 4 (2018): 553–82.

13. James D. Morrow, *Order within Anarchy: The Laws of War as an International Institution* (New York: Cambridge University Press, 2014).

14. American Red Cross, *Neuvième Conférence Internationale de la Croix-Rouge tenue à Washington du 7 au 17 Mai 1912, Compte rendu* (Washington, DC: American Red Cross, 1912), 45.

15. Robert Craigie, quoted in Federal Political Department of Switzerland, *Final Record*, vol. 2-B, 11.

16. Howard S. Levie, ed., *Protection of War Victims: Protocol 1 to the 1949 Geneva Conventions*, vol. 1 (Dobbs Ferry, NY: Oceana, 1979), 7–8.

17. Howard S. Levie, *The Law of Non-international Armed Conflict: Protocol II to the 1949 Geneva Conventions* (Leiden: Martinus Nijhoff, 1987), 21–134.

18. William Schabas, *The International Criminal Court: A Commentary on the Rome Statute* (Oxford: Oxford University Press, 2010), 18.

19. Jonathan Somer, "Jungle Justice: Passing Sentence on the Equality of Belligerents in Non-international Armed Conflict," *International Review of the Red Cross* 89, no. 867 (2008): 656.

20. ICRC, "Convention (I) for Amelioration of the Condition of the Wounded and Sick in Armed Forces in the Field, Geneva, August 12, 1949, Article 3: Conflicts Not of an International Character" (webpage), https://ihl-databases.icrc.org/applic/ihl/ihl.nsf/Article.xsp?action=openDocument&documentId=BAA341028EBFF1E8C12563CD00519E66.

21. Interstate and national liberation war are formally known as "armed conflicts in which peoples are fighting against colonial domination and alien occupation and against racist régimes in the exercise of their right of self-determination." ICRC, "Protocol Additional to the Geneva Conventions of 12 August 1949, and relating to the Protection of Victims of International Armed Conflicts (Protocol I), 8 June 1977, Article 1: General Principles and Scope of Application" (webpage), https://ihl-databases.icrc.org/applic/ihl/ihl.nsf/Article.xsp?action=openDocument&documentId=6C86520D7EFAD527C12563CD0051D63C.

22. Debate remains among international lawyers about how demanding the scope of APII actually is. Sandesh Sivakumaran, *The Law of Non-International Armed Conflict* (New York: Oxford University Press, 2012), 182–92.

23. For the full text of the APs, see ICRC, "Treaties, States Parties and Commentaries" (web database), https://ihl-databases.icrc.org/ihl.

24. This has been noted in Monica Hakimi, "Constructing an International Community," *American Journal of International Law* 111, no. 2 (2017): 317–56.

25. Richard Bellamy, Markus Kornprobst, and Christine Reh, "Introduction: Meeting in the Middle," *Government and Opposition* 47, no. 3 (2012): 275–76.

26. Christine Reh, "Consensus, Compromise and 'Inclusive Agreement': Negotiating Supranational Governance," in *Arguing Global Governance: Agency, Lifeworld, and Shared Reasoning*, ed. Corneliu Bjola and Markus Kornprobst (London: Routledge, 2011), 185.

27. Reh, "Consensus, Compromise and 'Inclusive Agreement,'" 185.

28. Philip Allott, "The Concept of International Law," *European Journal of International Law* 10, no. 1 (1999): 43.

29. Bellamy, Kornprobst, and Reh, "Introduction."

30. Another tactic is issue linkage, as theorized by institutionalist scholars. See Robert O. Keohane, *After Hegemony: Cooperation and Discord in the World Political Economy* (Princeton, NJ: Princeton University Press, 1984).

31. Joost Pauwelyn, Ramses A. Wessel, and Jan Wouters, "When Structures Become Shackles: Stagnation and Dynamics in International Lawmaking," *European Journal of International Law* 25, no. 3 (2014): 733–63.

32. On so-called secondary structures, rules, and practices of rule making and norm change in IR, see Mark Raymond, *Social Practices of Rule-Making in World Politics* (New York: Oxford University Press, 2019); and Wayne Sandholtz and Kendall Stiles, *International Norms and Cycles of Change* (New York: Oxford University Press, 2009).

33. Tine Hanrieder, "The False Promise of the Better Argument," *International Theory* 3, no. 3 (2011): 390–415; Antje Wiener, *The Invisible Constitution of Politics: Contested Norms and International Encounters* (New York: Cambridge University Press, 2008); Antje E. Wiener, *Constitution and Contestation of Norms in Global International Relations* (New York: Cambridge University Press, 2018).

34. H. Richard Friman, ed., *The Politics of Leverage in International Relations: Name, Shame, and Sanction* (New York: Palgrave Macmillan, 2015).

35. Jennifer Mitzen, "Ontological Security in World Politics: State Identity and the Security Dilemma," *European Journal of International Relations* 12, no. 3 (2006): 341–70; Brent J. Steele, *Ontological Security in International Relations: Self-Identity and the IR State* (London: Routledge, 2008); Richard Ned Lebow, *A Cultural Theory of International Relations* (New York: Cambridge University Press, 2008); Rebecca Adler-Nissen, "Stigma Management in International Relations: Transgressive Identities, Norms, and Order in International Society," *International Organization* 68, no. 1 (2014): 143–76; Ayse Zarakol, *After Defeat: How the East Learned to Live with the West* (New York: Cambridge University Press, 2011); Janice B. Mattern and Ayse Zarakol, "Hierarchies in World Politics," *International Organization* 70, no. 3 (2016): 623–54; Ann E. Towns, "Norms and Social Hierarchies: Understanding International Policy Diffusion 'from Below,'" *International Organization* 66, no. 2 (2012): 179–209; Ann E. Towns and Bahar Rumelili, "Taking the Pressure: Unpacking the Relation between Norms, Social Hierarchies, and Social Pressures on States," *European Journal of International Relations* 23, no. 4 (2017): 756–79; Ayse Zarakol, ed., *Hierarchies in World Politics* (New York: Cambridge University Press, 2017).

36. Giovanni Mantilla, "Social Pressure and the Making of Wartime Legal Protections for Civilians," *European Journal of International Relations* 26, no. 2 (2020): 443–68. Giovanni Mantilla, "Forum Isolation: Social Opprobrium and the Origins of the International Law of Internal Conflict," *International Organization* 72, no. 2 (2018): 317–49.

37. Alastair Iain Johnston has perhaps done more than anyone else to flesh out connections between social psychology and important outcomes in international institutions. See Alastair Iain Johnston, "Treating International Institutions as Social Environments," *International Studies Quarterly* 45, no. 4 (2001): 487–515; and Alastair Iain Johnston, *Social States: China in International Institutions, 1980–2000* (Princeton, NJ: Princeton University Press, 2008). I follow in his footsteps here but also make some key departures. Like Johnston, I am interested in the effects of social influence in multilateral interactions. Yet our focus is different; while Johnston's framework seeks to understand how "novice" states are socialized into existing norms of international society, I am interested in *how new norms emerge and crystallize* in the form of law.

38. For a sample of an ever growing interdisciplinary literature, see Jochen von Bernstorff and Philipp Dann, eds., *The Battle for International Law: South-North Perspectives on the Decolonization Era* (New York: Oxford University Press, 2019); Mark Mazower, *No*

Enchanted Palace: The End of Empire and the Ideological Origins of the United Nations (Princeton, NJ: Princeton University Press, 2009); Adom Getachew, *Worldmaking after Empire: The Rise and Fall of Self-Determination* (Princeton, NJ: Princeton University Press, 2019); Susan Pedersen, *The Guardians: The League of Nations and the Crisis of Empire* (Oxford University Press, 2015); Arnulf Becker Lorca, *Mestizo International Law: A Global Intellectual History, 1842–1933* (New York: Oxford University Press, 2014); Jennifer Pitts, *Boundaries of the International: Law and Empire* (Cambridge, MA: Harvard University Press, 2018); Mark Mazower, *Governing the World: The History of an Idea, 1815 to the Present* (New York: Penguin, 2012); Quinn Slobodian, *Globalists: The End of Empire and the Birth of Neoliberalism* (Cambridge, MA: Harvard University Press, 2019); Martti Koskenniemi, *The Gentle Civilizer of Nations: The Rise and Fall of International Law, 1870–1960* (Cambridge: Cambridge University Press, 2002); Guy Fiti Sinclair, *To Reform the World: International Organizations and the Making of Modern States* (New York: Oxford University Press, 2017); Martti Koskenniemi, Walter Rech, and Manuel Jiménez Fonseca, eds., *International Law and Empire: Historical Explorations* (New York: Oxford University Press, 2017); and Sundhya Pahuja, *Decolonising International Law: Development, Economic Growth and the Politics of Universality* (New York: Cambridge University Press, 2011).

39. Burke, *Decolonization and the Evolution of International Human Rights*; Jensen, *The Making of International Human Rights.*

40. Jensen, *The Making of International Human Rights*, 1–17.

41. Notable works include Timothy Dunne and Christian Reus-Smit, *The Globalization of International Society* (Oxford: Oxford University Press, 2017); Barry Buzan and George Lawson, *The Global Transformation: History, Modernity and the Making of International Relations* (New York: Cambridge University Press, 2015); Amitav Acharya and Barry Buzan, *The Making of Global International Relations: Origins and Evolution of IR at Its Centenary* (New York: Cambridge University Press, 2019); Julian Go and George Lawson, eds., *Global Historical Sociology* (New York: Cambridge University Press, 2017); Zarakol, *After Defeat*; Ann E. Towns, *Women and States: Norms and Hierarchies in International Society* (New York: Cambridge University Press, 2010); and Jennifer Mitzen, *Power in Concert: The Nineteenth-Century Origins of Global Governance* (Chicago: University of Chicago Press, 2013).

42. The single best book on the legal scholarship on the IHL that I theorize here is Sandesh Sivakumaran, *The Law of Non-international Armed Conflict.*

1. SOCIAL PRESSURE IN INTERNATIONAL LAWMAKING

1. My argument explains treaty-based IHL, not customary IHL. However, this book's conclusion reflects on the turn to customary IHL after 1977.

2. One could also cite the Rome Statute of the International Criminal Court (1998) and a host of weapons-related treaties.

3. Stephen D. Krasner, "Sovereignty, Regimes, and Human Rights," in *Regime Theory and International Relations*, ed. Volker Rittberger (Oxford: Clarendon, 1993), 139–67; Chris af Jochnick and Roger Normand, "The Legitimation of Violence: A Critical History of the Laws of War," *Harvard International Law Journal* 35, no. 1 (1994): 49–95; Naeem Inayatullah and David L. Blaney, "The Dark Heart of Kindness: The Social Construction of Deflection," *International Studies Perspectives* 13, no. 2 (2012): 164–75.

4. Many Third World countries relied heavily on this argument in the 1970s to oppose the creation of APII.

5. James D. Morrow, "The Laws of War, Common Conjectures, and Legal Systems in International Politics," *Journal of Legal Studies* 31, no. 1 (2002): 541–60.

6. Andrew Moravcsik, "Liberal Theories of International Law," in *Interdisciplinary Perspectives on International Law and International Relations: The State of the Art*, ed. Jeffrey L. Dunoff and Mark A. Pollack (New York: Cambridge University Press, 2013), 83–118; Thomas Risse-Kappen, "Ideas Do Not Float Freely: Transnational Coalitions, Domestic Structures, and the End of the Cold War," *International Organization* 48, no. 2 (1994): 185–214.

7. Martha Finnemore and Kathryn Sikkink, "International Norm Dynamics and Political Change," *International Organization* 52, no. 4 (1998): 887–917. This has become the standard argument, although other constructivist arguments exist in the IR literature, including: Wayne Sandholtz and Kendall Stiles, *International Norms and Cycles of Change* (New York: Oxford University Press, 2009).

8. Rudra Sil and Peter J. Katzenstein, *Beyond Paradigms: Analytic Eclecticism in the Study of World Politics* (New York: Palgrave Macmillan, 2010); Jeffrey T. Checkel, "Theoretical Pluralism in IR: Possibilities and Limits," in *Handbook of International Relations*, ed. Walter Carlsnaes, Thomas Risse, and Beth A. Simmons, 2nd ed. (Thousand Oaks, CA: Sage, 2012), 220–41.

9. My definition of politics encompasses the idiographic, purposive, ethical, and instrumental aspects discussed in Christian Reus-Smit, "Introduction," and Christian Reus-Smit, "The Politics of International Law," in *The Politics of International Law*, ed. Christian Reus-Smit (New York: Cambridge University Press, 2004), 1–44. See also Philip Allott, "The Concept of International Law," *European Journal of International Law* 10, no. 1 (1999): 46–47. Contrast this approach with the "rational design" school of international legalization; see Barbara Koremenos, *The Continent of International Law* (New York: Cambridge University Press, 2016).

10. Christian Reus-Smit, *The Moral Purpose of the State: Culture, Social Identity, and Institutional Rationality in International Relations* (Princeton, NJ: Princeton University Press, 1999); Jennifer Mitzen, "From Representation to Governing: Diplomacy and the Constitution of International Public Power," in *Diplomacy and the Making of World Politics*, ed. Ole Jacob Sending, Vincent Pouliot, and Iver B. Neumann (New York: Cambridge University Press, 2015).

11. Mark Raymond, *Social Practices of Rule-Making in World Politics* (New York: Oxford University Press, 2019).

12. Neta C. Crawford, *Argument and Change in World Politics* (New York: Cambridge University Press, 2002).

13. Timothy Dunne and Christian Reus-Smit, *The Globalization of International Society* (Oxford: Oxford University Press, 2017); Amitav Acharya and Barry Buzan, *The Making of Global International Relations: Origins and Evolution of IR at Its Centenary* (New York: Cambridge University Press, 2019).

14. Martha Finnemore, *The Purpose of Intervention: Changing Beliefs about the Use of Force* (Ithaca, NY: Cornell University Press, 2003), chap. 3.

15. Margaret E. Keck and Kathryn Sikkink, *Activists beyond Borders* (Ithaca, NY: Cornell University Press, 1998); Ian Clark, *International Legitimacy and World Society* (New York: Oxford University Press, 2007).

16. Louis B. Sohn, "Voting Procedures in United Nations Conferences for the Codification of International Law," *American Journal of International Law* 69, no. 2 (1975): 310–53; Robbie Sabel, *Procedure at International Conferences: A Study of the Rules of Procedure at the UN and at Inter-Governmental Conferences* (New York: Cambridge University Press, 2006); Martha Finnemore and Michelle Jurkovich, "Getting a Seat at the Table: The Origins of Universal Participation and Modern Multilateral Conferences," *Global Governance* 20, no. 3 (2014): 361–73.

17. Keck and Sikkink, *Activists beyond Borders*; Finnemore and Sikkink, "International Norm Dynamics and Political Change"; H. Richard Friman, ed., *The Politics of Leverage in International Relations: Name, Shame, and Sanction* (New York: Palgrave Macmillan, 2015); Ann E. Towns and Bahar Rumelili, "Taking the Pressure: Unpacking the Relation between Norms, Social Hierarchies, and Social Pressures on States," *European Journal of International Relations* 23, no. 4 (2017): 756–79.

18. Frank Schimmelfennig, "The Community Trap: Liberal Norms, Rhetorical Action, and the Eastern Enlargement of the European Union," *International Organization* 55, no. 1 (2001): 47–80; Ann E. Towns, "Norms and Social Hierarchies: Understanding International Policy Diffusion 'from Below,'" *International Organization* 66, no. 2 (2012) : 179–209; Judith G. Kelley, *Scorecard Diplomacy: The Power of Reputation to Influence States* (New York: Cambridge University Press, 2017); Judith G. Kelley and Beth A. Simmons, "Politics by Number: Indicators as Social Pressure in International Relations," *American Journal of Political Science* 59, no. 1 (2015): 55–70; Rebecca Adler-Nissen, "Stigma Management in International Relations: Transgressive Identities, Norms, and Order in International Society," *International Organization* 68, no. 1 (2014): 143–76; Ayşe Zarakol, "What Made the Modern World Hang Together: Socialisation or Stigmatisation?," *International Theory* 6, no. 2 (2014): 311–32.

19. Clarification on the connection between "status" and "reputation," especially what some IR work now labels *social reputation*, seems important. *Reputation* is commonly defined in rationalist IR scholarship as a judgment about an actor's past behavior that is used to predict (credible) future behavior. *Social reputation*, in turn, highlights two aspects that are often lost in rationalist IR theories of reputation: first, that reputational judgments are anchored in social communities which attach historically variable value to practices, attitudes, or statements of belief and identity, and second, that reputations carry within them legitimacy assessments within and between groups. Status and social reputation are thus similar; both turn on perceptions and comparisons of rightfulness and virtuosity. Yet they also differ in subtle ways, particularly insofar as status denotes rank in hierarchy. Generally I find the concept of status more powerful in explanatory terms, but given primary evidence of states' concern for *both* status and social reputation during negotiations, I avoid drawing strong artificial distinctions throughout the book. See also: Jennifer Erickson, *Dangerous Trade: Arms Exports, Human Rights, and International Reputation* (New York: Columbia University Press, 2015).

20. Keck and Sikkink, *Activists beyond Borders*; Joshua W. Busby, *Moral Movements and Foreign Policy* (New York: Cambridge University Press, 2010).

21. For sophisticated new conceptual work on norms, see Michelle Jurkovich, "What Isn't a Norm? Redefining the Conceptual Boundaries of 'Norms' in the Human Rights Literature," *International Studies Review*, online, 2019, https://doi.org/10.1093/isr/viz040.

22. For the connection between opprobrium and legitimacy, see Finnemore and Sikkink, "International Norm Dynamics and Political Change"; Martha Finnemore, "Legitimacy, Hypocrisy, and the Social Structure of Unipolarity: Why Being a Unipole Isn't All It's Cracked Up to Be," *World Politics* 61, no. 1 (2009): 58–85; and Hedley Bull, *The Anarchical Society: A Study of Order in World Politics* (New York: Palgrave Macmillan, 1977). *Legitimacy* has been defined as "a generalized perception or assumption that the actions of an entity are desirable, proper, and appropriate within some socially constructed system of norms, values, beliefs, and definitions"; see Mark C. Suchman, "Managing Legitimacy: Strategic and Institutional Approaches," *Academy of Management Review* 20, no. 3 (1995): 574. *Legitimation* refers to the practice, usually pursued through discourse, of seeking legitimacy for oneself or for one's preferred positions, decisions, or institutions, to be granted by others; see Christian Reus-Smit, "International Crises of Legitimacy," *International Politics* 44, nos. 2–3 (2007): 159.

23. On shame as a cognitive-affective phenomenon, see Christina H. Tarnopolsky, *Prudes, Perverts, and Tyrants: Plato's Gorgias and the Politics of Shame* (Princeton, NJ: Princeton University Press, 2010). As Christian Reus-Smit, *Individual Rights and the Making of the International System* (New York: Cambridge University Press, 2013), 62, notes, "because the development of an individual's social identity is so dependent on the recognition of others, denials or withdrawal of recognition . . . threatens basic self-understandings and esteem." For similar arguments, see also Richard Ned Lebow, *A Cultural Theory of International Relations* (New York: Cambridge University Press, 2008); and Jörg Friedrichs, "An Intercultural Theory of International Relations: How Self-Worth Underlies Politics among Nations," *International Theory* 8, no. 1 (2016): 63–96.

24. For a critical take on the politics behind early law-of-war codification, see Eyal Benvenisti and Doreen Lustig, "Monopolizing War: Codifying the Laws of War to Reassert Governmental Authority, 1856–1874," *European Journal of International Law* (forthcoming 2020).

25. Finnemore and Sikkink, "International Norm Dynamics and Political Change."

26. Keck and Sikkink, *Activists beyond Borders*; Sarah S. Stroup and Wendy H. Wong, *The Authority Trap: Strategic Choices of International NGOs* (Ithaca, NY: Cornell University Press, 2017).

27. For a useful review, see Charli Carpenter, *"Lost" Causes: Agenda Vetting in Global Issue Networks and the Shaping of Human Security* (Ithaca, NY: Cornell University Press, 2014), 39–41. See also Jennifer Hadden, *Networks in Contention: The Divisive Politics of Climate Change* (New York: Cambridge University Press, 2015); and Wendy Wong, *Internal Affairs: How the Structure of NGOs Transforms Human Rights* (Ithaca, NY: Cornell University Press, 2012).

28. This was the case especially after the Hague Conference of 1907. Despite some exceptions with regard to the law of weapons in conflict (including the 1925 Geneva Protocol on asphyxiating gases) the ICRC tended to centralize debate about the development of IHL.

29. As I mention in chapter 2, this was not so in the broader field of peacetime humanitarian activity.

30. Ilya Gaiduk, *Divided Together: The United States and the Soviet Union in the United Nations, 1945–1965* (Stanford, CA: Stanford University Press, 2013); Mary Ann Heiss, "Exposing 'Red Colonialism': U.S. Propaganda at the United Nations, 1953–1963," *Journal of Cold War Studies* 17, no. 3 (2015): 82–115.

31. Adom Getachew, *Worldmaking after Empire: The Rise and Fall of Self-Determination* (Princeton, NJ: Princeton University Press, 2019); Georges Abi-Saab, "The Third World and the International Legal Order," *Revue Egyptienne de Droit International* 29 (1973): 27–66; Georges Abi-Saab, "The Newly Independent States and the Rules of International Law: An Outline," *Howard Law Journal* 8, no. 2 (1962): 95–121.

32. Of course, these mechanisms may operate jointly (or alongside other mechanisms) to produce outcomes. My point is that the analytical distinctions should be maintained.

33. Schimmelfennig, "The Community Trap," 64. Entrapment is similar to hypocrisy exposure. On hypocrisy in international politics, see Finnemore, "Legitimacy, Hypocrisy, and the Social Structure of Unipolarity," 74.

34. Adler-Nissen, "Stigma Management," 146, 171.

35. Alastair Iain Johnston, *Social States: China in International Institutions, 1980–2000* (Princeton, NJ: Princeton University Press, 2008), 80, emphasis added, and, for the overall discussion of "social influence," chap. 3.

36. Johnston, *Social States*, 86.

37. Joseph P. Forgas and Kipling D. Williams, eds., *Social Influence: Direct and Indirect Processes* (Philadelphia: Psychology Press, 2001); Robert B. Cialdini and Noah J. Goldstein,

"Social Influence: Compliance and Conformity," *Annual Review of Psychology* 55 (2004): 607; Hans-Peter Erb, Gerd Bohner, Susanne Rank, and Sabine Einwiller, "Processing Minority and Majority Communications: The Role of Conflict with Prior Attitudes," *Personality and Social Psychology Bulletin* 18, no. 9 (2002): 1172–82; Barbara David and John C. Turner, "Self-Categorization Principles Underlying Majority and Minority Influence," in *Social Influence: Direct and Indirect Processes*, ed. Joseph P. Forgas and Kipling D. Williams (Philadelphia: Psychology Press, 2001), 297–310; Robin Martin and Miles Hewstone, "Determinants and Consequences of Cognitive Processes in Majority and Minority Influence," in *Social Influence: Direct and Indirect Processes*, ed. Joseph P. Forgas and Kipling D. Williams (Philadelphia: Psychology Press, 2001), 316.

38. David and Turner, "Self-Categorization Principles," 297.

39. Martin and Hewstone, "Determinants and Consequences," 316.

40. David and Turner, "Self-Categorization Principles," 310.

41. Ryan Goodman and Derek Jinks, *Socializing States: Promoting Human Rights through International Law* (Oxford: Oxford University Press, 2013).

42. Adler-Nissen, "Stigma Management."

43. Jonathan Renshon, "Status Deficits and War," *International Organization* 70, no. 3 (2016): 513–50; Allan Dafoe, Jonathan Renshon, and Paul Huth, "Reputation and Status as Motives for War," *Annual Review of Political Science* 17 (2014): 374.

44. Towns and Rumelili, "Taking the Pressure."

45. The literature on status makes two core assumptions: state (delegates) "care" about status (they have expectations as to how others should perceive them) and they strive to maintain or "upgrade" their status in a relevant hierarchy. Under certain conditions, as Renshon, "Status Deficits and War," notes, state officials may feel "dissatisfied" with their status or perceive it as threatened, encouraging the pursuit of tactics to address dissatisfaction, including war.

46. Deborah Welch Larson and Alexei Shevchenko, "Status Seekers: Chinese and Russian Responses to U.S. Primacy," *International Security* 34, no. 4 (2010): 63–95; Deborah Welch Larson and Alexei Shevchenko, "Status Concerns and Their Role in Cooperation and Conflict," Paper Presented at the 2015 Annual Convention of the International Studies Association, New Orleans, February 18–21, 2015; T. V. Paul, Deborah Welch Larson, and William C. Wohlforth, eds., *Status in World Politics* (New York: Cambridge University Press, 2014). The literature on status, status recognition, struggle, and revisionism is rapidly growing; see, for example, Marina G. Duque, "Recognizing International Status: A Relational Approach," *International Studies Quarterly* 62, no. 3 (2018): 577–92; Steven Ward, *Status and the Challenge of Rising Powers* (New York: Cambridge University Press, 2017); Michelle Murray, *The Struggle for Recognition in International Relations: Status, Revisionism, and Rising Powers* (New York: Oxford University Press, 2018); and Jonathan Renshon, *Fighting for Status: Hierarchy and Conflict in World Politics* (Princeton, NJ: Princeton University Press, 2017).

47. The link between legitimacy and universality is broadly accepted not just in constructivist but also realist and institutionalist accounts; see Richard H. Steinberg, "In the Shadow of Law or Power? Consensus-Based Bargaining and Outcomes in the GATT/WTO," *International Organization* 56, no. 2 (2002): 345. This institutional form and practice is distinctly modern; see Reus-Smit, *The Moral Purpose of the State*; and Finnemore and Jurkovich, "Getting a Seat at the Table."

48. Phillip Y. Lipscy, "Explaining Institutional Change: Policy Areas, Outside Options, and the Bretton Woods Institutions," *American Journal of Political Science* 59, no. 2 (2015): 341–56.

49. Risse, Thomas, Stephen C. Ropp, and Kathryn Sikkink, eds. *The Persistent Power of Human Rights: From Commitment to Compliance* (New York: Cambridge University Press, 2013); Friman, *The Politics of Leverage*; Snyder, Jack. "Backlash against Human Rights

Shaming: Emotions in Groups." *International Theory*, online (Cambridge University Press, 2019). https://doi.org/10.1017/S1752971919000216.

50. An implicit institutional condition facilitating the operation of shaming via isolation is a legislative or "codification" mandate. While some institutional environments are formally built or informally conceived as talking shops—that is, forums from which no authoritative outcome is necessarily expected to ensue—others bear an explicit mandate to produce such an outcome, to "legislate." In the latter, efforts exert social pressure in codification contexts will be especially acute. I consider this condition to be "implicit" because international negotiations are by definition expected to generate concrete outcomes, and pressures to achieve results are thus usually inherent to them.

51. As Schimmelfennig, "The Community Trap," 65, notes, "The actors under social pressure (usually) do not change their interests; they only refrain from illegitimate behavior."

52. Koremenos, *The Continent of International Law*, 158–91.

53. See Katerina Linos and Tom Pegram, "The Language of Compromise in International Agreements," *International Organization* 70, no. 3 (2016): 587–621. Interestingly, this aspect of the argument also comports with critical international legal scholarship concerning the politics and production of indeterminacy and ambiguity in international law; see Martti Koskenniemi, *From Apology to Utopia: The Structure of International Legal Argument* (New York: Cambridge University Press, 2005), 590–96.

54. Neta C. Crawford, "*Homo Politicus* and Argument (Nearly) All the Way Down: Persuasion in Politics," *Perspectives on Politics* 7, no. 1 (2009): 103–24; Stacie E. Goddard and Ronald R. Krebs, "Rhetoric, Legitimation, and Grand Strategy," *Security Studies* 24, no. 1 (2015): 5–36; Ronald R. Krebs and Patrick Thaddeus Jackson, "Twisting Tongues and Twisting Arms: The Power of Political Rhetoric," *European Journal of International Relations* 13, no. 1 (2007): 35–66. Crawford, "*Homo Politicus*," 120, acknowledges that "some forms of argument are more or less coercive. We have to look at particular instances of behavior and the arrangement of institutions in world politics to understand the scope and limits of argument and persuasion. What should be clear, however, is that the tendency to dichotomize between persuasion and argument on the one hand, and the use of force on the other, is unsustainable conceptually if one pays careful attention to the historical processes of world politics." I agree, and take on this task throughout the book.

55. Monica Hakimi, "Constructing an International Community," *American Journal of International Law* 111, no. 2 (2017): 317–56; Antje E. Wiener, *Constitution and Contestation of Norms in Global International Relations* (New York: Cambridge University Press, 2018).

2. NORMATIVE GATEKEEPING (1863–1921)

1. Mark Mazower, *Governing the World: The History of an Idea, 1815 to the Present* (New York: Penguin, 2012), 3–93; Ian Clark, *Legitimacy in International Society* (Oxford: Oxford University Press, 2007), 85–108.

2. In this section, I rely heavily on Stephen C Neff, *War and the Law of Nations: A General History* (New York: Cambridge University Press, 2005); and Lindsay Moir, *The Law of Internal Armed Conflict* (New York: Cambridge University Press, 2007).

3. Neff, *War and the Law of Nations*, 251–76.

4. Some cite instances in which Islamic law during the Middle Ages sought to depart from this strict division and to create a space for "doctrine-based" struggles as different from sheer criminality. This seems to have been an isolated position, however. See Neff, *War and the Law of Nations*, 251.

5. Neff, *War and the Law of Nations*. My discussion here has a narrow focus on the prevailing ideas and norms about civil war or internal conflicts. For this reason, I do not mention other crucial sources of the laws of war writ large, such as the chivalric codes.

6. Neff, *War and the Law of Nations*, 255.

7. Emerich de Vattel, quoted in Moir, *The Law of Internal Armed Conflict*, 3, emphasis added. See also Pablo Kalmanovitz, *The Laws of War in International Thought* (New York: Oxford University Press, 2020).

8. Moir, *The Law of Internal Armed Conflict*, 3, emphasis added.

9. A systematic assessment of this claim has not been conducted, perhaps due to reasons of data availability. For a longer discussion, however, see Hersch Lauterpacht, *Recognition in International Law* (New York: Cambridge University Press, 1947); and Moir, *The Law of Internal Armed Conflict*, chap. 1.

10. Moir, *The Law of Internal Armed Conflict*, 7–8.

11. That recognition of insurgency was in fact automatic remains disputed. See Neff, *War and the Law of Nations*, 273.

12. Neff, *War and the Law of Nations*, 260.

13. Neff, *War and the Law of Nations*, 262.

14. Neff, *War and the Law of Nations*, 268. Other major powers followed Britain's example, such as France and Russia toward the Greeks in the 1820s and France, the Netherlands, and Spain in the 1860s. The United States also employed it vis-a-vis the South American republics seeking independence from Spain in the 1810s and in the case of Texas's struggle for independence from Mexico in 1836. Neff, *War and the Law of Nations*, 267; Moir, *The Law of Internal Armed Conflict*, 6; Lauterpacht, *Recognition in International Law*.

15. See Martha Finnemore, *The Purpose of Intervention: Changing Beliefs about the Use of Force* (Ithaca, NY: Cornell University Press, 2003), chap. 3; and Gary J. Bass, *Freedom's Battle: The Origins of Humanitarian Intervention* (New York: Knopf Doubleday, 2008).

16. Moir, *The Law of Internal Armed Conflict*, 17, emphasis in the original.

17. Alejandro Valencia Villa, *La Humanización de la Guerra: Derecho Internacional Humanitario y Conflicto Armado en Colombia* (Bogota: Tercer Mundo Editores, 1991); Sandesh Sivakumaran, *The Law of Non-international Armed Conflict* (New York: Oxford University Press, 2012).

18. Geoffrey Best, *Humanity in Warfare* (New York: Columbia University Press, 1980), 170. For a prominent account, see John Fabian Witt, *Lincoln's Code: The Laws of War in American History* (New York: Free Press, 2012).

19. Francis Lieber, *Guerrilla Parties Considered with References to the Laws and Usages of War* (New York: D. Van Nostrand, 1862).

20. Major General H. W. Halleck to Francis Lieber, August 6, 1862, in Lieber, *Guerrilla Parties*, 3.

21. Lieber, *Guerrilla Parties*, 21.

22. Burrus M. Carnahan, "Lincoln, Lieber and the Laws of War: The Origins and Limits of the Principle of Military Necessity," *American Journal of International Law* 92, no. 2 (1998): 213–31, claims that in the prewar period the U.S. Army consisted of thirteen thousand professional fighters. These figures appeared to have risen to a million for the Civil War, prompting Lincoln's concern.

23. Lieber was the major author. The rest of the committee members reportedly only briefly edited his draft. Gary D Solis, *The Law of Armed Conflict: International Humanitarian Law in War* (New York: Cambridge University Press, 2010).

24. Francis Lieber, *Instructions for the Government of Armies of the United States in the Field* (New York: D. Van Nostrand, 1863). See also David Armitage, *Civil War: A History in Ideas* (New York: Knopf, 2018), chap. 5.

25. Lieber, *Instructions for the Government of Armies*, 43.

26. Michael Barnett, *Empire of Humanity: A History of Humanitarianism* (Ithaca, NY: Cornell University Press, 2011), 49–94. On the enthusiasm for international law among

liberal "internationalists" in Europe and the United States around this time, see Martti Koskenniemi, *The Gentle Civilizer of Nations: The Rise and Fall of International Law, 1870–1960* (New York: Cambridge University Press, 2002). On war reporting and its historical impact, see Paul L. Moorcraft, *Shooting the Messenger: The Political Impact of War Reporting* (Lincoln, NE: Potomac Books, 2008). On the eventual symbiosis between the Red Cross movement and growing war-prone nationalism in Europe, see John F. Hutchinson, *Champions of Charity: War and the Rise of the Red Cross* (Boulder, CO: Westview, 1996).

27. The name of the committee varied in its early period. It was first named the Société Genevoise d'Utilité Publique (Geneva Society for Public Welfare), and later the Comité International de Secours aux Blessés (International Committee of Relief to the Wounded), among other slight variations. Eventually, in 1875, the ICRC name was adopted.

28. Although a declaration on war at sea had been signed in 1856 in Paris at the end of the Crimean War, its contents were limited to protecting neutral maritime trade. See Dietrich Schindler and Jiri Toman, eds., *The Laws of Armed Conflicts: A Collection of Conventions, Resolutions, and Other Documents*, 4th ed. (Leiden: Martinus Nijhoff, 2004), 1055.

29. See, for example, David P. Forsythe, *The Humanitarians: The International Committee of the Red Cross* (New York: Cambridge University Press, 2005) and James Crossland, *War, Law and Humanity: The Campaign to Control Warfare, 1853–1914* (London: Bloomsbury Publishing, 2018). For an ICRC historian's account of this early period of the movement, see Pierre Boissier, *From Solferino to Tsushima* (Geneva: Institut Henry Dunant, 1985). More critical histories are provided in Hutchinson, *Champions of Charity*; and Caroline Moorhead, *Dunant's Dream: War, Switzerland and the History of the Red Cross* (New York: Carroll and Graf, 1998).

30. Henry Dunant, *A Memory of Solferino* (Geneva: ICRC, 1986). The other towering figure was Florence Nightingale in the United Kingdom; see Best, *Humanity in Warfare*, 148–49; and Hutchinson, *Champions of Charity*, 19.

31. Boissier, *From Solferino to Tsushima*, 49–53.

32. Hutchinson, *Champions of Charity*, 21, 22, 23.

33. According to Stacie E. Goddard, "Brokering Change: Networks and Entrepreneurs in International Politics," *International Theory* 1, no. 02 (2009): 257, in social network theory brokers are political entrepreneurs "who bridge structural holes in fragmented networks; they maintain ties with actors who would otherwise remain unconnected." And "by bridging structural holes, brokers occupy central positions in a network structure, acting as nodes through which the multiple transactions coalesce." To this basic definition I would add that brokers not only attack existing "structural holes" but can and often do *make them evident* by pursuing a number of different tactics. These tactics are ultimately geared toward providing a common interpretive terrain and a focal point for action. The theoretical approach I adopt here pays substantive attention to brokers as agents of change but maintains that the conditions under which entrepreneurs as agents succeed ultimately depend on the structural position they occupy.

34. A fifth idea was added later: relief workers should be considered neutral by combatants and could not be targeted. The primary use of the Red Cross emblem was initially reserved for military medics, something that helps explain why initial governmental and army resistance to these new humanitarian standards soon subsided and transformed into a forceful embrace.

35. For the text of the First Geneva Convention, see ICRC, "Convention for the Amelioration of the Condition of the Wounded in Armies in the Field" (webpage), https://ihl-databases.icrc.org/applic/ihl/ihl.nsf/INTRO/120?opendocument. The political negotiations of the First Geneva Convention in 1863 and 1864 were arduous, however. For contrasting explanations of its origins, see Martha Finnemore, "Norms and War: The International Red Cross and the Geneva Conventions," in *National Interests in Interna-*

tional Society (Ithaca, NY: Cornell University Press, 1996); and Hutchinson, *Champions of Charity*, 33–56.

36. This is a bare-bones description of the Red Cross movement in its early period. For more, see Forsythe, *The Humanitarians*, 316; and François Bugnion, *The International Committee of the Red Cross and the Protection of War Victims* (Oxford: Macmillan Education, 2003). For brevity I often use the singular "Red Cross" and the plural "national Red Cross societies," but note that many national societies are actually named societies of the Red Crescent, and in the case of Israel, Red Crystal. The entire movement is officially known as the International Red Cross and Red Crescent movement.

37. The First International Conference took place in Paris in 1867. Originally called the International Conference of Red Cross Societies, the switch to International Conference of the Red Cross offered greater accuracy. These meetings included not just national societies but also the ICRC, state parties to the Geneva Convention, and, eventually, the League of Red Cross and Red Crescent Societies (now the International Federation of Red Cross and Red Crescent Societies). Richard Perruchoud, *Les Resolutions des Conferences Internationales de la Croix-Rouge* (Geneva: Institut Henry Dunant, 1979).

38. Best, *Humanity in Warfare*, 163. See also Ian Clark, *International Legitimacy and World Society* (New York: Oxford University Press, 2007), chap. 3.

39. Schindler and Toman, *The Laws of Armed Conflicts*, 91.

40. For the text of the Brussels Declaration, see Schindler and Toman, *The Laws of Armed Conflicts*, 21. For accounts of the origins of the Institute of International Law, see Romain Yakemtchouk, *Les Origines de L'Institut de Droit International* (Paris: Éditions A. Pedone, 1973); and Koskenniemi, *The Gentle Civilizer of Nations, 1870–1960.*

41. On the Hague Conferences, see James Brown Scott, *The Hague Peace Conferences of 1899 and 1907*, vol. 1 (Charleston, NC: Nabu, 2010); and James Brown Scott, *The Hague Peace Conferences of 1899 and 1907*, vol. 2 (Neuilly-sur-Seine, France: Ulan, 2012). For international relations analyses highlighting important outcomes of these events, see Reus-Smit, *The Moral Purpose of the State: Culture, Social Identity, and Institutional Rationality in International Relations* (Princeton, NJ: Princeton University Press, 1999), chap. 6; Clark, *International Legitimacy and World Society*, chap. 3; and Maartje Abbenhuis, *The Hague Conferences and International Politics, 1898–1915* (London: Bloomsbury Publishing, 2019). On the Permanent Court of Arbitration and its face-saving function, see Andrei Mamolea, "Saving Face: The Political Work of the Permanent Court of Arbitration," in *Experiments in International Adjudication: Historical Accounts*, ed. Ignacio de la Rasilla and Jorge E. Viñuales (New York: Cambridge University Press, 2019), 193–210.

42. Later in this chapter, however, I will cite two expert meetings of the IIL that considered the subject but failed to produce a humanitarian code.

43. Henry Dunant, *Mémoires* (Geneva: Institut Henry Dunant, 1971), 71; Rosemary Abi-Saab, *Droit Humanitaire et Conflits Internes: Origines et Évolution de la Réglementation Internationale* (Geneva: Institut Henry Dunant, 1986), 30–31; Jean-François Pitteloud, ed., *Procès-Verbaux des Séances du Comité International de la Croix-Rouge: 17 Février 1863–28 Août 1914* (Geneva: Société Henry Dunant / ICRC, 1999), 20.

44. Dunant, *Mémoires*, 71, my translation, emphasis added; Abi-Saab, *Droit Humanitaire et Conflits Internes*, 30–31, my translation; Pitteloud, *Procès-Verbaux*, 20, my translation.

45. Gustave Moynier, quoted in Abi-Saab, *Droit Humanitaire et Conflits Internes*, 31, my translation.

46. Moynier, quoted in Abi-Saab, *Droit Humanitaire et Conflits Internes*, 31, my translation.

47. On the long history of the ICRC's work on political prisoners in internal troubles, see Jacques Moreillon, *Le Comité International de la Croix-Rouge et la Protection Des Détenus Politiques* (Geneva: Institut Henry-Dunant / Éditions L'Âge d'Homme, 1973).

48. Some national societies acted out of their own volition, including during the uprising on the island of Candia (now Crete) in 1868 and during the Paris Commune in 1871. François Bugnion. *The International Committee of the Red Cross and the Protection of War Victims*. (Oxford: Macmillan Education, 2003), 246.

49. Moreillon, *Le Comité International de la Croix-Rouge*, 25.

50. Boissier, *From Solferino to Tsushima*, 297.

51. It was later renamed the *Bulletin International des Sociétés de la Croix Rouge*.

52. Moreillon, *Le Comité International de la Croix-Rouge*, 26.

53. Boissier, *From Solferino to Tsushima*, 298.

54. Moreillon, *Le Comité International de la Croix-Rouge*, 28–29. It appears that the ICRC also reminded the other national societies in the countries receiving refugee flows from the internal conflict of their right and duty to aid such victims, irrespective of the side they supported, scolding the Austrian Red Cross for refusing to provide such help to wounded refugees thought to be insurgents.

55. I do not claim that things worked much better in the context of international war, particularly during its early years. Moynier's language, however, seems to indicate his belief that that the situation of the Red Cross in civil wars was especially grim, and I take his declaration seriously.

56. Gustave Moynier. *La Croix Rouge: Son Passé et Son Avenir* (Paris: Sandoz et Thuillier, 1882), 169–80.

57. Moynier, *La Croix Rouge*, 171, my translation, emphasis in the original.

58. Moynier, *La Croix Rouge*, 178–79.

59. Moynier, *La Croix Rouge*, 178–79. His specific proposals were, first, that national Red Cross societies should offer their services to *all* combatants irrespective of the side they were on; second, national societies would be called to cooperate with one another during civil war but should refrain from establishing any links with rebels; and third, foreign national societies had to completely refrain from intervening in countries torn by civil conflict where the Red Cross had no presence at all.

60. See "Annexe a la 52me Circulaire du Comité International de la Croix-Rouge, 25 Janvrier 1884, Liste de Sujets Proposés pour les Délibérations de la Conférence Internationale des Sociétés de la Croix-Rouge qui devait se tenir à Vienne," *Bulletin International des Sociétés de Secours aux Militaires Blessés* 15, no. 57 (1884): 9–27.

61. This procedure changed in 1884 when a special commission was formed to prepare the organization for the international conferences. This so-called council of delegates has since been composed of the ICRC, the national Red Cross societies, and eventually, the League (now International Federation) of Red Cross and Red Crescent Societies. See Perruchoud, *Les Resolutions des Conferences Internationales de la Croix-Rouge*.

62. Count de Beaufort to Gustave Moynier, April 17, 1884, A AF Carton 7, Document 1888, ICRC Archives, my translation.

63. Pitteloud, *Procès-Verbaux*, 479.

64. According to the Dutch Red Cross, differences should be made between relief originating from within the conflict-ridden state and that coming from abroad. In the former context, the concerned national Red Cross society could, but was not obliged to, provide relief to the insurgent wounded and sick. In the latter situation, the Dutch Red Cross declared, "serious doubts should be raised" and more careful steps had to be taken. These steps were, first, that foreign relief had to be channeled through the concerned Red Cross, because direct flow of aid risked forfeiting the neutrality of the Red Cross cause as a whole; second, aid had to be provided only to *military* wounded and sick; and third, relief should in general follow a strict observance of the Geneva Convention so as to preserve the neutrality of the Red Cross. See *Quatrième Conférence Internationale des Sociétés de la Croix-Rouge tenue à Calrsuhe du 22 au 27 Septembre 1887, Compte rendu* (Geneva: ICRC, 1887), 239–40.

65. *Quatrième Conférence Internationale des Sociétés de la Croix-Rouge*, 147.

66. Clark, *Revolutionary and Legitimate Orders*; Finnemore, *The Purpose of Intervention*, 108–24.

67. David Strang, "Contested Sovereignty: The Social Construction of Colonial Imperialism," in *State Sovereignty as a Social Construct*, ed. Thomas Biersteker and Cynthia Weber (New York: Cambridge University Press, 1996), 27.

68. Thomas Biersteker and Cynthia Weber, "The Social Construction of State Sovereignty," in *State Sovereignty as a Social Construct*, eds. Thomas Biersteker and Cynthia Weber (New York: Cambridge University Press, 1996), 11.

69. Christian Reus-Smit, "Struggles for Individual Rights and the Expansion of the International System," *International Organization* 65, no. 2 (2011): 207–42.

70. Strang, "Contested Sovereignty," 25.

71. Michael W. Doyle, *Empires* (Ithaca, NY: Cornell University Press, 1986), 45. For a historical and conceptual discussion, see: Duncan Bell, "Empire and Imperialism," in *The Cambridge History of Nineteenth Century Political Thought*, eds. Gregory Claeys and Gareth Stedman Jones (New York: Cambridge University Press, 2011), 864–92.

72. Gerrit W. Gong, *The Standard of "Civilization" in International Society* (Oxford: Clarendon, 1984), 74.

73. I borrow the term *episteme* from John Gerard Ruggie, who borrows it from Michel Foucault. By *social episteme*, Ruggie means "a dominant way of looking at social reality, a set of shared symbols and references, mutual expectations and a mutual predictability of intention." See John Gerard Ruggie, *Constructing the World Polity: Essays on International Institutionalization* (London: Routledge, 1998), 55.

74. Boissier, *From Solferino to Tsushima*, 12, 8.

75. Barnett, *Empire of Humanity*, 82.

76. Gustave Moynier, quoted in Boissier, *From Solferino to Tsushima*, 277. The quote continues with Moynier stating that "if we preach to them pity for the enemy wounded and respect for a symbol of charity on the battlefields, they would not understand what we were talking about because, for them, the law of war does not allow of such consideration; and as for associations for helping the victims, that would seem to them non-sense." Similar anecdotes and quotes exist that denote frank derision toward countries such as China, India, Japan, Persia, and Turkey. Archival evidence gathered during my own research confirms these views.

77. See Hutchinson, *Champions of Charity*; and Forsythe, *The Humanitarians*, chap. 1.

78. Hutchinson, *Champions of Charity*, 150, 175, 176.

79. Barnett, *Empire of Humanity*, 81, following others, highlights the probably exclusionary role exerted by the ICRC founders' ardent Christian faith.

80. Bugnion, *The International Committee of the Red Cross and the Protection of War Victims*, 248.

81. Florence Nightingale famously expressed the latter critique.

82. See Hutchinson, *Champions of Charity*, chaps. 2–3.

83. Moynier, quoted in Hutchinson, *Champions of Charity*, 90.

84. Hutchinson, *Champions of Charity*, 105–28.

85. In 1872 Moynier proposed the creation of an international judicial institution formed by notable and impartial figures appointed by states to judge individual cases of wartime atrocities. Such a plan, however, was either ignored or coolly dismissed by many of his fellow legal luminaries in Europe and the United States at the time. Gustave Rolin-Jaequemyns, "Note sur le Projet de M. Moynier, Relatif a l'établissement d'une Institution Judiciaire Internationale Protectrice de la Convention," *Revue de Droit International et de Legislation Comparée* 2 (1872): 325–46; Katharina Neureiter, "'Too Radical for Its Time'? Gustave Moynier and His Proposal for an International Criminal

Court around 1872" (master's thesis, London School of Economics and Political Science, 2012).

86. Forsythe, *The Humanitarians*, 24.

87. Hutchinson, *Champions of Charity*, 157. The limits set by governments to humanitarian ideals at any given time, however, are never entirely clear nor fixed, and it is upon this unclear "frontier" that the ICRC has historically operated when trying to move the humanitarian agenda forward.

88. For references to this aspect with regard to the First Geneva Convention, see Boissier, *From Solferino to Tsushima*, 119.

89. Abi-Saab, *Droit Humanitaire et Conflits Internes*, 25, my translation.

90. Abi-Saab, *Droit Humanitaire et Conflits Internes*, 25, my translation.

91. Abi-Saab, *Droit Humanitaire et Conflits Internes*, 25, my translation.

92. For the texts of these declarations, see Emilio Brusa and Ludwig von Bar, rapporteurs, *Règlement sur la Responsabilité des Etats à raison des Dommages soufferts par des Étrangers en cas d'Émeute, d'Insurrection ou de Guerre Civile* (Geneva: Institute of International Law, 1900), http://www.idi-iil.org/app/uploads/2017/06/1900_neu_01_fr.pdf; and Arthur Desjardins and Marquis de Olivart, rapporteurs, *Droits et Devoirs des Puissances Étrangères, au cas de Mouvement Insurrectionnel, envers les Gouvernements établis et reconnus qui sont aux prises avec l'Insurrection* (Geneva: Institute of International Law, 1900), http://www.idi-iil.org/app/uploads/2017/06/1900_neu_02_fr.pdf.

93. Clara Barton to Gustave Moynier, October 17, 1895, A AF Carton 5, Document 284, ICRC Archives.

94. Gustave Moynier to Clara Barton, October 31, 1895, A AF Livre 14, Document 290, ICRC Archives, my translation.

95. Forsythe, *The Humanitarians*, 30, cites additional examples of this attitude in the case of the Spanish-American War in the Philippines. I also collected others in my own fieldwork. Bugnion, *The International Committee of the Red Cross*, 247, concurs with this assessment.

96. This episode is well told in Boissier, *From Solferino to Tsushima*, 365–84.

97. Neville Wylie, "Muddied Waters: The Influence of the First Hague Conference on the Evolution of the Geneva Conventions of 1864 and 1906," in *War, Peace and International Order? The Legacies of the Hague Conferences of 1899 and 1907*, eds. Maartje Abbenhuis, Christopher Ernest Barber, and Annalise R. Higgins (London: Routledge, 2017), 52–68.

98. Boissier, *From Solferino to Tsushima*, 383–84.

99. André Durand, *From Sarajevo to Hiroshima: History of the International Committee of the Red Cross* (Geneva: Henry Dunant Institute, 1984), 10.

100. Various histories of the American Red Cross attest to the intricate relationship between the U.S. government and the Red Cross during this time. See Foster Rhea Dulles, *The American Red Cross: A History* (New York: Harper and Brothers, 1950), 81–101; and Gwendolyn C. Shealy, *A Critical History of the American Red Cross, 1882–1945: The End of Noble Humanitarianism* (Lewiston, NY: Edwin Mellen, 2003).

101. Joshua R. Clark Jr., "Functions of Red Cross when Civil War or State of Insurrection Exists," report of a committee appointed by the International Relief Board of the American Red Cross, to be read as a part of the paper to be presented at the Ninth International Conference, Washington DC, April 1, 1912, A AF Carton 31 Dossier 2, ICRC Archives.

102. For an initial analysis, see Jean Siotis, *Le Droit de la Guerre et Les Conflits Armés d'un Caractère Non-International* (Paris: Librairie générale de droit et de jurisprudence, 1958), 136–42.

103. Dulles, *The American Red Cross*; Shealy, *A Critical History*; Justin Hart, *Empire of Ideas: The Origins of Public Diplomacy and the Transformation of U.S. Foreign Policy*

(Oxford: Oxford University Press, 2013); Benjamin Allen Coates, *Legalist Empire* (Oxford: Oxford University Press, 2016); Jane Burbank and Frederick Cooper, *Empires in World History: Power and the Politics of Difference* (Princeton, NJ: Princeton University Press, 2010), 321–24.

104. Bugnion, *The International Committee of the Red Cross*, 249.

105. For two biographies of Joshua Reuben Clark Jr., see Frank W. Fox, *J. Reuben Clark: The Public Years* (Provo, UT: Brigham Young University Press, 1980); and Stephen S. Davis, "J. Reuben Clark, Jr., Statesman and Counselor," in *Counselors to the Prophets*, ed. Michael K. Winder (Salt Lake City: Eborn Books, 2001).

106. Dulles, *The American Red Cross*, 127–30.

107. Aside from its efforts during the Mexican Revolution of 1910, the American Red Cross sent missions during uprisings in the Dominican Republic (1903 and 1906), Venezuela (1903), Nicaragua (1909), Honduras (1911), and China (1912). Bugnion, *The International Committee of the Red Cross*, 247.

108. I thank Andrei Mamolea for this observation; Andrei Mamolea, "The Mexican Protectorate," unpublished manuscript.

109. American Red Cross, *Neuvième Conférence Internationale de la Croix-Rouge tenue à Washington du 7 au 17 Mai 1912, Compte rendu* (Washington DC: American Red Cross, 1912), 45.

110. American Red Cross, *Neuvième Conférence*, 45.

111. William Quentin Maxwell, *Lincoln's Fifth Wheel: The Political History of the United States Sanitary Commission* (Longmans, Green, 1956).

112. American Red Cross, *Neuvième Conférence*, 203, 45.

113. Bugnion, *The International Committee of the Red Cross*, 250.

114. Durand, *From Sarajevo to Hiroshima*, 99, 110.

115. The Red Cross societies from Austria-Hungary, Bulgaria, Germany, and Turkey also attended in an advisory capacity.

116. Moreillon, *Le Comité International de la Croix-Rouge*, 44–47; Durand, *From Sarajevo to Hiroshima*, 97–123; Bugnion, *The International Committee of the Red Cross*, 250–58.

117. Durand, *From Sarajevo to Hiroshima*, 138.

118. Durand, *From Sarajevo to Hiroshima*, 132–33.

119. Durand, *From Sarajevo to Hiroshima*, 138.

120. Letter from an unidentified member of the ICRC to Buch [representative, Danish Red Cross in Kiev], February 4, 1919, B CR-22, ICRC Archives.

121. Georges Lodygensky to the ICRC, May 8, 1920, B CR 22/1, ICRC Archives.

122. Gustave Ador to Georges Lodygensky, May 21, 1920, B CR 22/1, ICRC Archives.

123. Georges Lodygensky to Gustave Ador, May 24, 1920, B CR 22/1, ICRC Archives. Lodygensky's reports from July 1920 were his effort to prevent the issue from stalling within the ICRC, after a special fact-finding mission sent by the committee could not enter Russia. For the remainder of the correspondence, see B CR 22/1, ICRC Archives.

124. Kimberly A. Lowe, "Humanitarianism and National Sovereignty: Red Cross Intervention on Behalf of Political Prisoners in Soviet Russia, 1921–3," *Journal of Contemporary History* 49, no. 4 (2014): 652–74.

125. Moreillon, *Le Comité International de la Croix-Rouge*, 52–63.

126. *Dixième Conférence Internationale de la Croix-Rouge tenue à Genève du 30 Mars au 7 Avril 1921, Compte Rendu* (Geneva: ICRC, 1921).

127. Lowe, "Humanitarianism and National Sovereignty." Lowe is, in part, quoting the report of the Italian Red Cross.

128. *Dixième Conférence*, 217–18.

129. In addition to the analysis of the conference presented here, see Siotis, *Le Droit de la Guerre*, 142–45.

130. *Dixième Conférence*, 66–67.

131. Moreillon, *Le Comité International de la Croix-Rouge*, 59, hints at this underlying concern and the political dilemma it created.

132. Moreillon, *Le Comité International de la Croix-Rouge*, 59.

3. SQUARING THE CIRCLE

1. Jean S. Pictet, ed., *Commentary on the First Geneva Convention for the Amelioration of the Condition of the Wounded and Sick Armed Forces in the Field, August 12, 1949* (Geneva: ICRC, 1952), 48; G.I.A.D. Draper, *The Red Cross Conventions* (Praeger, 1958).

2. *XVII Conférence de la Croix-Rouge, Stockholm, Août 1948, Commission juridique, Sténogramme des séances* (Geneva: ICRC, 1948), 44.

3. All these cases contain interesting elements. The Upper Silesia conflict, for instance, was peculiar in that it occurred in an area whose formal status had not been decided. The Polish and Montenegro cases were pursued after private individuals or groups made public denunciations about state persecution for political reasons but not in the context of overt armed conflict. See Jacques Moreillon, *Le Comité International de la Croix-Rouge et la Protection des Détenus Politiques* (Geneva: Institut Henry Dunant, 1973), 65–96; André Durand, *From Sarajevo to Hiroshima: History of the International Committee of the Red Cross* (Geneva: Institut Henry Dunant, 1984), chaps. 5–7; and François Bugnion, *The International Committee of the Red Cross* (Oxford: Macmillan Education, 2003), 263–66.

4. This applied, in this case, to France and Spain. See Durand, *From Sarajevo to Hiroshima*, 239.

5. Moreillon, *Le Comité International de la Croix-Rouge*, 65–96.

6. Bugnion, *The International Committee of the Red Cross*, 282–83.

7. For this portrayal I draw mainly on Durand, *From Sarajevo to Hiroshima*, 317–68. See also Bugnion, *The International Committee of the Red Cross*, 266–83.

8. Durand, *From Sarajevo to Hiroshima*, 322.

9. For more detail, see Durand, *From Sarajevo to Hiroshima*, 317–68; and Bugnion, *The International Committee of the Red Cross*, 266–83.

10. Durand, *From Sarajevo to Hiroshima*, 323.

11. Durand, *From Sarajevo to Hiroshima*, 268.

12. Bugnion, *The International Committee of the Red Cross*, 283.

13. Walter Yung, "Le Rôle et l'Action de la Croix-Rouge en Temps de Guerre Civile," *Revue Internationale de la Croix-Rouge* 20 (1938): 97–113, my translation.

14. Bugnion, *The International Committee of the Red Cross*, 285.

15. ICRC, *Compte-rendu de la 2ème commission Londres*, B CRI-19, ICRC Archives.

16. ICRC, *Compte-rendu de la 2ème commission Londres*, B CRI-19, ICRC Archives.

17. ICRC, *Sixteenth International Red Cross Conference, London* (Geneva: ICRC, 1938), 82–83.

18. Giovanni Mantilla, "The Origins and Evolution of the 1949 Geneva Conventions and the 1977 Additional Protocols," in *Do the Geneva Conventions Matter?*, ed. Matthew Evangelista and Nina Tannenwald (Oxford: Oxford University Press, 2017), 35–68.

19. For simplicity, I refer to the first two conventions collectively as the Wounded and Sick Conventions, and to the third and fourth as the POW Convention and the Civilians Convention. The Wounded and Sick Conventions had been updated in 1929 and the POW Convention was created that same year. A key precedent to the Civilians Convention had been an earlier draft treaty known as the Tokyo Project of 1934. For more on that instrument, see ICRC, "Draft International Convention on the Condition and Protection of Civilians of Enemy Nationality Who Are on Territory Belonging to or Occupied by a Belligerent, Tokyo, 1934" (webpage), https://ihl-databases.icrc.org/ihl/INTRO/320?OpenDocument.

20. Giovanni Mantilla, "Social Pressure and the Making of Wartime Legal Protections for Civilians," *European Journal of International Relations* 26, no. 2 (2020): 443–68.

21. Catherine Rey-Schyrr, *De Yalta à Dien Bien Phu: Histoire Du Comité International de la Croix-Rouge, 1945–1955* (Geneva: Georg Éditeur, 2007), 242–44.

22. ICRC, *Manuel Chronologique pour l'histoire Générale de la Croix-Rouge, 1863–1899* (Geneva: Imprimerie I. Soullier, 1900), 3.

23. Durand, *From Sarajevo to Hiroshima*, 187.

24. Hans Haug, *Humanity for All: The International Red Cross and Red Crescent Movement* (Geneva: Institut Henry Dunant, 1993), 165; Rey-Schyrr, *De Yalta à Dien Bien Phu*, 27.

25. ICRC, *Report on the Work of the Preliminary Conference of National Red Cross Societies for the Study of the Conventions and of Various Problems Relative to the Red Cross, Geneva, July 26–August 3, 1946* (Geneva: ICRC, 1946).

26. ICRC, *Conférence Préliminaire des Sociétés de la Croix-Rouge pour l'Étude des Conventions et des Divers Problèmes Ayant Trait à la Croix-Rouge, Genève, 26 Juillet–3 Août 1946, Procès-Verbaux*, vol. 2 (Geneva: ICRC, 1946), 3. Jean Pictet is a towering figure in the history of IHL and the ICRC. It should suffice to note here that he was the main architect of the Geneva Conventions of 1949, and remained central to the evolution of the law and the principles of the Red Cross moving forward.

27. ICRC, *Conférence Préliminaire*, 4–7.

28. ICRC, *Conférence Préliminaire*, 7–15; ICRC, *Report on the Work of the Preliminary Conference of National Red Cross Societies*, 70.

29. Apparently unaware of the ICRC's invitation (which had gone to the U.S Department of State), the U.S. War Department in fact decided in August 1945 to write a report of the gaps faced in the application of the conventions during the war. When the War Department staff learned of the ICRC's plans, it was willing and able to participate in the discussions.

30. Boyd van Dijk, "'The Great Humanitarian': The Soviet Union, the International Committee of the Red Cross, and the Geneva Conventions of 1949," *Law and History Review* 37, no. 1 (2019): 209–35.

31. Files of Colonel R. McDonald Gray Relating to the U.S. Interdepartmental Committee on Prisoners of War, Gray's Reports, Administrative Division, Mail and Records Branch, Geneva Convention 1946–1949, Box 670, Entry A1 437, Record Group 389, U.S. National Archives.

32. Projet de Convention Relative au Traitement des Prisonniers de Guerres—Révision de la Convention de Genève du 27/07/1929, Art. 159, Cote 4-17, Unions Internationales 1944–1964, Ministère des Affaires Étrangères, Direction des Archives. Translation of the names of the different participating agencies is my own.

33. Revision of Geneva and Red Cross Conventions, FO 369/3592/K17356, UK National Archives.

34. Interdepartmental Committee on the Revision of the Geneva Conventions, FO 369/3796/K11724, UK National Archives.

35. This documentation was based on the ICRC draft conventions, produced partly on the conclusions of the 1946 meeting of national Red Cross societies. Its late arrival annoyed some governments since it gave them less time to think through the ICRC proposals.

36. ICRC, *Report on the Work of the Conference of Government Experts for the Study of the Conventions for the Protection of War Victims, Geneva, April 14–26, 1947* (Geneva: ICRC, 1947).

37. *Conférence d'Experts Gouvernementaux pour l'étude des Conventions protégeant les victimes de la guerre, Genève, 14–16 avril 1947, Procès-Verbaux, Assemblées Plénières*, vol. 1 (Geneva: ICRC, 1947), 32.

38. ICRC, *Report on the Work of the Conference of Government Experts*, 8.

39. *Conférence d'Experts Gouvernementaux*, 32.

40. Projet de Convention pour la Protection de la Population Civile en Temps de Guerre, subfolder P. Mollard (Personnel), Art. 159, Cote 4-17, Unions Internationales, 1944–1964, Ministère des Affaires Étrangères, Direction des Archives, my translation.

41. Eric Beckett on Harold Satow's report, June 13, 1947, FO 369/3794/K8146, UK National Archives.

42. *Report of Proceeding of the US Delegation to the Meeting of Gov. Experts re the Revision of the Geneva Conv.*,1947, Records Relating to the International Committee of the Red Cross (ICRC), 1900–2005, Container 75, Entry P 108, Record Group 200, U.S. National Archives.

43. It may also be that the documents registering explicit French preparatory debates on this were not kept complete by archivists. I report here on what I could find.

44. Prisoners of War Committee minutes, January 10, 1949, POWC M104, Minutes, Box 673, Entry A1 437, Record Group 389, U.S. National Archives.

45. Interdepartmental Committee on the Revision of the Geneva Conventions, FO 369/3796/K11724, UK National Archives.

46. William Gardner to Harold Satow, September 17, 1947, FO 369/3796/K12857, UK National Archives.

47. Gardner also referenced the Nazi "resistance" forces, known as the Werewolves, after the fall of the Reich; Draft—Applications of the Conventions, FO 369/3796/K12857, UK National Archives. See also William I. Hitchcock, "Human Rights and the Laws of War: The Geneva Conventions of 1949," in *The Human Rights Revolution: An International History*, ed. Akira Iriye, Petra Goedde, and William I. Hitchcock (New York: Oxford University Press, 2012), 104.

48. Joyce Gutteridge to Francis Vallat, September 25, 1947, FO 369/3796/K12857, UK National Archives.

49. William Gardner to John W. O. Davidson, March 24, 1948, FO 369/3967/K4200, UK National Archives.

50. William Gardner to John W. O. Davidson, May 5, 1948, FO 369/3968/K5862, UK National Archives.

51. Interdepartmental Committee on the Revision of the Geneva Conventions, Report of the Chairman, FO 369/3968/K5862, UK National Archives.

52. Interdepartmental Committee on the Revision of the Geneva Conventions, Report of the Chairman, FO 369/3968/K5862, UK National Archives.

53. ICRC, *Draft Revised or New Conventions for the Protection of War Victims* (Geneva: ICRC, 1948), 6.

54. The Greek delegate represented both his country's national society and the government. The French delegate spoke for the national Red Cross society, while the American Red Cross and U.S. government delegates shared views and worked together.

55. *XVII Conférence de la Croix-Rouge, Stockholm*, 39–45, 46.

56. *XVII Conférence de la Croix-Rouge, Stockholm*, 46.

57. *XVII Conférence de la Croix-Rouge, Stockholm*, 49, 52–53, 57, 64. See also ICRC, *Draft Revised or New Conventions*, 71–72. Swedish government representatives were publicly opposed to inserting conditional reciprocity in the POW Convention.

58. United States draft for the revision of the Geneva Convention Relative to the Treatment of Prisoners of War, POWC D-43, March 4, 1949, Box 673, Entry A1 437, Record Group 389, U.S. National Archives.

59. William Gardner to John W. O. Davidson, September 1, 1948, FO 369/3969/K10003, UK National Archives.

60. The comparative importance and prioritization with which various British cabinets approached revisions of IHL relative to other treaty-making exercises or domestic

political concerns deserves further reflection elsewhere. Similarly, further research is desirable on the relative influence of the bureaucratic cultures, practices, and interests of the British civil service and how these interact, constrain, or channel the preferences and policies of varying UK governments of different political persuasions.

61. William Gardner to John W. O. Davidson, October 48, 1949, FO 369/3970/K11941, UK National Archives.

62. Memorandum proposed for submission to the Swiss Government for circulation to other Governments in anticipation of the Diplomatic Conference, FO 369/3970/K11941, UK National Archives.

63. Memorandum proposed for submission to the Swiss Government for circulation to other Governments in anticipation of the Diplomatic Conference, FO 369/3970/K11941, UK National Archives.

64. First Revise of the Draft Brief on the Civil War Provisions in Article 2 of the I.C.R.C. Draft, FO 369/3970/K13445, UK National Archives.

65. William P. Speake to David J. Mill Irving, January 3, 1949, FO 369/4142/K406, emphasis added.

66. First Revise of the Draft Brief on the Civil War Provisions in Article 2 of the I.C.R.C. Draft, FO 369/3970/K11941, UK National Archives. The only possible way out of this impasse for the HO team was to accept the possibility for states to strike ad hoc agreements with the armed opposition based on reciprocity and facilitated by the ICRC. Eventually, however, even this was found unacceptable. Alternatively, the HO team suggested the proper place for this genre of clauses was the UN "Human Rights Charter," not humanitarian law.

67. Transmission of correspondence to Robert Craigie concerning the two most serious outstanding difficulties in the existing drafts of the Civilian Convention, FO 369/3970/K13445, UK National Archives.

68. Minutes of a Meeting of Ministers held at No. 10, Downing Street, S.W.1., on Monday, 28th March, 1949, at 10.15 a.m., CAB 130/46/281, UK National Archives.

69. Notes of a Meeting held in the Attorney General's room at the House of Commons on Monday, 11th April, 1949, to discuss war crimes, FO 369/4148/3905, UK National Archives.

70. Odd Arne Westad, "The Cold War and the International History of the Twentieth Century," in *The Cambridge History of the Cold War*, vol. 1, *Origins*, ed. Odd Arne Westad and Melvyn P. Leffler (New York: Cambridge University Press, 2010), 13. See also David C. Engerman, "Ideology and the Origins of the Cold War, 1917–1962," in *The Cambridge History of the Cold War*, vol. 1, *Origins*, ed. Odd Arne Westad and Melvyn P. Leffler (New York: Cambridge University Press, 2010), 20.

71. Erik Ringmar, "The Recognition Game: Soviet Russia against the West," *Cooperation and Conflict* 37, no. 2 (2002): 115–36; Avi Shlaim, "Britain's Quest for a World Role," *International Relations* 5, no. 1 (1975): 838–56; Edward A. Kolodziej, *French International Policy under De Gaulle and Pompidou: The Politics of Grandeur* (Ithaca, NY: Cornell University Press, 1974).

72. Shlaim, "Britain's Quest for a World Role," 839.

73. Charles de Gaulle, quoted in Gadi Heimann, "What Does It Take to Be a Great Power? The Story of France Joining the Big Five," *Review of International Studies* 41, no. 1 (2014): 199.

74. Heimann, "What Does it Take?," 199.

75. Ringmar, "The Recognition Game," 128.

76. Engerman, "Ideology and the Origins of the Cold War," 41, 23, 33.

77. Robert Jervis, "Identity and the Cold War," in *The Cambridge History of the Cold War*, vol. 2, *Crisis and Détente*, ed. Melvyn P. Leffler and Odd Arne Westad (New York: Cambridge University Press, 2010), 33.

78. Anne Deighton, "Britain and the Cold War, 1945–1955," in *The Cambridge History of the Cold War*, vol. 1, *Origins*, ed. Odd Arne Westad and Melvyn P. Leffler (New York: Cambridge University Press, 2010), 112, 119, 113–14, 119–20.

79. Mark Philip Bradley, "Decolonization, the Global South, and the Cold War, 1919–1962," in *The Cambridge History of the Cold War*, vol. 1, *Origins*, ed. Odd Arne Westad and Melvyn P. Leffley (New York: Cambridge University Press, 2010), 473.

80. Deighton, "Britain and the Cold War," 147.

81. Christopher N. J. Roberts, *The Contentious History of the International Bill of Human Rights* (New York: Cambridge University Press, 2014), 70, 128, 134.

82. Robert H. Jackson, "The Weight of Ideas in Decolonization: Normative Change in International Relations," in *Ideas and Foreign Policy: Beliefs, Institutions and Political Change*, ed. Judith Goldstein and Robert O. Keohane (Ithaca, NY: Cornell University Press, 1993); Ilya Gaiduk, *Divided Together: The United States and the Soviet Union in the United Nations, 1945–1965* (Stanford, CA: Stanford University Press, 2013); Mary Ann Heiss, "Exposing 'Red Colonialism': U.S. Propaganda at the United Nations, 1953–1963," *Journal of Cold War Studies* 17, no. 3 (2015): 82–115.

83. Harold Karan Jacobson, "The United Nations and Colonialism: A Tentative Appraisal," *International Organization* 16, no. 1 (1962): 39.

84. David M. McCourt, *Britain and World Power since 1945: Constructing a Nation's Role in International Politics* (Ann Arbor: University of Michigan Press, 2014).

85. Christopher Hill, "Powers of a Kind: The Anomalous Position of France and the United Kingdom in World Politics," *International Affairs* 92, no. 2 (2016): 393–414.

86. See Giovanni Mantilla, "The Protagonism of the USSR and Socialist States in the Revision of International Humanitarian Law (IHL)," *Journal of the History of International Law* 21, no. 2 (2019): 181–211; and Van Dijk, "'The Great Humanitarian.'"

87. Federal Political Department of Switzerland, *Final Record of the Diplomatic Conference of Geneva of 1949*, vol. 2-B (Bern: Federal Political Department of Switzerland, 1963), 10.

88. Albert Lamarle, quoted in Federal Political Department of Switzerland, *Final Record*, vol. 2-B, 11.

89. Robert Craigie, quoted in Federal Political Department of Switzerland, *Final Record*, vol. 2-B, 11.

90. Federal Political Department of Switzerland, *Final Record*, vol. 2-B, 11. The Mexican delegation was explicitly counseled to show "categorical" support for the extension of the conventions to civil war "out of a progressive and humanitarian spirit," denouncing great powers' resistance to any advancement in international law as being rooted in their material and political interest to retain their colonial possessions by force, "sometimes using procedures that violate the most elementary humanitarian norms to repress any liberation movement." "Instrucciones a la Legación Mexicana," Vicente Sánchez Gavito to Embajador Pedro de Alba, April 13, 1949, Folder III-2552-1, Acervo Histórico Genaro Estrada, Secretaría de Relaciones Exteriores, my translation.

91. Federal Political Department of Switzerland, *Final Record*, vol. 2-B, 12–13.

92. General Nikolai Vassilievitch Slavin, quoted in Federal Political Department of Switzerland, *Final Record*, vol. 2-B, 14.

93. Slavin, quoted in Federal Political Department of Switzerland, *Final Record*, vol. 2-B, 14.

94. Soviet POWs also suffered harshly in the hands of their German captors during World War II, but the connection between this specific concern and the issue of civil war is at best tenuous.

95. Federal Political Department of Switzerland, *Final Record*, vol. 2-B, 16.

96. Albert Lamarle to the Ministry of Foreign Affairs, April 28, 1949, Art. 161, Cote 4-17, Unions Internationales, 1944–1964, Ministère des Affaires Étrangères, Direction des Archives.

97. John Alexander to Christopher Kemball, April 30, 1949, FO 369/4149/K4555, UK National Archives, underlining in the original.

98. "Inter Arma Caritas," *Times* (London), April 21, 1949. *Le Journal de Genève* ran two articles remarking upon the extension of the conventions to internal conflict, noting the conservative attitude of the British, on the same day; see "Les principes de Croix-Rouge sont valables pour tous," *Le Journal de Genève*, April 28, 1949; and "L'application des conventions aux cas des guerres civiles et aux conflits coloniaux," *Le Journal de Genève*, April 28, 1949.

99. Henry Strutt to Frank Newsam, FO 369/4149/K4590, UK National Archives.

100. John Alexander to Christopher Kemball, FO 369/4149/K4555, UK National Archives, emphasis added.

101. Memorandum on developments in the Conference on the subject of the application of the Conventions to Civil War, FO 369/4149/K4720, UK National Archives.

102. Harold Strutt to Frank Newsam, FO 369/4149/K4555, UK National Archives.

103. Federal Political Department of Switzerland, *Final Record*, vol. 2-B, 45.

104. The First Working Party comprised Australia, France, Norway, Switzerland, the United Kingdom, and the United States.

105. Federal Political Department of Switzerland, *Final Record*, vol. 2-B, 46–47.

106. Note by Christopher Kemball, FO 369/4149/K4555, UK National Archives.

107. Note by Christopher Kemball, FO 369/4149/K4720, UK National Archives.

108. Note by Eric Beckett, FO 369/4149/K4555, UK National Archives.

109. Note by Eric Beckett, FO 369/4149/K4720, UK National Archives.

110. Robert Craigie to Harold Caccia, FO 369/4149/K4720, UK National Archives, emphasis added.

111. Notes on a Meeting between Mr. Christopher Mayhew, Parliamentary Under Secretary for Foreign Affairs and Sir Robert Cragie, FO 369/4151/K5239, UK National Archives, emphasis added.

112. Robert Craigie to Harold Caccia, FO 369/4149/K4720, UK National Archives.

113. Robert Craigie to Harold Caccia, FO 369/4149/K4720, UK National Archives.

114. Application to Civil War of Geneva Conventions on War Victims, Report by Official Working Party, CAB 130/46/281, UK National Archives.

115. Minutes of a Meeting of Ministers held in the Prime Minister's Room, House of Commons, S.W.1. on Monday, 23rd May, 1949, at 3.30 p.m., CAB 130/46/281, UK National Archives.

116. Albert Lamarle to the Ministry of Foreign Affairs, May 13, 1949, Art. 161, Cote 4-17, Unions Internationales, 1944–1964, Ministère des Affaires Étrangères, Direction des Archives.

117. Albert Lamarle to Ministry of Foreign Affairs, May 25, 1949, Art. 161, Cote 4-17, Unions Internationales, 1944–1964, Ministère des Affaires Étrangères, Direction des Archives; Robert Craigie to Harold Caccia, May 9, 1949, FO 369/4151/K5239, UK National Archives.

118. Robert Craigie to Harold Caccia, June 3, 1949, FO 369/4152/K5437, UK National Archives.

119. Craigie to Caccia, June 3, 1949.

120. Note from Ministry of Foreign Affairs to French Delegation in Geneva, June 4, 1949, Art. 161, Cote 4-17, Unions Internationales, 1944–1964, Ministère des Affaires Étrangères, Direction des Archives.

121. Note from Ministry of Foreign Affairs, June 4, 1949. Curiously, British delegates perceived the new French instructions as a "hardening" of their previous position, since it

no longer allowed for the application of the majority of the provisions of the Conventions, just general principles. See FO 369/4152/K5437, UK National Archives.

122. David J. Mill Irving to Christopher Kemball, FO 369/4154/K5812.

123. Notes of the 41st United Kingdom Delegation Meeting held on Friday 17th June, 1949, FO 369/4155/K6172, UK National Archives.

124. Notes of the 43rd United Kingdom Delegation Meeting held on Tuesday 21st June, 1949, FO 369/4156/K6348, UK National Archives.

125. Albert Lamarle, quoted in Federal Political Department of Switzerland, *Final Record*, vol. 2-B, 84.

126. Federal Political Department of Switzerland, *Final Record*, vol. 2-B, 95.

127. Federal Political Department of Switzerland, *Final Record*, vol. 2-B, 103.

128. Catherine Rey-Schyrr, *De Yalta à Dien Bien Phu*, 648–57.

129. Federal Political Department of Switzerland, *Final Record*, vol. 2-B, 103.

130. Notes of the 57th United Kingdom Delegation Meeting held on Saturday 9th July, 1949, FO 369/4157/K6841, UK National Archives. This seemed to them a more effective option than protesting the vote in the Special Committee, since voting rules required a two-thirds majority to approve a reopened topic.

131. Robert Craigie to Harold Caccia, FO 369/4158/K6948, UK National Archives.

132. Robert Craigie to Harold Caccia, FO 369/4158/K6948, UK National Archives.

133. Notes of the 59th United Kingdom Delegation Meeting held on Tuesday 12th July, 1949, FO 369/4158/K7107, UK National Archives.

134. Notes of the 67th United Kingdom Delegation Meeting held on Thursday 21st July, 1949, FO 369/4160/K7627, UK National Archives.

135. Federal Political Department of Switzerland, *Final Record*, vol. 2-B, 129.

136. Platon Dmitrievitch Morosov, quoted in Federal Political Department of Switzerland, *Final Record*, vol. 2-B, 325, 326.

137. General Tun Hla Oung, quoted in Federal Political Department of Switzerland, *Final Record*, vol. 2-B, 328–29.

138. Plinio Bolla, quoted in Federal Political Department of Switzerland, *Final Record*, vol. 2-B, 335.

139. Oung, quoted in Federal Political Department of Switzerland, *Final Record*, vol. 2-B, 337.

140. War Office comments on the draft of the Common Articles Memorandum, FO 369/4163/ K10223, UK National Archives.

141. Minutes of the Meeting of May 19, 1949, PV Conseil de la Présidence 1949–1950, ICRC Archives.

4. A WINDING ROAD TO THE ADDITIONAL PROTOCOLS (1950–1968)

1. France ratified the conventions in 1951, the United States in 1955, and the United Kingdom in 1957. On the British and American decisions to commit, see Giovanni Mantilla, "Conforming Instrumentalists: Why the USA and the United Kingdom Joined the 1949 Geneva Conventions," *European Journal of International Law* 28, no. 2 (2017): 483–511. Argentina and Portugal lodged reservations regarding CA3 upon signature, but withdrew them upon ratification.

2. Procès-Verbaux de la Commission Juridique et documentation y relative, Nos 36 à 60, vol. 2, ICRC Archives, my translation.

3. Fabian Klose, "The Colonial Testing Ground: The International Committee of the Red Cross and the Violent End of Empire," *Humanity* 2, no. 1 (2011): 107–26.

4. Unlike in political science, where scholars have agreed on some numerical thresholds to characterize a situation as armed conflict—twenty-five battle-related deaths, for example—in international law there is no such clear, accepted equivalent.

5. See, for example, Fabian Klose, *Human Rights in the Shadow of Colonial Violence: The Wars of Independence in Kenya and Algeria* (Philadelphia: University of Pennsylvania Press, 2013).

6. Giovanni Mantilla, "Social Pressure and the Making of Wartime Legal Protections for Civilians," *European Journal of International Relations* 26, no. 2 (2020): 443–68.

7. See ICRC, "Draft Rules for the Limitation of the Dangers incurred by the Civilian Population in Time of War: ICRC, 1956" (webpage), http://www.icrc.org/applic/ihl/ihl.nsf/INTRO/420?OpenDocument.

8. Jean S. Pictet, *Commentary on the First Geneva Convention for the Amelioration of the Condition of the Wounded and Sick Armed Forces in the Field, August 12, 1949* (Geneva: ICRC, 1952), 50. However, note that in Jean S. Pictet, ed., *Commentary on the Fourth Geneva Convention Relative to the Protection of Civilian Persons in War, August 12, 1949* (Geneva: ICRC, 1958), 36, Pictet added, "Speaking generally, it must be recognized that the conflicts referred to in Article 3 are armed conflicts, with armed forces on either side engaged in hostilities—conflicts, in short, which are in many respects similar to an international war, but take place within the confines of a single country. In many cases, each of the Parties is in possession of a portion of the national territory, and there is often some sort of front." Despite a slight change in tone, Pictet still viewed territorial control and the existence of frontlines as optional, not obligatory elements.

9. Jacques Moreillon, *Le Comité International de la Croix-Rouge et la Protection Des Détenus Politiques* (Geneva: Institut Henry Dunant, 1973), 130–35; Françoise Perret and François Bugnion, *De Budapest a Saigon: Histoire Du Comité International de La Crox-Rouge 1956-1965* (Geneva: Georg Editeur, 2009), 259–68.

10. Perret and Bugnion, *De Budapest à Saigon*, 264; Klose, "The Colonial Testing Ground." Perret and Bugnion usefully cite the words of British international lawyer Gerald Draper, who asserted that Britain's decision against recognizing that violence in Kenya or in other British territories like Cyprus or Malaya fell under the scope of CA3 was political, not one "determined by an objective assessment of the facts." Draper's words are important because he was not particularly progressive with regard to advancing IHL for internal conflicts, as we will see in chapter 5, which discusses his official actions as expert delegate for the United Kingdom in the 1960s and 1970s.

11. Brian Drohan, *Brutality in an Age of Human Rights: Activism and Counterinsurgency at the End of the British Empire* (Ithaca, NY: Cornell University Press, 2017).

12. Moreillon, *Le Comité International*, 126–30; Catherine Rey-Schyrr, *De Yalta à Dien Bien Phu: Histoire Du Comité International de la Croix-Rouge, 1945–1955* (Geneva: Georg Éditeur, 2007), 687–98. Some ICRC prison visits were possible in Morocco but were facilitated through personal contacts, not on the basis of legal instruments.

13. Sahr Conway-Lanz, *Collateral Damage: Americans Noncombatant Immunity and Atrocity After World War II* (Abingdon, UK: Routledge, 2006), 168–70.

14. Perret and Bugnion, *De Budapest à Saigon*, 51–83.

15. David P. Forsythe, "Legal Regulation of Internal Conflicts: The 1977 Protocol on Non-International Armed Conflicts," *American Journal of International Law* 72, no. 2 (1978): 272–95, took an important first step in this direction, yet systematic research on this important topic is still lacking.

16. James Edward Bond, *The Rules of Riot: Internal Conflict and the Law of War* (Princeton, NJ: Princeton University Press, 1974), 60; Lindsay Moir, *The Law of Internal Armed Conflict* (New York: Cambridge University Press, 2007), 67–88.

17. ICRC historians and members have recognized the committee's ambivalence and hesitation vis-à-vis internal troubles and tensions before and after World War II. See Moreillon, *Le Comité International*; François Bugnion, *The International Committee of the Red Cross and the Protection of War Victims* (Oxford: Macmillan Education,

2003); Rey-Schyrr, *De Yalta à Dien Bien Phu*; and Perret and Bugnion, *De Budapest à Saigon*.

18. This concern was not new for the ICRC. Among other concerns, its interest about the effects of warfare on civilians had previously been recorded in the form of a resolution (resolution 5) issued during the Fourteenth International Conference of the Red Cross in 1930, from which a series of expert consultations followed. ICRC, *Final Record concerning the Draft Rules for the Limitation of Dangers Incurred by the Civilian Population in Time of War, XIXth International Conference of the Red Cross* (Geneva: ICRC, 1958), 8; Rey-Schyrr, *De Yalta à Dien Bien Phu*, 290.

19. In an annex, one of the Hague Conventions of 1907 (convention 4) contained general principles regarding civilians, but these were not phrased to induce restraint in the use of "imprecise" or "indiscriminate" weapons and methods of war (as the ICRC referred to them), such as bombing from the air or launching nuclear warheads.

20. The only treaty signed since 1907 dealing with weapons was a protocol prohibiting gas and bacteriological warfare, negotiated in 1925 and revised in 1993. See ICRC, "Protocol for the Prohibition of the Use of Asphyxiating, Poisonous or Other Gases, and of Bacteriological Methods of Warfare, Geneva, 17 June 1925" (webpage), https://ihl-databases.icrc.org/applic/ihl/ihl.nsf/Article.xsp?action=openDocument&documentId=58A096110540867AC12563CD005187B9.

21. As chapter 2 illustrated, practical concern for the victims of internal violence, especially for detained persons, had earlier roots in the ICRC. In this sense, debates in the 1950s were resuming conversations that had begun earlier. See Moreillon, *Le Comité International*, 94–95.

22. Moreillon, *Le Comité International*, 118.

23. A first step was taken in 1952 at the Eighteenth International Conference of the Red Cross in Toronto. Participants there, including not only national Red Cross societies but also the ICRC, the League of Red Cross Societies, and governments' delegates adopted the revised Statutes of the International Red Cross and Red Crescent Movement, which recognized the ICRC as a "neutral institution whose humanitarian activity is exerted especially in cases of civil war and internal troubles [where] it strives at all times to ensure protection and assistance to military and civilian victims of said conflicts and their direct results" (my translation). See the entire text of the revised 1952 statutes in Richard Perruchoud, *Les Resolutions des Conferences Internationales de la Croix-Rouge* (Geneva: Institut Henry Dunant, 1979), 451. This recognition was important given governmental acquiescence at the international Red Cross conference that approved the statutes, but it did not rise to the level of binding international law and was often ignored by states. It was strengthened later, in 1986 and 1995, adding reference to what is known as the ICRC's "right of humanitarian initiative" in any situation or question it may deem to come within its purview (Art. 5). For the latest version, see ICRC, *Statutes of the International Red Cross and Red Crescent Movement* (Geneva: ICRC, 2007), http://www.icrc.org/eng/resources/documents/misc/statutes-movement-220506.htm.

24. Rey-Schyrr, *De Yalta à Dien Bien Phu*, 317.

25. See also the report written on this issue by R. J. Wilhelm, legal expert at the ICRC, in the Minutes for the Meeting of December 22, 1952 (and the related document D. 252), Procès-Verbaux de la Commission Juridique et documentation y relative, Nos 36 à 60, vol. 2, ICRC Archives.

26. Moreillon, *Le Comité International*, 120–21.

27. The Eighteenth International Conference in 1952, like the one that followed in 1957 in New Delhi, featured bitter debates over the participation of the two Chinas as the legitimate representatives of the Republic of China. Both meetings ended with the abrupt walking out of various delegations.

28. Rey-Schyrr, *De Yalta à Dien Bien Phu*, 320.

29. Rey-Schyrr, *De Yalta à Dien Bien Phu*, 318, 666–83. See also the Minutes for the Meetings of January 12 and January 22, 1953 and the related document D. 250. Procès-Verbaux de la Commission Juridique et documentation y relative, Nos 36 à 60, vol. 2, ICRC Archives.

30. ICRC, *Commission of Experts for the Examination of the Question of Assistance to Political Detainees, Geneva, June 9–11, 1953* (Geneva: ICRC, 1953). The invited experts were Maurice Bourquin, a professor in Geneva; Roberto Córdova, the Mexican ambassador to Switzerland; Nihat Erim, a professor and former Turkish minister; Gilbert Gidel, a French professor; Jean Graven, a professor in Geneva; Max Huber, then honorary ICRC president and former judge on the Permanent International Court of Justice; Caracciolo Parra-Pérez, a Venezuelan diplomat; Emil Sandstroem, the Swedish president of the Governing Council of the League of National Red Cross Societies; Giuseppe Saragat, an Italian politician; and Carlo Schmid, a West German parliamentarian.

31. Moreillon, *Le Comité International*, 124.

32. Moreillon, *Le Comité International*, 125; Rey-Schyrr, *De Yalta à Dien Bien Phu*, 320–23.

33. The Guatemalan government also eventually accepted the application of CA3 to the conflict in 1954.

34. ICRC, *Commission of Experts for the Study of the Question of the Application of Humanitarian Principles in the Event of Internal Disturbances, Geneva, October 3–8, 1955* (Geneva, ICRC, 1955). In attendance were Paul Cornil, president of the International Criminal Law Association; Gilbert Gidel, France; Max Huber, Switzerland; Julio López-Olivan, Spanish diplomat; Mohan Sinha Mehta, the Indian ambassador in Bern; Abbas-Naficy, former vice president of the Council of Iran and vice president of the Red Crescent and Lion; Nihat Erim, Turkey; Caracciolo Parra-Pérez, Venezuela; M. Pilotti, president of the European Coal and Steel Community Court of Justice; Alejandro Quijano and M. de Rueda, Mexican Red Cross; W. E. Rappard, a professor in Geneva; Emil Sandstroem, Sweden; and Carlo Schmid, West Germany. See also Moreillon, *Le Comité International*, 137.

35. The experts also cited the UDHR, the European Convention on Human Rights, and the then emerging work of the UN on the prevention of crime and the treatment of delinquents as normative basis for action. Moreillon, *Le Comité International*, 138.

36. Rey-Schyrr, *De Yalta à Dien Bien Phu*, 294–96.

37. Other government legal advisers shared this pessimistic view. See R. J. Wilhelm's mention of his encounter with Lauterpacht in the Minutes for the Meeting of January 22, 1953. Procès-Verbaux de la Commission Juridique et documentation y relative, Nos 36 à 60, vol. 2, ICRC Archives. Note that aside from World War II, aerial bombardment was also used to cruel effects in cities like Durango, Guernica, and Málaga during the Spanish Civil War, and in Algeria and Cuba, among other places. Michel Veuthey, *Guerrilla et Droit Humanitaire* (Geneva: Institut Henry Dunant, 1976), 97–102.

38. ICRC, *Commission of Experts for the Legal Protection of Civilian Populations and Victims of War from the Danger of Aerial Warfare and Blind Weapons, Geneva, April 6–13, 1954, Documents and Summary Records* (Geneva: ICRC, 1954). The experts in attendance were Major Richard Baxter, Judge Advocate General's Office, U.S. State Department; Maurice Bourquin, Belgium; Georges Cahen-Salvador, council of state, France; Erik Castrén, law professor, Finland; André Costedoat, surgeon general, France; Juji Enomoto, former law professor, Japan; Captain Cyril Betham Palls, former Oxford University history of war professor, United Kingdom; S.E. Gundevia, Indian ambassador to Switzerland; Radmilc Jovanovic, surgeon general, Yugoslavia; Giorgio La Pira, former senator, Italy; M. W. Mouton, Dutch Royal Navy, Netherlands; Hans Rumpf, West Germany; Major General E. D. Tobiessen, chief of civilian defense, Norway; Masao Tsuzuki, professor emeritus in Medi-

cine, Japan; Raymond Yingling, legal adviser, U.S. State Department; and R. J. E. M. van Zinnicq-Bergman, royal court marshal, Dutch Air Force, Netherlands.

39. The ICRC's initial desired mix consisted of China, France, India, the United Kingdom, the United States, the USSR, two South American countries, an Arab country, and two neutral states, Finland and Sweden. See the Minutes for the Meeting of April 16, 1953 (and the related document D. 273). Procès-Verbaux de la Commission Juridique et documentation y relative, Nos 36 à 60, vol. 2, ICRC Archives.

40. Minutes for the Meeting of April 29, 1955, and the related documents D. 384, D. 385, and D. 386. Procès-Verbaux de la Commission Juridique et documentation y relative, Nos 36 à 60, vol. 2, ICRC Archives. For more on the Draft Rules, see: ICRC, *Commission of Experts for the Legal Protection of Civilian Populations and Victims of War from the Danger of Aerial Warfare and Blind Weapons, Geneva, April 6–13, 1954, Documents and Summary Records* (Geneva: ICRC, 1954). See also the related documents housed in the ICRC Archives: ICRC B AG 051/Pj. I also consulted the minutes of the Council of the ICRC Presidency for this entire period (1952–65): *Procès-Verbaux de la Conseil de la Présidence*, ICRC Archives.

41. The full name was the Draft Rules for the Protection of Civilian Population against the Dangers of Indiscriminate Warfare. The decision to urge the ICRC to complete these gaps in the 1949 Geneva Conventions came from a meeting of the Board of Governors of the League of National Red Cross Societies, which took place in Oslo in May 1954. Rey-Schyrr, *De Yalta à Dien Bien Phu*, 301–3.

42. For the complete text of the Draft Rules, see ICRC, "Draft Rules."

43. For the text of Article 14, see ICRC, "Draft Rules."

44. Raymond Yingling was a legal adviser to the State Department who had attended the Diplomatic Conference of Geneva in 1949 as part of the American delegation, as well as the prior April 1954 meeting on the issue of warfare regulations. Richard Baxter was a judge advocate at the time and later became a celebrated international lawyer and military expert, holding a faculty position at Harvard Law School and eventually representing the United States at the Diplomatic Conference on the Reaffirmation and Development of IHL Applicable in Armed Conflicts, 1974–77, which will be explored in chapter 5.

45. "Material Relating to the Geneva Conventions and the Yingling-Baxter Comments on the Draft Rules (1952 & 1957)," Container 56, Entry P 108, Record Group 200, U.S. National Archives.

46. "Material Relating to the Geneva Conventions."

47. Correspondance échangée avec le colonel Gerald I.A.D. Draper, expert juridique britannique concernant le Projet de Règles, B AG 051/Pj-021.04, ICRC Archives. For Draper's analysis (in apparent agreement with an FO lawyer, likely Joyce Gutteridge), see the untitled document signed by Draper, October 27, 1955, WO 32/15875, UK National Archives.

48. Minutes for the Meeting of March 22, 1956. *Procès-Verbaux de la Conseil de la Présidence*, ICRC Archives.

49. Twelve national Red Cross societies were represented, from Belgium, East Germany, France, India, Japan, Mexico, the Netherlands, Norway, Poland, Switzerland, West Germany, and Yugoslavia. Rey-Schyrr, *De Yalta à Dien Bien Phu*, 304.

50. "Protection juridique des populations civiles—1952–1967," B AG 051/Pj, ICRC Archives. The precise document I refer to is identified as SP 146.

51. Folder "ICRC—Draft Rules of Warfare for the Protection of the Civilian Population, RTY," in Box 1, "Rev of U.S. Policy on Treatment of P.O.W.s to XXth Int'l Conf of the Red Cross," Record Group 59, U.S. National Archives.

52. The United States drafted projected attendance and voting charts to make its decision and to figure out who it had to influence prior to the conference to ensure its desired outcome.

53. Folder "ICRC—Draft Rules."

54. François Bugnion, "The International Conference of the Red Cross and Red Crescent: Challenges, Key Issues and Achievements," *International Review of the Red Cross* 91, no. 876 (2010): 681–84.

55. The ICRC organized initial conversations with high-level interlocutors from the United States (General Alfred Gruenther, then president of the American Red Cross and the former supreme allied commander in Europe / commander-in-chief of the U.S. European Command until 1956), and the United Kingdom (the aforementioned British lawyer Colonel Gerald Draper, then a lecturer in law at the University of London, adviser to the UK government, and former military prosecutor at the war crimes tribunals in Germany). These contacts revealed once again the utter distaste of the UK and U.S. governments for the Draft Rules and the unlikelihood of their approval. Conversations also took place with Japanese and West German officials, and though less disappointing, they did not give confidence to ICRC jurists that the project had legs. Finally, a meeting of national Red Cross societies in Athens in November 1959, where the Draft Rules received only lukewarm support from few Red Crosses, confirmed the lack of enthusiasm by a majority of states. See "Entretien avec le général Gruenther, président de la Croix-Rouge américaine, le 26 septembre 1958, concernant le 'Projet de Règles,'" B AG 051/Pj-021.07, ICRC Archives.

56. "Suite de travaux relatifs au Projet de reglés. Groupe de juristes, procès-verbaux", B AG 051/Pj-024, ICRC Archives; see especially the Minutes of the Legal Commission sessions held on November 30, 1959, and February 29, 1960.

57. Keith Suter, *An International Law of Guerilla Warfare: The Global Politics of Law-Making* (New York: St. Martin's, 1984), 96.

58. Minutes of the Legal Commission sessions held on November 30, 1959, and February 29, 1960, "Suite de travaux relatifs au Projet de reglés. Groupe de juristes, procès-verbaux", B AG 051/Pj-024, ICRC Archives. In addition, the New Delhi Conference had issued a general "invitation" to the ICRC to continue making efforts toward the protection of the civilian population against the evils of war. ICRC lawyers took this as a basis for their continued work.

59. Minutes of the Legal Commission sessions held on November 30, 1959, and February 29, 1960, "Suite de travaux relatifs au Projet de reglés. Groupe de juristes, procès-verbaux", B AG 051/Pj-024, ICRC Archives.

60. Moreillon, *Le Comité International*, 151–56; Perret and Bugnion, *De Budapest à Saigon*, 443–44.

61. In 1961, during a meeting of its board of governors, the Yugoslavian Red Cross proposed a resolution urging the ICRC to focus on improving the legal protection and relief for victims of internal conflicts. The resolution was approved and served as the basis for the continued work of the ICRC on this subject. See ICRC, *Protection of Victims of Non-International Conflict (Item 6 of the Provisional Agenda of the International Humanitarian Law Commission), Report Submitted by the International Committee of the Red Cross, XXth International Conference of the Red Cross, Vienna, October 1965* (Geneva: ICRC, 1965), 5.

62. ICRC, *Commission of Experts for the Study of the Question of Aid to the Victims of Internal Conflicts, Geneva, October 25–30, 1962* (Geneva: ICRC, 1962). The experts in attendance were Robert Argo, professor, Italy; Frede Castberg, professor, Norway; Paul Cornil, Belgium; Jean Graven, Switzerland; Nihat Erim, Turkey; Roger Pinto, professor, France; Georges Tenekides, professor, Greece; Erik Husfeldt, professor, Danish Red Cross; J. J. G. de Rueda, Mexican Red Cross; and Bosco Jakovljevic, Yugoslavia. Gerald Draper of the United Kingdom and Carlo Schmid of West Germany could not attend but approved the final report.

63. ICRC, *Commission of Experts.*

64. Nine experts came to this meeting. Three were public opinion leaders: Hubert Beuve-Mery, director of the French Newspaper *Le Monde*; Major Adalbert Weinstein, mil-

itary journalist for the West German newspaper *Frankfurter Allgemeine Zeitung*; and Urs Schwarz of the Swiss newspaper *Neue Zurcher Zeitung*. Four were military strategists: Admiral A. Buzzard of the United Kingdom; Professor T. C. L. Halle of the Graduate Institute in Geneva; Thomas Schelling, a professor at Harvard University; and Colonel F. C. Miksche of the French military. Two were prominent legal experts: Colonel Gerald Draper, United Kingdom; and one Professor François, Netherlands. The ICRC also attempted to consult with Arab, Asian, and Soviet experts, but reportedly to no avail. See ICRC, *Protection Juridique des Populations Civiles, Rapport sur le consultations menées par le CICR depuis 1962 sur le thème "Opportunité et Possibilité de Limiter les Maux de la Guerre dans le Monde Actuel," rapport réservé à l'usage interne, Genève, Janvrier 1965, SP 488* (Geneva, ICRC, 1965.) A microfilmed version of this internal ICRC report can be found in the Minutes of the Meeting of January 21, 1965, *Procès-Verbaux de la Conseil de la Présidence*, ICRC Archives.

65. There are interesting exceptions. Thomas Schelling was a steadily skeptical voice, doubting that belligerents waging total war could actually respect the principle of distinction. Regardless, Schelling reportedly recognized the humanitarian value in reaffirming the principle.

66. ICRC, *The Legal Protection of Civilian Populations against the Dangers of Indiscriminate Warfare (Item 5a of the Provisional Agenda of the International Humanitarian Law Commission), Report Submitted by the International Committee of the Red Cross, XXth International Conference of the Red Cross, Vienna, October 1965, Geneva, March 1965* (Geneva: ICRC, 1965), 7.

67. ICRC, *The Legal Protection of Civilian Populations*, 8.

68. Peter Haas, "Introduction: Epistemic Communities and International Policy Coordination," *International Organization* 46, no. 1 (1992): 1–35; Jutta Brunnée and Stephen J. Toope, *Legitimacy and Legality in International Law: An Interactional Account* (New York: Cambridge University Press, 2010).

69. The ICRC considered directly submitting a draft resolution reaffirming the basic principles on the protection of civilian populations supported by the experts. However, fearing backlash, it was content to simply include the passing of such a resolution as a recommendation of the experts that national Red Cross societies could then either adopt or set aside. Various national societies from neutral and socialist countries (Austria, Czechoslovakia, East Germany, Switzerland, the USSR, and Vietnam), however, introduced their own resolutions reaffirming the basic principles. These were eventually merged into one resolution, which received almost unanimous approval with a vote of 128–0 (with three abstentions). The votes were not recorded, but the abstainers probably included the United Kingdom and the United States. See ICRC, *XX International Conference of the Red Cross, Report, Vienna, October 2–9, 1965* (Geneva: ICRC, 1965), 86–87.

70. See the resulting resolution (resolution 28) in ICRC, *XX International Conference*, 108–9.

71. Correspondence between the U.S. Defense and State Departments on this position paper was interesting. Both agreed on the same conclusion, that this type of regulative work was not desirable, yet each department's reasoning differed; while State Department legal adviser Raymond Yingling argued that the rules of warfare were not the province of the ICRC, Defense Department assistant general counsel Benjamin Forman pointed out that this was "debatable" and suggested instead using the argument about the impossibility of actually respecting the principle of distinction. Folder "'XXth Int'l Conference of the Red Cross,' The Legal Protection of Civilian Populations against the Dangers of Indiscriminate Warfare, L/SFP," in Box 1, "Rev of U.S. Policy on Treatment of P.O.W.s to XXth Int'l Conf of the Red Cross," Record Group 59, U.S. National Archives. Note that instead of new rules, the only alternative acceptable for the United States to ameliorate the fate of

civilians was the introduction of neutralized zones, as contemplated by the Fourth Geneva Convention.

72. "Protection of Victims of Non-International Conflict, September 25, 1965" (U.S. position paper), in *Briefing Book for the XXth International Conference of the Red Cross*, in Box 1, "Rev of U.S. Policy on Treatment of P.O.W.s to XXth Int'l Conf of the Red Cross," Record Group 59, U.S. National Archives.

73. ICRC, *XX International Conference of the Red Cross, Report, Vienna, October 2–9, 1965* (Geneva: ICRC, 1965), 80–81.

74. Folder "'XXth Int'l Conference of the Red Cross.'"

75. The final vote tally was 115–7 (with six abstentions). ICRC, *XX International Conference*, 87. For British instructions on the conference, see FO 369/5777.

76. The final vote tally was 123–73 (with twenty-four abstentions). ICRC, *XX International Conference*, 90.

77. The final vote tally was 124–0 (with five abstentions). ICRC, *XX International Conference*, 90.

78. ICRC, *XX International Conference*, 108–109.

79. For details, see ICRC, *Reaffirmation and Development of the Laws and Customs Applicable in Armed Conflicts, Report Submitted by the International Commission of the Red Cross, XXI International Conference of the Red Cross, Istanbul, September 1969* (Geneva: ICRC, 1969), 16–17.

80. ICRC, *Reaffirmation and Development*, 17.

81. ICRC, *Reaffirmation and Development*, 17.

82. ICRC, *Reaffirmation and Development*, 18.

83. This was the case until the late 1950s and mid-1960s. In its 1969 report, the ICRC for the first time recognized that there existed "several private national and international institutions showing active concern with this problem, holding meetings on the subject," adding that it was "only too pleased to witness the interest appearing in numerous circles on a subject too long left aside." Among the organizations showcased by the ICRC in this report was the Institute of International Law, which since 1956 had reportedly been working on the reconsideration of the principles of the laws of war. ICRC, *Reaffirmation and Development*, 15.

84. For a new reading of their relationship, see Boyd van Dijk, "Human Rights in War: On the Entangled Foundations of the 1949 Geneva Conventions," *American Journal of International Law* 112, no. 4 (2018): 553–82. I say *almost* because the ICRC was mindful of the progress made on the human rights front but did not dare to publicly or officially mix the two under the belief that IHL applied to times of armed conflict and amid low levels of violence, while human rights law applied chiefly during peacetime.

85. This summary draws heavily from Howard Tolley Jr.'s work, as well as from Keith Suter. See Howard B. Tolley, *The International Commission of Jurists: Global Advocates for Human Rights* (Philadelphia: University of Pennsylvania Press, 1994); and Suter, *An International Law of Guerilla Warfare.*

86. Tolley, *The International Commission of Jurists*, 92.

87. Suter, *An International Law of Guerilla Warfare*, 24.

88. Suter, *An International Law of Guerilla Warfare*, 24.

89. For a brief biography of MacBride, see Nobel Prize, "Seán MacBride: Facts" (webpage), https://www.nobelprize.org/prizes/peace/1974/macbride/facts/.

90. Tolley, *The International Commission of Jurists*, 100. See also Amanda Alexander, "A Short History of International Humanitarian Law," *European Journal of International Law* 26, no. 1 (2015): 118–19.

91. Tolley, *The International Commission of Jurists*, 100.

92. In 1963 the UNGA had declared 1968 the first International Year of Human Rights.

93. United Nations, *Proclamation of Teheran, Final Act of the International Conference on Human Rights, Teheran, 22 April to 13 May 1968*, UN Doc. A/CONF. 32/41 (New York: United Nations, 1968), 3.

94. Suter, *An International Law of Guerilla Warfare*, 25.

95. Suter, *An International Law of Guerilla Warfare*, 27, 28.

96. Seán MacBride, quoted in Suter, *An International Law of Guerilla Warfare*, 29.

97. MacBride, quoted in Suter, *An International Law of Guerilla Warfare*, 29.

98. Suter, *An International Law of Guerilla Warfare*, 31.

99. Suter, *An International Law of Guerilla Warfare*, chap. 2; Roland Burke, *Decolonization and the Evolution of International Human Rights* (Philadelphia: University of Pennsylvania Press, 2010), chap. 4; Samuel Moyn, *The Last Utopia: Human Rights in History* (Cambridge, MA: Harvard University Press, 2010).

100. The United States proposed, successfully, a resolution on respect for prisoner of war protections at the 1965 ICRC Conference in Vienna. The U.S. delegation admitted in its report to Secretary of State Dean Rusk that "from a purely political viewpoint" this was the most important international legal issue for the United States. *Report of the United States Delegation to the XXth International Conference of the Red Conference, Vienna, Austria, October 2–9*, in Box 1, "Rev of U.S. Policy on Treatment of P.O.W.s to XXth Int'l Conf of the Red Cross," Record Group 59, U.S. National Archives.

101. State Department Telegram, subject "Tehran HR Conference," 511–04.10, in folder "ICRC Conferences on Humanitarian Law (1972)," POW/Civilian Internee Information Center, Confidential Records, Box 11, P 2, Record Group 389, U.S. National Archives.

102. "Statement by Jean Picker, United States Representative in Committee III on Human Rights in Armed Conflicts, December 10, 1968," in folder "Human Rights in Armed Conflicts (1968)," POW/Civilian Internee Information Center, Confidential Records, Box 9, P 2, Record Group 389, U.S. National Archives.

103. This section relies heavily on the authoritative work of Howard Levie. See Howard Levie "Maltreatment of Prisoners of War in Vietnam," in *The Vietnam War and International Law*, vol. 2, ed. Richard A. Falk (Princeton, NJ: Princeton University Press, 1969), 361–97.

104. Levie, "Maltreatment of Prisoners," 364–65.

105. All three states had ratified the Geneva Conventions. CA3 arguably bound the Vietcong, since it operated on the territory of states that were party to the conventions, but this interpretation was not shared by the Vietcong itself. The ICRC letters to North Vietnam, South Vietnam, and the United States were published in "Application of Geneva Conventions in Viet-Nam: Letter of International Committee of the Red Cross, and Replies of the United States and Republic of Viet-Nam" *International Legal Materials* 4, no. 6 (1965): 1171–74.

106. "Application of Geneva Conventions."

107. Tran Van Do, quoted in "Application of Geneva Conventions."

108. Levie, "Maltreatment of Prisoners," 362.

109. For a variety of sources, see U.S. National Archives, "Military Resources: Vietnam War" (webpage), http://www.archives.gov/research/alic/reference/military/vietnam-war.html.

110. Assistant Secretary of Defense, Memorandum for the Deputy Secretary of Defense, in folder "Report on the PW Problem (1968)," in Box 33, P 2, Record Group 389, U.S. National Archives. As noted earlier, lack of information about POWs and personnel missing in action was only one of the American problems.

111. Assistant Secretary of Defense, Memorandum for the Deputy Secretary of Defense.

112. Department of the Army, Memorandum for Chief of Staff, Subject "Prisoner of War Study (U)," December 31, 1967, in folder "Prisoner of War Study (1967)," in Box 33, P 2, Record Group 389, U.S. National Archives.

113. In regard to the international law section, the U.S. Army confided that "the in-house expertise for a study of this kind is highly limited. The resources of the Judge Advocate General and to a lesser extent those of the Provost Marshal General which could be applied to the study effort are inadequate to undertake a study of the magnitude visualized and to continue to meet the day-to-day operational requirements." Although I could not find the final international law report, it appears it was completed *after* the in-house portion—that is, after November 1968. See Department of the Army, Memorandum for Chief of Staff. See also Enclosure F, in folder "Prisoner of War Study (1967)," Box 33, P 2, Record Group 389, U.S. National Archives.

114. Enclosure F. A fourth problem included in the Army review and worth reproducing at length stemmed from the fact that the conventions

> are documents primarily in the Judeo/Christian tradition in their respect for human life and dignity. To the United States and other Western nations, good treatment of prisoners is part of their national character. It would take place whether this and other western countries were signatories to the Geneva Convention or not. To most other signatory countries, however, the spirit of the conventions is miles apart from their ideology and national character. It should be possible to conduct cultural studies of each of these [potential enemy] nations with these objectives in mind: a. To determine to what extent can the nation be expected to deviate from the Geneva Conventions, considering its culture, character, ideology, and traditions. This information would be of immense value in the training programs of all services; conversely, it could be used in the training and indoctrination of prisoners from the nation under study. b. To identify the psychological Achilles heel of potential and actual enemy nations. The objective of this information is to secure correct treatment of captured U.S. personnel. The traditional methods of persuading an enemy country to provide good treatment, such as appeals to world public opinion, publication of 'White Papers,' protests to various embassies and the International Committee of the Red Cross do not work too well with such Communist powers as Red China, North Korea and North Vietnam. On the other hand, psychological attacks aimed at losing face or otherwise wounding the national character may bring about the desired good treatment. We are now in our third war during which prisoners have suffered at the hands of oriental captors who were signatories to international agreements. More sophisticated methods than those traditionally employed must be used in obtaining better treatment for our people.

Enclosure E, in folder "Prisoner of War Study (1967)," Box 33, P 2, Record Group 389, U.S. National Archives.

115. Enclosure F.

116. Not all of the new states (i.e., Israel) were former colonies.

117. Data taken from David A. Kay, *The New Nations in the United Nations, 1960–1967* (New York: Columbia University Press, 1970).

118. Kay, *The New Nations*, 45; Georges Abi-Saab, "The Newly Independent States and the Rules of International Law: An Outline," *Howard Law Journal* 8, no. 2 (1962): 95–121; Georges Abi-Saab, "The Third World and the International Legal Order," *Revue Egyptienne de Droit International* 29 (1973): 27–66; Mohammed Bedjaoui, *Law and the Algerian Revolution* (Brussels: International Associations of Democratic Lawyers, 1961).

119. Amitav Acharya and Barry Buzan, *The Making of Global International Relations: Origins and Evolution of IR at Its Centenary* (New York: Cambridge University

Press, 2019), 112–37; Adom Getachew, *Worldmaking after Empire: The Rise and Fall of Self-Determination* (Princeton, NJ: Princeton University Press, 2019), 71–106; Mark Mazower, *Governing the World: The History of an Idea, 1815 to the Present* (New York: Penguin, 2012), 250–72; Burke, *Decolonization and the Evolution of International Human Rights*; Steven L. B. Jensen, *The Making of International Human Rights: The 1960s, Decolonization and the Reconstruction of Global Values* (New York: Cambridge University Press, 2016).

120. Kay, *The New Nations*, 85.

121. For classic IR takes on this debate, see Robert H. Jackson, "The Weight of Ideas in Decolonization: Normative Change in International Relations," in *Ideas and Foreign Policy: Beliefs, Institutions and Political Change*, ed. Judith Goldstein and Robert O. Keohane (Ithaca, NY: Cornell University Press, 1993); Neta C. Crawford, *Argument and Change in World Politics* (New York: Cambridge University Press, 2002); and Christian Reus-Smit, "Struggles for Individual Rights and the Expansion of the International System," *International Organization* 65, no. 2 (2011): 207–42.

122. Inis Claude, "Collective Legitimization as a Political Function of the United Nations," *International Organization* 20, no. 3 (1966): 369.

123. On this debate, see Jan Eckel, "Essay-Review: Human Rights and Decolonization: New Perspective and Open Questions," *Humanity* 1, no. 1 (2010): 111–35.

124. Louis Henkin, "The United Nations and Human Rights," *International Organization* 19, no. 3 (1965): 512.

125. On Jamaica, see Jensen, *The Making of International Human Rights*, 69–101. On Uganda, see Suter, *An International Law of Guerilla Warfare*, 51.

126. Burke, *Decolonization and the Evolution of International Human Rights*, 103.

127. Burke, *Decolonization and the Evolution of International Human Rights*, 103. See also Mary L. Dudziak, *Cold War Civil Rights: Race and the Image of American Democracy* (Princeton, NJ: Princeton University Press, 2011).

128. Burke, *Decolonization and the Evolution of International Human Rights*, 104.

129. Burke, *Decolonization and the Evolution of International Human Rights*, 108, emphasis added.

130. Kay, *The New Nations in the United Nations*, 83.

5. A REVOLUTION IN LAWMAKING? (1968–1977)

1. For a useful overview of the "battle for international law" during the era of decolonization, see Jochen von Bernstorff and Philipp Dann, "The Battle for International Law: An Introduction," in *The Battle for International Law: South-North Perspectives on the Decolonization Era*, ed. Jochen von Bernstorff and Philipp Dann (New York: Oxford University Press, 2019), 1–31.

2. ICRC, "Protocol Additional to the Geneva Conventions of 12 August 1949, and Relating to the Protection of Victims of International Armed Conflicts (API), 8 June 1977" (webpage), http://www.icrc.org/ihl.nsf/full/470?opendocument.

3. During the drafting of API the article on POWs was numbered 42. The final treaty reorganized the text and it became Article 44. In this chapter, I refer to it as Article 42 in keeping with the drafting history.

4. Other analyses of the politics of the CDDH are Jessica Whyte, "The 'Dangerous Concept of the Just War': Decolonization, Wars of National Liberation, and the Additional Protocols to the Geneva Conventions," *Humanity* 9, no. 3 (2019): 313–41; Amanda Alexander, "International Humanitarian Law, Postcolonialism and the 1977 *Geneva Protocol I*," *Melbourne Journal of International Law* 17, no. 1 (2016): 15–50; Helen M. Kinsella, *The Image before the Weapon: A Critical History of the Distinction between Combatant and Civilian* (Ithaca, NY: Cornell University Press, 2011), chap. 6; Helen M. Kinsella, "Superfluous

Injury and Unnecessary Suffering: National Liberation and the Laws of War," *Political Power and Social Theory* 32 (2017): 205–31.

5. Guided by protagonists' own use of the term, by "Western" I refer to North America and Western Europe. As we will see, however, at times the Western Group extended to Australia, New Zealand, and even Japan and Turkey. I identify those occasions whenever possible. Latin American states, though located in the Western Hemisphere, usually constituted a separate, semicohesive group during discussions about IHL.

6. Keith Suter, *An International Law of Guerilla Warfare: The Global Politics of Law-Making* (New York: St. Martin's, 1984), 50. The five governments were Czechoslovakia, Egypt (then the United Arab Republic), India, Jamaica, and Uganda.

7. U Thant to Séan MacBride, April 25, 1968. On file with author.

8. The states involved were Afghanistan, Denmark, Finland, India, Indonesia, Iraq, Jamaica, Jordan, Morocco, Norway, Philippines, Sweden, Uganda, United Arab Republic (Egypt), Yugoslavia, and Zambia. The Indian delegate rightly presented this mix as "a cross-section of the membership of the United Nations" representing "the widespread concern felt throughout the world for the preservation of human rights in armed conflict." Suter, *An International Law of Guerilla Warfare*, 53.

9. In attendance was a combination of experts from Western, newly decolonized, Third World, and socialist states. For details, see ICRC, *Reaffirmation and Development of the Laws and Customs Applicable in Armed Conflicts, Report Submitted by the International Commission of the Red Cross, XXI International Conference of the Red Cross, Istanbul, September 1969* (Geneva: ICRC, 1969), 25–26.

10. ICRC, *Reaffirmation and Development*, 32. In the end, due to time constraints, the experts focused on the specific issues of weapons, protection of civilians, noninternational conflicts, and guerrilla warfare.

11. ICRC, *Reaffirmation and Development*, 21.

12. ICRC, *Reaffirmation and Development*, 98.

13. See ICRC, *XXI International Conference of the Red Cross, Report, Istanbul, September 6–13, 1969* (Geneva: ICRC, 1969).

14. ICRC, *Reaffirmation and Development*, 100.

15. ICRC, *Reaffirmation and Development*, 101.

16. ICRC, *Reaffirmation and Development*, 110.

17. This proposed complementarity between IHL and human rights is prescient of current debates on the interaction between the two legal regimes. Monica Hakimi, "The Theory and Practice at the Intersection between Human Rights and Humanitarian Law," *American Journal of International Law* 111, no. 4 (2017): 1063–74.

18. One idea that the ICRC circulated at the time was to draft a model agreement which parties to the conflict might sign on an ad hoc basis. CA3 encouraged this but provided no specific template, something that the ICRC thought should be remedied.

19. ICRC, *Reaffirmation and Development*, 102.

20. ICRC, *Reaffirmation and Development*, 103.

21. Beyond formal ICRC or UN meetings, experts' meetings organized by international law institutes began to take place, gathering individuals who sometimes acted as government legal advisers, including the United Kingdom's Gerald Draper or the United States' Richard Baxter.

22. For details on attendance, see United Nations General Assembly, *Respect for Human Rights in Armed Conflicts, Report of the Secretary-General*, UN Doc. A/8052 (New York: United Nations, 1970), 8.

23. This section is based on a sea of (mostly public) documentation produced by the ICRC in preparation for or as the outcome of the various meetings it sponsored in 1971–1973 (prior to the opening of the official Diplomatic Conference), as well as from the

Twenty-second International Conference of the Red Cross in 1973 in Teheran. It also relies on a deep study of the similarly voluminous confidential internal government documents relating to the preparatory process found in the archives of France, the United Kingdom, and the United States. Some key ICRC documents, all of which may be found at the ICRC Library in Geneva, are ICRC, *Conference of Government Experts on the Reaffirmation and Development of International IHL Applicable in Armed Conflicts (Geneva, 24 May–12 June 1971), Report on the Work of the Conference* (Geneva: ICRC, 1971); ICRC, *Conference of Government Experts on the Reaffirmation and Development of International IHL Applicable in Armed Conflicts, Second Session (Geneva, 3 May–3 June 1971), Report on the Work of the Conference*, vols. 1–2, *Geneva, July 1972* (Geneva: ICRC, 1972); ICRC, *Draft Additional Protocols to the Geneva Conventions of August 12, 1949, Commentary, Geneva, October 1973* (Geneva: ICRC, 1973); and ICRC, *XXII International Conference of the Red Cross, Report, Teheran, 8–15 November, 1973* (Geneva: ICRC, 1973). This list is not exhaustive, however. The list of government archives and the main coordinates for locating them is included in the bibliography. In other sections of this chapter, I cite relevant sources as regard precise statements.

24. I use these terms not as normative assessments of the merits or value of states' positions, but descriptively, referring to whether states wished to create or revise the law (construction), or prevent or boycott legal development (destruction).

25. On the history of POW protections under IHL, see Neville Wylie and Lindsey Cameron, "The Impact of World War I on the Law Governing the Treatment of Prisoners of War and the Making of a Humanitarian Subject," *European Journal of International Law* 29, no. 4 (2018): 1327–50.

26. Wherever states had decided to grant one or both to guerrilla fighters facing them (as the United States had done in Vietnam since 1967 or the French in Algeria in 1958), this was done on an ad hoc "policy" basis, without necessarily recognizing that the conflict was an international war. See Edwina Morgan, "The Protection of 'Irregular' Combatants: An Enduring Challenge for Humanitarian Action" (master's thesis, Geneva Center for Education and Research in Humanitarian Action, 2011).

27. Georges Abi-Saab, "Wars of National Liberation and the Laws of War," in *International Law: A Contemporary Perspective*, ed. Richard A. Falk, Friedrich V. Kratochwil, and Saul H. Mendlovitz (Boulder, CO: Westview, 1985), 410–37.

28. This distaste was not reserved for the idea of regulating troubles or disturbances, but also included efforts to complement the principles of CA3 in key areas such as the conduct of hostilities. In fact, during the Diplomatic Conference a radical fringe even opposed the idea of a protocol applying to high-level civil wars.

29. The staunchness of Norway's support of wide protections for liberation war remains somewhat unclear, but the general stance may be related to Norwegian delegate Hans Longva having been a student of Georges Abi-Saab.

30. David P. Forsythe, *The Politics of Prisoner Abuse: The United States and Enemy Prisoners After 9/11* (New York: Cambridge University Press, 2011), 18–19. See also George H. Aldrich, "Some Reflections on the Origins of the 1977 Geneva Protocols," in *Studies and Essays on International Humanitarian Law and Red Cross Principles in Honour of Jean Pictet*, ed. Christophe Swinarski (The Hague: Kluwer Law International, 1984).

31. House Subcommittee on International Organizations and Movements, *Human Rights in the World Community: A Call for U.S. Leadership: Report*, 93rd Congress, 2nd Sess., March 27, 1974 (Washington, DC: GPO, 1974), 33–37. In addition to the Fraser hearings, Senator Ted Kennedy (D-MA), sent with the American delegation a speech setting out the progressive congressional line before the first session of the Diplomatic Conference in 1974.

32. This list, for example, does not include the annual meetings of experts, including those acting as government delegates during the CDDH at the International Institute of

Humanitarian Law in Sanremo which were crucial not only for academic debate but for the negotiation of various articles of the protocols in the years 1974–77.

33. Folder "Proposed Agenda ICRC Conf on IHL (1971), POW/Civilian Internee Information Center, Confidential Records 511-02," in Box 1, "Letters concerning ICRC Activities 1971 to Misc Intelligence Reports, Records of the Provost Marshal General, 1941–," Entry P1, Record Group 389, U.S. National Archives.

34. Folder "Conférence d'Experts Gouvernementaux sur le Développement du Droit International Humanitaire: Genève, 24 mai à 12 juin 1971." Carton 1297, Cote S. 50.3.8.4.6, NUOI 1970–1973, Ministère des Affaires Étrangères, Direction des Archives.

35. Australia, Japan, New Zealand, and Turkey were sometimes invited.

36. Vincent Pouliot, *International Pecking Orders: The Politics and Practice of Multilateral Diplomacy* (New York: Cambridge University Press, 2016).

37. UK delegation report after 1972 ICRC meeting, December 4, 1972, FCO 66/422, doc. 74, UK National Archives, emphasis added.

38. UK delegation report after 1972 ICRC meeting, December 4, 1972.

39. Note, however, that it was again unclear the Soviets were being humanitarian solely out of strategic posturing. Implying that there may have been a measure of sincerity, David Forsythe, who was present, claimed at the end of the negotiations that "in the last analysis the Soviet Union went out of its way to engage in public debate with Third World opponents of the [APII], action indicating clear support for the Protocol especially when compared with the more general Soviet pattern of supporting the Third World on many issues related to API." See David P. Forsythe, "Legal Regulation of Internal Conflicts: The 1977 Protocol on Non-International Armed Conflicts," *American Journal of International Law* 72, no. 2 (1978): 280–81n38.

40. Giovanni Mantilla, "Social Pressure and the Making of Wartime Legal Protections for Civilians," *European Journal of International Relations*, online, 2019, https://journals.sagepub.com/doi/10.1177/1354066119870237.

41. In 1974 France still retained some colonies; in private communication, the French seemed especially worried about the Comoros and the French Territory of the Afars and the Issas (now Djibouti) because the national liberation movements from those territories demanded participation at the Diplomatic Conference. Britain worried mostly about Northern Ireland.

42. Guy Martin, "Continuity and Change in Franco-African Relations," *Journal of Modern African Studies* 33, no. 1 (1995): 1–20; Guia Migani, "De Gaulle and Sub-Saharan Africa: From Decolonization to French Development Policy, 1958–1963," in *Globalizing De Gaulle: International Perspectives on French Foreign Policies, 1958–1969*, ed. Christian Nuenlist, Anna Locher, and Garret Martin (Lanham, MD: Lexington Books, 2010), 251–70.

43. Edward A. Kolodziej, *French International Policy under De Gaulle and Pompidou: The Politics of Grandeur* (Ithaca, NY: Cornell University Press, 1974), 585–93.

44. Avi Shlaim, "Britain's Quest for a World Role," *International Relations* 5, no. 1 (1975): 850–56.

45. Mike Bowker and Phil Williams, *Superpower Détente: A Reappraisal* (London: Sage, 1988), chap. 3.

46. See generally: Odd Arne Westad, *The Global Cold War: Third World Interventions and The Making of Our Times* (New York: Cambridge University Press, 2005).

47. Robert J. McMahon, ed., *The Cold War in the Third World* (New York: Oxford University Press, 2013); Jürgen Dinkel, *The Non-Aligned Movement: Genesis, Organization and Politics (1927–1992)* (Leiden: Brill, 2019), 214–26.

48. Amitav Acharya, *Constructing Global Order: Agency and Change in World Politics* (New York: Cambridge University Press, 2018), 202.

49. Adom Getachew, *Worldmaking after Empire: The Rise and Fall of Self-Determination* (Princeton, NJ: Princeton University Press, 2019).

50. As mentioned, France also found pride in its good relations with the French-speaking world. Christopher Hill, "Powers of a Kind: The Anomalous Position of France and the United Kingdom in World Politics," *International Affairs* 92, no. 2 (2016): 393–414.

51. On Soviet vulnerability to bottom-up pressure linked to the Helsinki Accords, see Daniel C. Thomas, *The Helsinki Effect: International Norms, Human Rights, and the Demise of Communism* (Princeton, NJ: Princeton University Press, 2001).

52. Given its helpful reorganization of key CDDH materials regarding API, I have used mostly Howard S. Levie, ed., *Protection of War Victims: Protocol 1 to the 1949 Geneva Conventions*, vols. 1–2 (Dobbs Ferry, NY: Oceana, 1979, 1980). For the full CDDH records, see Federal Political Department of Switzerland, *Records of the Diplomatic Conference on the Reaffirmation and Development of IHL Applicable in Armed Conflicts, Geneva, 1974–1977*, vols. 1–17 (Bern: Federal Political Department of Switzerland, 1978).

53. Summary Record of First Plenary Meeting, paras. 28–33, in Federal Political Department of Switzerland, *Records of the Diplomatic Conference*, 5:12–13.

54. The United States rallied just enough votes against PRG admission. Guinea-Bissau was welcomed, prompting a Portuguese walkout.

55. Levie, *Protection of War Victims*, 1:3.

56. The two Western exceptions were Australia and Norway.

57. Levie, *Protection of War Victims*, 1:26–27.

58. Levie, *Protection of War Victims*, 1:7.

59. UK Mission Geneva to FCO, March 12, 1974, FCO 61/1232, doc. 89, UK National Archives.

60. Levie, *Protection of War Victims*, 1:8.

61. Electronic Telegram, 1974STATE047331, Secretary of State, Washington, to U.S. embassy in Canberra, March 8, 1974, Central Foreign Policy File, 1973–1976, Record Group 59, U.S. National Archives.

62. Levie, *Protection of War Victims*, 1:1–26.

63. UK Mission Geneva to FCO, March 19, 1974, FCO 61/1232, doc. 97, UK National Archives.

64. UK Mission Geneva to FCO, March 19, 1974.

65. UK Mission Geneva to FCO, March 19, 1974, emphasis added.

66. Thomas Keeble to Vincent Evans, March 21, 1974, FCO 61/1232, doc. W105, UK National Archives.

67. "International Humanitarian Law and National Liberation Movements", memorandum signed by Roger Martin, March 21, 1974, FCO 61/1232, doc. 105, UK National Archives, emphasis added.

68. UK Mission Geneva to FCO, March 19, 1974. The Canadian proposal was never seriously considered and the winning coalition even sought later to delete it from the record.

69. Levie, *Protection of War Victims*, 1:42. Voting in favor were Albania, Algeria, Argentina, Bangladesh, Bulgaria, Burundi, the Byelorussian Soviet Socialist Republic, Chad, China, Cuba, Cyprus, Czechoslovakia, the Democratic People's Republic of Korea, Democratic Yemen, El Salvador, Finland, Gabon, the German Democratic Republic, Ghana, Guinea-Bissau, Honduras, Hungary, India, Indonesia, Iran, Iraq, Ivory Coast, Jordan, the Khmer Republic, Kuwait, Lebanon, Liberia, the Libyan Arab Republic, Madagascar, Mali, Mauritania, Mexico, Mongolia, Morocco, Nigeria, Norway, Pakistan, Panama, Peru, Poland, Qatar, the Republic of Vietnam, Romania, Saudi Arabia, Senegal, Sri Lanka, Sudan, the Sultanate of Oman, Syrian Arab Republic, Thailand, Trinidad and Tobago, Tunisia, Uganda, the Ukrainian Soviet Socialist Republic, the United Arab Emirates, the United

Arab Republic (Egypt), the United Republic of Cameroon, the United Republic of Tanzania, the USSR, Venezuela, Yemen, Yugoslavia, Zaire, and Zambia. Voting against were Belgium, Canada, Denmark, the Federal Republic of Germany, France, Israel, Italy, Japan, Liechtenstein, Luxembourg, Monaco, New Zealand, the Netherlands, Portugal, the Republic of Korea, South Africa, Spain, Switzerland, the United Kingdom, the United States, and Uruguay. Abstaining were Australia, Austria, Brazil, Burma, Chile, Colombia, Greece, Guatemala, the Holy See, Ireland, Philippines, Sweden, and Turkey.

70. UK Mission Geneva to FCO, March 29, 1974, FCO 61/1232, doc. 122, UK National Archives.

71. UK embassy in Paris to FCO, July 24, 1974, FCO 61/1234, UK National Archives; copy of U.S. delegation report after 1974 session, June 10, 1974, FCO 61/1234, doc. W191, UK National Archives; UK delegation report after 1974 session, June 17, 1974, FCO 61/1233, doc. 165, UK National Archives.

72. Jane Beard (UK embassy in Switzerland), paraphrasing Swiss diplomat François Pictet, in a letter to Tessa Solesby, UN Department, FCO, May 22, 1974, FCO 61/1233, doc. 160, UK National Archives.

73. Gerald Draper, comments on draft UK report, May 5, 1974, FCO 61/1232, doc. 147, UK National Archives.

74. UK delegation report after 1974 session, June 17, 1974.

75. Lloyd Gruber, *Ruling the World: Power Politics and the Rise of Supranational Institutions* (Princeton, NJ: Princeton University Press, 2000); James Fearon, "Bargaining, Enforcement, and International Cooperation," *International Organization* 52, no. 2 (1998): 269–305.

76. UK delegation report after 1974 session, June 17, 1974, emphasis added.

77. UK delegation report after 1974 session, June 17, 1974, emphasis added.

78. United States Delegation report after 1974 session, FCO 61/1234, UK National Archives; "Classified Report of the United States Delegation to the Diplomatic Conference on the Reaffirmation and Development of IHL Applicable in Armed Conflicts, Geneva, Switzerland, February 20–March 29, 1974", on file with the author; hereafter cited as *Classified U.S. CDDH Report.*

79. Classified U.S. CDDH Report, 7.

80. Classified U.S. CDDH Report, 6. The United States, moreover, worried about the matter of individual criminal responsibility for violations of the protocols which many non-Western states threatened to insert without reference to "intent" or "fault," exposing troops to easy charges of abuse and to the withdrawal of POW benefits.

81. This was as noted by American delegates in their unclassified conference report. Copy of U.S. delegation 1974 conference report, June 10, 1974, FCO 61/1234, W191, UK National Archives.

82. Thomas Keeble to Vincent Evans, June 19, 1974, FCO 61/1233, doc. 166, UK National Archives.

83. Keeble to Evans, June 19, 1974.

84. "Bericht über die Meetings des 'Western-group' an der Diplomatischen Konferenz über das Humanitäre Kriegsvölkerrecht (London 2–3 September und 17–19 September 1974)," Département politique féderal, J2.111*, 1979/29_1, Swiss Federal Archives.

85. "Bericht über die Meetings des 'Western-group.'".

86. "Bericht über die Meetings des "Western-group.'"

87. Christian Girard to Secretary General, French Ministry of Foreign Affairs, January 20, 1975, Carton 1678, Cote F. 6.8.1.2, NUOI 1974–1979, Ministère des Affaires Étrangères, Direction des Archives. For the United States: George Aldrich. For France: Christian Girard and Col. Charles Fricaud-Chanaud. For the United Kingdom: John Freeland and Martin Eaton, FCO, and James Makin, MOD. For Canada: David Miller, Gerry

Olsen, and Col. Jack Wolfe. See Electronic Telegram, 1975OTTAWA00045, U.S. embassy in Paris to U.S. Embassies in Ottawa and London, January 7, 1975, Central Foreign Policy File, 1973–1976, Record Group 59, U.S. National Archives.

88. Report of meeting, January 20, 1975, FCO 61/1374, doc. 14, UK National Archives.

89. Report attached to UK embassy in Bonn to Robert Facey, UN Department, FCO, January 22, 1975, FCO 61/1374, doc. 29, UK National Archives. Although the struggles in Israel-Palestine, Rhodesia, and South Africa persisted alongside remaining overseas territories held by various European states, the likely downfall of a disgraced imperial Portugal clearly worked to allay the concerns of the West. A key reason buttressing the West's "cynical" line was tied to world political changes unfolding at the time. Portugal's Carnation Revolution at home in April 1974 indicated that that country's colonial holdings would soon attain independence, resolving one of the major sources of impetus behind the African initiatives. Attentive to these developments, the majority of the Western coalition believed that the issue of national liberation was temporary and soon to end, limiting the dangers of accepting Article 1 or the eventual ratification of API.

90. The Western Group comprised Australia, Austria, Belgium, Canada, Denmark, France, the Federal Republic of Germany, Ireland, Italy, Japan, Luxembourg, the Netherlands, Portugal, Switzerland, Turkey, the United Kingdom, and the United States.

91. "Humanitarian Law: Reception for Delegates to London Meeting of Western Group," memorandum signed by Peter Maxey, January 27, 1975, FCO 61/1374, doc. 34, UK National Archives.

92. The British volunteered this had again been partly due to the multiple (coffee-break and otherwise related) absences by African delegates while votes were being cast.

93. UK report after second CDDH session, August 5, 1975, FCO 61/1374, doc. 134, UK National Archives.

94. Mantilla, "Social Pressure and the Making of Wartime Legal Protections for Civilians."

95. Howard S. Levie, *The Law of Non-international Armed Conflict: Protocol II to the 1949 Geneva Conventions* (Leiden: Martinus Nijhoff, 1987), 57–58.

96. Levie, *The Law of Non-international Armed Conflict*, 57–58, emphasis in the original.

97. Levie, *The Law of Non-international Armed Conflict*, 57–58.

98. Copy of U.S. report after second CDDH session, July 18, 1975, FCO 61/1374, doc. 131, UK National Archives.

99. UK report after second CDDH session, August 5, 1975, FCO 61/1374, doc. 134, UK National Archives.

100. French delegation report after second CDDH session, May 30, 1975, Carton 1678, Cote F. 6.8.1.2, NUOI 1974–1979, Ministère des Affaires Étrangères, Direction des Archives.

101. West Germany had emerged as a helpful partner of Canada, the United Kingdom, and the United States during the IHL revisions process and a leader on the military implications of the protocols. Preventing German suspicions about backdoor dealings, the original Inner Core member states pretended this was the first of the restricted consultations.

102. UK report of meeting, November 28, 1975, FCO 61/1374, doc. 51, UK National Archives.

103. French report of November 17–18 meeting, Carton 1678, Cote F. 6.8.1.2, NUOI 1974–1979, Ministère des Affaires Étrangères, Direction des Archives; UK report of meeting, November 28, 1975.

104. French report of November 17–18, 1975, meeting, Carton 1678, Cote F. 6.8.1.2, NUOI 1974–1979, Ministère des Affaires Étrangères, Direction des Archives, my translation.

105. French report of March 15–17, 1976, meeting, Carton 1678, Cote F. 6.8.1.2, NUOI 1974–1979, Ministère des Affaires Étrangères, Direction des Archives.

106. Aldrich, "Some Reflections"; George H. Aldrich, "Prospects for United States Ratification of Additional Protocol I to the 1949 Geneva Conventions," *American Journal of International Law* 85, no. 1 (1991): 1–20; George H. Aldrich, "The Laws of War on Land," *American Journal of International Law* 94, no. 1 (2000): 42–63. On the role of the ICRC in persuading the French and the United States to treat and/or consider captured rebels as POWs in Algeria and Vietnam, respectively, and the importance of these experiences for the drafting of Article 42 of API, see Morgan, "The Protection of 'Irregular' Combatants," 49–50, 76–77.

107. UK delegation report after 1976 CDDH session, September 21, 1976, FCO 58/997, doc. 96, UK National Archives.

108. UK delegation report after 1976 CDDH session, September 21, 1976.

109. See various documents, beginning on June 7, 1976 in Département politique féderal, Consultations Presidentielles, J2.111*, 1979/29_1, Swiss Federal Archives.

110. Jean Pictet to Jean Humbert, July 15, 1976, Département politique féderal, J2.111*, 1979/29_1, Swiss Federal Archives.

111. Geoff Harris to UK Mission to NATO, January 12, 1977, FCO 58/1127, doc. 4, UK National Archives; Brussels to Paris, telegram, no. 20/25, January 7, 1977, Carton 1678, Cote F. 6.8.1.2, NUOI 1974–1979, Ministère des Affaires Étrangères, Direction des Archives.

112. Note of a Meeting held in Historic Room (MOD) on 21 December 1976 to discuss MOD views on Draft Protocol I to the Geneva Conventions, FCO/58/1127, enclosure to doc. 25, UK National Archives. Aldrich later recognized in print that given these ambiguities, "the protection accorded by this article to irregulars may be less than it seems because it is the captor Power and its tribunals that have to interpret them." See George H. Aldrich, "Progressive Development of the Laws of War: A Reply to Criticisms of the 1977 Geneva Protocol I," *Virginia Journal of International Law* 26, no. 3 (1986): 708.

113. Report of UK-Australia meeting, January 12, 1977, FCO 58/1127, doc. 1, and report of Western Liaison group meeting, March 1, 1977, FCO 58/1127, doc. 54, UK National Archives.

114. Report of Western Liaison group meeting, March 1, 1977.

115. Martin Eaton to John Freeland, March 8, 1977, FCO 58/1127, doc. W66, and memorandum by David Hughes-Morgan, March 8, 1977, FCO 58/1127, doc. 66, UK National Archives; report of Western Liaison group meeting, March 1, 1977.

116. Eaton to Freeland, March 8, 1977. This was Eaton's paraphrasing of his conversation with U.S. general Walter Reed on February 22, 1977.

117. Report of Western Weaponry Liaison meeting of February 22, 1977, FCO 58/1127, doc. 58, UK National Archives.

118. John Gutteridge to Geoff Harris, March 29, 1977, FCO 58/1125, doc. 64, UK National Archives.

119. Memorandum by Hughes-Morgan, March 8, 1977.

120. Eaton to Freeland, March 8, 1977.

121. Memorandum by Hughes-Morgan, March 8, 1977.

122. Report of Inner Core meeting of March 14, 1977, FCO 58/1127, doc. 76, UK National Archives.

123. Report of Inner Core meeting of March 14, 1977, FCO 58/1127, doc. 76, UK National Archives.

124. Report of Inner Core meeting of March 14, 1977. The British MOD instructed its defense staff in Washington to persuade the Pentagon to put pressure on Aldrich, hoping

to secure amendments to the text or to at least to insert interpretive statements in the negotiating record.

125. Record of meeting with Evan Luard, April 4, 1977, FCO 58/1125, doc. 72, UK National Archives. Interestingly, Luard displayed a far more humanitarian view than those under him toward APII, arguing that a high threshold including territorial control was an illogical demand in view of the reality of guerrilla warfare. Notwithstanding fears about the protocol's applicability to Northern Ireland, Luard thought the United Kingdom should support language that would apply to as many internal conflicts as possible. However, being reminded that at that stage of the negotiations the existing compromise was what seemed attainable, the delegation ultimately did not depart from it.

126. Brief for the UK delegation, April 7, 1977, FCO 58/1126, doc. 44, UK National Archives, emphasis added.

127. Levie, *Protection of War Victims*, 2:485–86. Voting in favor were Afghanistan, Algeria, Austria, Belgium, Bulgaria, the Byelorussian Soviet Socialist Republic, Costa Rica, Cuba, Cyprus, Czechoslovakia, the Democratic People's Republic of Korea, Ecuador, Egypt, the Federal Republic of Germany, Finland, France, the German Democratic Republic, Ghana, Greece, Honduras, Hungary, India, Indonesia, Iran, Ivory Coast, Jordan, Kuwait, Lebanon, Madagascar, Mali, Mauritania, Mexico, Mongolia, Morocco, the Netherlands, Nigeria, Norway, Oman, Pakistan, Panama, Peru, Poland, Qatar, the Republic of Korea, Romania, Saudi Arabia, Senegal, the Socialist People's Libyan Arab Jamahiriya, the Socialist Republic of Vietnam, Somalia, Sri Lanka, Sudan, Sweden, the Syrian Arab Republic, Tunisia, Turkey, Uganda, the Ukrainian Soviet Socialist Republic, United Arab Emirates, the United Republic of Cameroon, the United Republic of Tanzania, the United States, the USSR, Venezuela, Yugoslavia, and Zaire. Voting against were Brazil and Israel. Abstaining were Argentina, Australia, Bolivia, Canada, Chile, Colombia, Denmark, Guatemala, the Holy See, Ireland, Italy, Japan, New Zealand, Nicaragua, Spain, Thailand, the United Kingdom, and Uruguay.

128. Telegram DELFRA GENEVE to Paris, No 304/05, Carton 1678, Cote F. 6.8.1.2, NUOI 1974–1979, Ministère des Affaires Étrangères, Direction des Archives, my translation.

129. Levie, *Protection of War Victims*, 2:486–512.

130. Levie, *Protection of War Victims*, 1:62–80.

131. Voting in favor were Afghanistan, Algeria, Argentina, Australia, Austria, Bangladesh, Belgium, Brazil, Bulgaria, the Byelorussian Soviet Socialist Republic, Chile, Cyprus, Colombia, Costa Rica, Cuba, Czechoslovakia, the Democratic People's Republic of Korea, Democratic Yemen, Denmark, Egypt, Ecuador, Finland, the German Democratic Republic, Ghana, Greece, the Holy See, Honduras, Hungary, India, Indonesia, Iran, Iraq, Ivory Coast, Jamaica, Jordan, Kenya, Kuwait, Lebanon, the Libyan Arab Republic, Liechtenstein, Luxembourg, Madagascar, Mali, Malta, Mauritania, Mexico, Mongolia, Morocco, Mozambique, the Netherlands, New Zealand, Nicaragua, Nigeria, Norway, Oman, Pakistan, Panama, Peru, the Philippines, Poland, Portugal, Qatar, the Republic of Korea, Romania, Saudi Arabia, Senegal, the Socialist Republic of Vietnam, Somalia, Sudan, Sri Lanka, Sweden, Switzerland, the Syrian Arab Republic, Thailand, Tunisia, Turkey, Uganda, the Ukrainian Soviet Socialist Republic, the United Arab Emirates, the United Republic of Cameroon, the United Republic of Tanzania, Uruguay, the USSR, Venezuela, Yemen, Yugoslavia, and Zaire. Voting against was Israel. Abstaining were Canada, the Federal Republic of Germany, France, Guatemala, Ireland, Italy, Japan, Monaco, Spain, the United Kingdom, and the United States.

132. UK Mission Geneva to FCO, May 24, 1977 FCO 58/1124, doc. 128, UK National Archives.

133. Telegram DELFRA GENEVE to Paris No. 1604–10, Carton 1678, Cote F. 6.8.1.2, NUOI 1974–1979, Ministère des Affaires Étrangères, Direction des Archives, my translation, emphasis added.

134. Levie, *Protection of War Victims*, 2:514–45.

135. Voting in favor were Afghanistan, Algeria, Austria, Bangladesh, Belgium, Bulgaria, the Byelorussian Soviet Socialist Republic, Cuba, Cyprus, Czechoslovakia, Democratic Yemen, Denmark, Ecuador, Egypt, Finland, France, the German Democratic Republic, Ghana, Greece, the Holy See, Hungary, India, Indonesia, Iran, Iraq, Ivory Coast, Jamaica, Jordan, Kenya, Kuwait, Lebanon, Luxembourg, Madagascar, Mali, Malta, Mauritania, Mexico, Mongolia, Morocco, Mozambique, the Netherlands, Nigeria, Norway, Oman, Pakistan, Panama, the People's Democratic Republic of Korea, Peru, Poland, Qatar, the Republic of Korea, Romania, Saudi Arabia, Senegal, the Socialist People's Libyan Arab Jamahiriya, the Socialist Republic of Vietnam, Sri Lanka, Sudan, Sweden, the Syrian Arab Republic, Tunisia, Turkey, Uganda, the Ukrainian Soviet Socialist Republic, the United Arab Emirates, the United Republic of Cameroon, the United Republic of Tanzania, the United States, the USSR, Venezuela, Yemen, Yugoslavia, and Zaire. Voting against was Israel. Abstaining were Argentina, Australia, Brazil, Canada, Chile, Colombia, the Federal Republic of Germany, Guatemala, Honduras, Ireland, Italy, Japan, New Zealand, Nicaragua, the Philippines, Portugal, Spain, Switzerland, Thailand, the United Kingdom, and Uruguay.

136. UK Mission Geneva to FCO and MOD, May 26, 1977 DEFE 24/1345, doc. E45, UK National Archives. The handwritten comments seem to belong to John Gutteridge.

137. Summary Record of the Fifty-Sixth Plenary Meeting, in Federal Political Department of Switzerland, *Records of the Diplomatic Conference*, 7:191–94.

138. UK Mission Geneva to FCO, June 7, 1977, FCO 58/1124, doc. 153, UK National Archives.

139. Telegram DELFRA-GENEVE to Paris No. 450/54, Carton 1678, Cote F. 6.8.1.2, NUOI 1974–1979, Ministère des Affaires Étrangères, Direction des Archives.

140. Telegram DELFRA-GENEVE to Paris No. 1878–83, Carton 1678, Cote F. 6.8.1.2, NUOI 1974–1979, Ministère des Affaires Étrangères, Direction des Archives, my translation, emphasis added.

141. My paraphrasing here is an amalgamation of paragraphs 2 and 3 of the text, emphasis added. National liberation movements are not named as such, but rather referred to as an "authority representing a people engaged against a High Contracting Party in an armed conflict of the type referred to in Article 1, paragraph 4." For the original text, see Article 96, "Treaty relations upon entry into force of this Protocol," at ICRC, "Protocol Additional to the Geneva Conventions of 12 August 1949, and Relating to the Protection of Victims of International Armed Conflicts (API), 8 June 1977" (webpage), http://www.icrc.org/ihl.nsf/INTRO/470?OpenDocument.

142. Various states issued explanations of their vote. Some, such as Canada, Israel, the Netherlands, and the United Kingdom, wished to emphasize that only declarations made in good faith by groups truly implementing the law in practice could be valid, while West Germany clarified that until this type of declaration was made CA3 applied. Howard S. Levie, ed., *Protection of War Victims: Protocol 1 to the 1949 Geneva Conventions*, vol. 4 (Dobbs Ferry, N.Y.: Oceana, 1981), 481–500.

143. Telegram DELFRA-GENEVE No. 1864–69, Carton 1678, Cote F. 6.8.1.2, NUOI 1974–1979, Ministère des Affaires Étrangères, Direction des Archives.

144. Levie, *The Law of Non-international Armed Conflict*, 4.

145. Judge Mushtaq Hussain, quoted in Levie, *The Law of Non-international Armed Conflict*, 5.

146. Levie, *The Law of Non-international Armed Conflict*, 74.

147. Notable articles retained (in modified form) due to pressure from the ICRC, Austria, the Holy See, and Scandinavian states were those related to the protection of the civilian population, the protection of objects indispensable to the survival of the civilian population and the protection of works and installations containing dangerous forces.

148. Federal Political Department of Switzerland, *Records of the Diplomatic Conference*, 1:110.

149. Summary Record of the Fifty-Sixth Plenary Meeting.

150. Stephen D. Krasner, *Structural Conflict: The Third World Against Global Liberalism* (Berkeley: University of California Press, 1985), 10.

151. Mantilla, "Social Pressure and the Making of Wartime Legal Protections for Civilians."

CONCLUSION

1. Monica Hakimi, "Constructing an International Community," *American Journal of International Law* 111, no. 2 (2017): 317–56.

2. Sandesh Sivakumaran, "Re-envisaging the International Law of Internal Armed Conflict," *European Journal of International Law* 22, no. 1 (2011): 225.

3. Theodor Meron, "The Continuing Role of Custom in the Formation of International Humanitarian Law," *American Journal of International Law* 90, no. 2 (1996): 238–49; Jean-Marie Henckaerts, "Study on Customary International Humanitarian Law: A Contribution to the Understanding and Respect for the Rule of Law in Armed Conflict," *International Review of the Red Cross* 87, no. 857 (2005): 175–212.

4. Jonathan Somer, "Jungle Justice: Passing Sentence on the Equality of Belligerents in Non-international Armed Conflict," *International Review of the Red Cross* 89, no. 867 (2008): 656. Note that if this seemed true in 2008, this is doubly the case in 2020.

5. Michael N. Schmitt and Sean Watts, "State Opinio Juris and International Humanitarian Law Pluralism," *International Law Studies* 91 (2015): 171–215. For a thoughtful, balanced take on this debate, see Sandesh Sivakumaran, "Making and Shaping the Law of Armed Conflict," *Current Legal Problems* 71, no. 1 (2018): 119–60.

6. See, however, Matthew Evangelista and Nina Tannenwald, eds., *Do the Geneva Conventions Matter?* (New York: Oxford University Press, 2017); and Hyeran Jo, *Compliant Rebels: Rebel Groups and International Law in World Politics* (New York: Cambridge University Press, 2015). On the law of interstate conflict, see James D. Morrow, *Order within Anarchy: The Laws of War as an International Institution* (New York: Cambridge University Press, 2014).

7. Note that this argument is historically conditional. The third condition no longer seems necessary, as we have seen important international treaties survive negotiation and exert influence even without the support of great powers. See Adam Bower, *Norms without the Great Powers: International Law and Changing Social Standards in World Politics* (New York: Oxford University Press, 2017); and Richard Price, "Reversing the Gun Sights: Transnational Civil Society Targets Land Mines," *International Organization* 52, no. 3 (1998): 613–44.

8. Beyond mentioning the International Commission of Jurists' connection to Amnesty International in the mid-1960s, and the work of Seán MacBride in Tehran at the 1968 UN International Conference on Human Rights, I have not systematically reflected on the strengthening of human rights norms and discourse at this time nor on their broader direct or indirect influence on the development of IHL, yet clearly this was occurring and merits further research. See Steven L. B. Jensen, *The Making of International Human Rights: The 1960s, Decolonization and the Reconstruction of Global Values* (New York: Cambridge University Press, 2016); and Ann Marie Clark, *Diplomacy of Conscience:*

Amnesty International and Changing Human Rights Norms (Princeton, NJ: Princeton University Press, 2001).

9. Antonio Cassese, "A Tentative Appraisal of the Old and the New Humanitarian Law of Armed Conflict," in *The New Humanitarian Law of Armed Conflict*, ed. Antonio Cassese (Naples: Editoriale scientifica, 1979), 500–501.

10. Antonio Cassese, "The Geneva Protocols of 1977 on the Humanitarian Law of Armed Conflict and Humanitarian Law," *UCLA Pacific Basin Law Journal* 3, nos. 1–2 (1984): 55–118.

11. Notably, both Cassese and Meron were involved in the 1970s APs diplomatic process: Meron acted as legal adviser for Israel at one of the ICRC preparatory conferences, while Cassese was a member of the Italian delegation throughout.

12. Michael J. Matheson, "The United States Position on the Relation of Customary International Law to the 1977 Protocols Additional to the 1949 Geneva Conventions," *American University International Law Review* 2, no. 2 (1987): 419–31.

13. The Prosecutor v. Dusko Tadic, Decision on the Defence Motion for Interlocutory Appeal on Jurisdiction, IT-94-1-A, October 2, 1995, International Criminal Tribunal Yugoslavia; Colin Warbrick and Peter Rowe, "The International Criminal Tribunal for Yugoslavia: The Decision of the Appeals Chamber on the Interlocutory Appeal on Jurisdiction in the *Tadic* Case," *International and Comparative Law Quarterly* 45, no. 3 (1996): 691–701.

14. I expand on this in Giovanni Mantilla, "Under (Social) Pressure: The Historical Regulation of Internal Armed Conflicts through International Law" (PhD diss., University of Minnesota, 2013), chap. 5.

15. This idea was proposed in a January 1995 meeting of the Intergovermental Expert Group and endorsed at the International Conference of the Red Cross and Red Crescent later that year.

16. François Bugnion, "Customary International Humanitarian Law," *African Yearbook of International Law* (2008): 59–99.

17. The ICRC found insufficient evidence to consider as custom the rule that armed actors in internal conflict should, when in doubt during their military operations, assume that persons were civilians and thus refrain from attacking them. Other provisions dealing with civilian protection and combatant or prisoner of war status were also left untouched. Henckaerts, "Study on Customary International Humanitarian Law."

18. Jean Marie Henckaerts and Louise Doswald-Beck, *Customary International Humanitarian Law: Rules*, vol. I. (Cambridge: Cambridge University Press, 2005); Elizabeth Wilmshurst and Susan Breau, eds., *Perspectives on the ICRC Study on Customary International Humanitarian Law* (Cambridge: Cambridge University Press, 2007). Note that some of the experts praising the report had participated in its elaboration process. For a ringing endorsement, see Theodor Meron, "Revival of Customary Humanitarian Law," *American Journal of International Law* 99, no. 4 (2005): 817–34. For a crucial, more skeptical view, see George H. Aldrich, "International Customary Humanitarian Law—An Interpretation on Behalf of the International Committee of the Red Cross," *British Yearbook of International Law* 76, no. 1 (2006): 503–24.

19. Jean-Marie Henckaerts, "The International Committee of the Red Cross and Customary Humanitarian Law," in *Humanizing the Laws of War: The Red Cross and the Development of International Humanitarian Law*, ed. Robin Geiß, Andreas Zimmermann, and Stefanie Haumer (Cambridge: Cambridge University Press, 2017), 83–112; Linus Mührel, "The Authority of Interpretations and Law-Ascertainments of the International Committee of the Red Cross in the Course of Times" (paper presented at Paths Panel II: The Authority of Legal Instruments: Perspectives from IHL and Environmental Law, Graduate Institute of International and Development Studies, Geneva, May 16, 2019).

20. From these, the U.S. response was the most robust, both recognizing the value of the customary law study and critiquing its method and conclusions. See John B. Bellinger III and William J. Haynes II, "A US Government Response to the International Committee of the Red Cross Study *Customary International Humanitarian Law*," *International Review of the Red Cross* 89, no. 866 (2007): 443–71. Among various aspects of the study, Bellinger and Haynes decried the experts' tendency to privilege military manuals as evidence of practice supportive of custom, as well as the choice to include nonbinding resolutions of the UN General Assembly and nongovernmental organization statements as authoritative sources. Instructions contained in manuals, U.S. advisers argued, often represented policy decisions that did not amount to widely accepted binding law. They also claimed that the experts behind the ICRC study had not paid "counterpractice" enough attention—that is, practice contradicting the rules that it held to be customary, and especially the counterpractice of states that were not parties to certain treaties. The ICRC responded swiftly to these and other critiques, standing its ground. See Jean-Marie Henckaerts, "Customary International Humanitarian Law: A Response to US Comments," *International Review of the Red Cross* 76, no. 866 (2007): 259–70. For reactions by some of the states mentioned, see ICRC, *Report of the XXX International Conference of the Red Cross and the Red Crescent, Geneva 23–30 November 2007* (Geneva: ICRC, 2007).

21. George H. Aldrich, "Establishing Legal Norms through Multilateral Negotiation: The Laws of War," *Case Western Reserve Journal of International Law* 9 (1977): 15, emphasis added.

22. This is why, after all, so much IR and legal scholarship puzzles around the questions of states' compliance with, and more generally the influence and effectiveness of, international law.

23. Although I do not engage in explicit ethical reasoning here, my view may correspond to a "pragmatic constructivist ethic"; see Jason Ralph, "What Should Be Done? Pragmatic Constructivist Ethics and the Responsibility to Protect," *International Organization* 72, no. 1 (2018): 173–203. None of this is to argue that "more law" represents "better law," let alone better protection for the victims of armed conflict. As I reiterate later in this conclusion, we do not yet know with precision how influential IHL has been in internal conflict. However, the normative wager concerning IHL—and most law—is that by creating standards of appropriate conduct we generate pressures to comply and to conform, which may work to reduce atrocity, however imperfectly and unevenly.

24. Ian Clark, Sebastian Kaempf, Christian Reus-Smit, and Emily Tannock, "Crisis in the Laws of War? Beyond Compliance and Effectiveness," *European Journal of International Relations* 24, no. 2 (2018): 319–43.

25. Both may redound in greater respect for IHL. Sivakumaran, "Re-envisaging the International Law of Internal Armed Conflict"; Tanisha M. Fazal, *Wars of Law: Unintended Consequences of the Regulation of Armed Conflict* (Ithaca, NY: Cornell University Press, 2018), 245–49; Hyeran Jo, "Compliance with International Humanitarian Law by Non-State Armed Groups: How Can It Be Improved?," in *Yearbook of International Humanitarian Law*, vol. 19, *2016*, ed. Terry D. Gill, Tim McCormack, Robin Geiß, Heike Krieger, and Christophe Paulussen (The Hague: T.M.C. Asser, 2018), 63–88.

26. The U.S. Army revised its *Commander's Handbook on the Law of Land Warfare* in 2019, apparently omitting or bringing in ambiguity concerning rules of IHL that it previously accepted. While it is unclear whether this is a response to the customary law study, it signals a subtle but potentially consequential form of pushback against certain portions of IHL it previously accepted as binding.

27. Jelena Pejić, "Strengthening Compliance with IHL: The ICRC-Swiss Initiative," *International Review of the Red Cross* 98, no. 901 (2016): 315–30. For a skeptical take, see Giulio Bartolini, "The 'Compliance Track' on a Track to Nowhere," *EJIL Talk!* (blog),

European Journal of International Law, January 22, 2016, https://www.ejiltalk.org/the-compliance-track-on-a-track-to-nowhere/.

28. IR work on the IHL of interstate conflict began appearing only around 2006. They include James D. Morrow, "When Do States Follow the Laws of War?," *American Political Science Review* 101, no. 3 (2007): 559–72; Benjamin Valentino, Paul Huth, and Sarah Croco, "Covenants without the Sword: International Law and the Protection of Civilians in Times of War," *World Politics* 58, no. 3 (2006): 339–77; and Alexander B Downes, *Targeting Civilians in War* (Ithaca, NY: Cornell University Press, 2008).

29. Helen M. Kinsella and Giovanni Mantilla, "Contestation before Compliance: History, Politics, and Power in International Humanitarian Law," *International Studies Quarterly*, 2020, https://doi.org/10.1093/isq/sqaa032.

30. Helen M. Kinsella, *The Image before the Weapon: A Critical History of the Distinction between Combatant and Civilian* (Ithaca, NY: Cornell University Press, 2011); Jo, *Compliant Rebels*; Jessica A. Stanton, *Violence and Restraint in Civil War: Civilian Targeting in the Shadow of International Law* (New York: Cambridge University Press, 2016); Tanisha M. Fazal and Brooke C. Greene, "A Particular Difference: European Identity and Civilian Targeting," *British Journal of Political Science* 45, no. 04 (2015): 829–51.

31. See, however, Hyeran Jo and Catarina P. Thomson, "Legitimacy and Compliance with International Law: Access to Detainees in Civil Conflicts, 1991–2006," *British Journal of Political Science* 44, no. 2 (2014): 323–55.

32. Dustin Tingley and Barbara F. Walter, "Can Cheap Talk Deter? An Experimental Analysis," *Journal of Conflict Resolution* 55, no. 6 (2011): 996–1020.

33. Thomas Risse, Stephen C. Ropp, and Kathryn Sikkink, *The Power of Human Rights: International Norms and Domestic Change* (New York: Cambridge University Press, 1999); Heather Smith-Cannoy, *Insincere Commitments: Human Rights Treaties, Abusive States, and Citizen Activism* (Washington, DC: Georgetown University Press, 2012); Thomas Risse, Stephen C. Ropp, and Kathryn Sikkink, eds., *The Persistent Power of Human Rights: From Commitment to Compliance* (New York: Cambridge University Press, 2013); Beth A. Simmons, *Mobilizing for Human Rights: International Law in Domestic Politics* (New York: Cambridge University Press, 2009).

34. Ryan Goodman and Derek Jinks, *Socializing States: Promoting Human Rights through International Law* (Oxford: Oxford University Press, 2013). On the politics of interpretation in international law, see Ingo Venzke, *How Interpretation Makes International Law: On Semantic Change and Normative Twists* (New York: Oxford University Press, 2012).

35. Philip Allott, "The Concept of International Law," *European Journal of International Law* 10, no. 1 (1999): 46, emphasis added.

36. Giovanni Mantilla, "Conforming Instrumentalists: Why the USA and the United Kingdom Joined the 1949 Geneva Conventions," *European Journal of International Law* 28, no. 2 (2017): 483–511. For a political theory of international law promise making which looks beyond nonfulfillment and hypocrisy, see Emma Mackinnon, "Promise-Making and the History of Human Rights: Reading Arendt with Danto," *Humanity* 9, no. 2 (2018): 193–217.

37. For a legal argument about addressing indeterminacy in IHL, see Adil Ahmad Haque, "Indeterminacy in the Law of Armed Conflict," *International Law Studies* 95 (2019): 118–60.

38. Fabian Klose, *Human Rights in the Shadow of Colonial Violence: The Wars of Independence in Kenya and Algeria* (Philadelphia: University of Pennsylvania Press, 2013); Brian Drohan, *Brutality in an Age of Human Rights: Activism and Counterinsurgency at the End of the British Empire* (Ithaca, NY: Cornell University Press, 2017).

39. Drohan, *Brutality in an Age of Human Rights*, calls this partial effect "cooperative manipulation" by states.

40. David P. Forsythe, "Legal Regulation of Internal Conflicts: The 1977 Protocol on Non-International Armed Conflicts," *American Journal of International Law* 72, no. 2 (1978): 277; Jelena Pejić, "Status of Armed Conflicts," in *Perspectives on the ICRC Study on Customary International Humanitarian Law*, ed. Elizabeth Wilmshurst and Susan Breau (Cambridge: Cambridge University Press, 2007), 85; Jelena Pejić, "The Protective Scope of Common Article 3: More than Meets the Eye," *International Review of the Red Cross* 93, no. 881 (2011): 189–225.

41. Katerina Linos and Tom Pegram, "The Language of Compromise in International Agreements," *International Organization* 70, no. 3 (2016): 587–621.

42. Barbara Koremenos, *The Continent of International Law* (New York: Cambridge University Press, 2016); Alexander Thompson, "Rational Design in Motion: Uncertainty and Flexibility in the Global Climate Regime," *European Journal of International Relations* 16, no. 2 (2010): 269–96; Erik Voeten, "Making Sense of the Design of International Institutions," *Annual Review of Political Science* 22, no. 1 (2019): 147–63; Martha Finnemore and Stephen J. Toope, "Alternatives to 'Legalization': Richer Views of Law and Politics," *International Organization* 55, no. 3 (2001): 743–58.

43. See ICRC, "Customary IHL, III: Military Manuals" (web database), https://ihl-databases.icrc.org/customary-ihl/eng/docs/src_iimima; and U.S. Naval War College, "Stockton e-Portal: Military Legal Manuals" (web database), https://usnwc.libguides.com/c.php?g=86619&p=557511; and Jo, "Compliance with International Humanitarian Law."

44. Sandesh Sivakumaran, *The Law of Non-international Armed Conflict* (New York: Oxford University Press, 2012), 107–54. See also Ezequiel Heffes, "Compliance with IHL by Non-state Armed Groups: Some Practical Reflections at the 70th Anniversary of the 1949 Geneva Conventions," *EJIL Talk!* (blog), *European Journal of International Law*, August 21, 2019, http://www.ejiltalk.org/compliance-with-ihl-by-non-state-armed-groups-some-practical-reflections-at-the-70th-anniversary-of-the-1949-geneva-conventions/.

45. ICRC, "Colombia Peace Agreement" (webpage), https://casebook.icrc.org/case-study/colombia-peace-agreement.

46. Eve La Haye, *War Crimes in Internal Armed Conflicts* (Cambridge: Cambridge University Press, 2008). See also ICRC, "Customary IHL, IV: National Legislation" (web database), https://ihl-databases.icrc.org/customary-ihl/eng/docs/src_ivnale.

47. Hamdan v. Rumsfeld, 548 U.S. 557 (2006).

48. Giovanni Mantilla, "Social Pressure and the Making of Wartime Legal Protections for Civilians," *European Journal of International Relations* 26, no. 2 (2020): 443–68; Giovanni Mantilla, "The Origins and Evolution of the 1949 Geneva Conventions and the 1977 Additional Protocols," in *Do the Geneva Conventions Matter?*, ed. Matthew Evangelista and Nina Tannenwald (Oxford: Oxford University Press, 2017), 35–68.

49. A. W. Brian Simpson, "Britain and the Genocide Convention," *British Yearbook of International Law* 73, no. 1 (2002): 5–64; Karen E. Smith, "Acculturation and the Acceptance of the Genocide Convention," *Cooperation and Conflict* 48, no. 3 (2013): 358–77; Christopher N. J. Roberts, *The Contentious History of the International Bill of Human Rights* (New York: Cambridge University Press, 2014); Christian Reus-Smit, *Individual Rights and the Making of the International System* (New York: Cambridge University Press, 2013), 156; Darren Hawkins, "Explaining Costly International Institutions: Persuasion and Enforceable Human Rights Norms," *International Studies Quarterly* 48, no. 4 (2004): 779–804.

50. David Scheffer, *All the Missing Souls: Personal History of the War Crimes Tribunals* (Princeton, NJ: Princeton University Press, 2013), 220–26; Price, "Reversing the Gun Sights"; Jennifer Erickson, *Dangerous Trade: Arms Exports, Human Rights, and International Reputation* (New York: Columbia University Press, 2015); Margarita H. Petrova, "Rhetorical Entrapment and Normative Enticement: How the United Kingdom Turned

from Spoiler into Champion of the Cluster Munition Ban," *International Studies Quarterly* 60, no. 3 (2016): 387–99.

51. John S. Odell and Susan K. Sell, "Reframing the Issue: The WTO Coalition on Intellectual Property and Public Health," in *Negotiating Trade: Developing Countries in the WTO and NAFTA*, ed. John S. Odell (Cambridge: Cambridge University Press, 2006); Richard H. Steinberg, "In the Shadow of Law or Power? Consensus-Based Bargaining and Outcomes in the GATT/WTO," *International Organization* 56, no. 2 (2002): 339–74.

52. On the civilizing power of hypocrisy, see Jon Elster, "Deliberation and Constitution-Making," in *Deliberative Democracy*, ed. Jon Elster (Cambridge: Cambridge University Press, 1998), 97, 111.

53. Rebecca Adler-Nissen, "Stigma Management in International Relations: Transgressive Identities, Norms, and Order in International Society," *International Organization* 68, no. 1 (2014): 143–76.

54. Mantilla, "Social Pressure and the Making of Wartime Legal Protections for Civilians"; Risse, Ropp, and Sikkink, *The Persistent Power of Human Rights*, 287–90; Daniel C. Thomas, *The Helsinki Effect: International Norms, Human Rights, and the Demise of Communism* (Princeton, NJ: Princeton University Press, 2001). See also Jeff Colgan and Nicholas Miller, "Rival Hierarchies and the Origins of Nuclear Technology Sharing," *International Studies Quarterly* 63, no. 2 (2019): 310–21.

55. Giovanni Mantilla, "Conforming Instrumentalists."

56. Others will judge how successful this book is on both counts, but this was my intention nevertheless.

57. Beyond the archives of France, Switzerland, the United Kingdom, and United States, and the ICRC, I consulted those of Colombia, Ireland, and Mexico. However, my research there did not lead to much discovery.

APPENDIX

1. On configurational explanations, see Andrew Bennett, "Causal Mechanisms and Typological Theories in the Study of Civil Conflict," in *Transnational Dynamics of Civil War*, ed. Jeffrey T. Checkel (New York: Cambridge University Press, 2013), 206; and Patrick Thaddeus Jackson, *The Conduct of Inquiry in International Relations: Philosophy of Science and Its Implications for the Study of World Politics* (Abingdon, UK: Routledge, 2010).

2. Andrew Bennett and Jeffrey T. Checkel, eds., *Process Tracing: From Metaphor to Analytic Tool* (Cambridge: Cambridge University Press, 2014), 3–4.

Archival Sources

UNITED KINGDOM

UK National Archives, Kew Gardens, London
- Cabinet (CAB)
- Foreign and Commonwealth Office (FCO)
- Foreign Office (FO)
- Home Office (HO)
- Ministry of Defence (DEFE)
- War Office (WO)

UNITED STATES

U.S. National Archives, College Park, MD
- Record Group 59: General Records of the Department of State, 1763–2002.
  - Central Foreign Policy File, 1970–1973, SOC 3 Red Cross, Boxes 3011–13, Entry 1613.
  - Electronic Telegrams, Central Foreign Policy Files, 1973–1979. (Accessible online at http://aad.archives.gov/aad/series-description.jsp?s=4073; search term: "humanitarian law.")
  - Records Relating to the Red Cross and the Geneva Conventions, Textual Records from the Department of State, Office of the Legal Adviser (07/01/1931). Boxes 1–18, Entry A1 5210.
- Record Group 200: Records Relating to the International Committee of the Red Cross (ICRC); 1900–2005, Entry P 108, Boxes 1, 3, 4, 56.
- Record Group 389: Records of the Office of the Provost Marshal General, 1920–1975.
  - POW/Civilian Information Center, Confidential Records, Entries P 1 (Boxes 1–44) and P 2 (Boxes 1–25.)
  - Subject Files Relating to the Preparation of the Geneva Conventions, compiled 1946–1949, documenting the period 1917–1949. Entry A1 437, Boxes 669–79.

FRANCE

Ministère des Affaires Étrangères, Direction des Archives, La Courneuve
- Nations-Unies et Organisations Internationales (NUOI) 1970–1973, Cartons 1296–97, Cote S. 50.3.8.4.6.
- Nations-Unies et Organisations Internationales (NUOI) 1974–1979, Conférence Diplomatique sur la Réaffirmation et le Développement du Droit International Humanitaire Applicable dans les Conflits Armés, Carton 1678, Cote F. 6.8.1.2.
- Unions Internationales 1944–1964, Arts. 159–63, Cotes 4-17, 4-18, 4-19.

SWITZERLAND

International Committee of the Red Cross (ICRC), Geneva
Swiss Federal Archives, Bern

Conférence Diplomatique sur la Réaffirmation et le Développement du Droit International Humanitaire Applicable dans les Conflits Armés (1973–1979), J2.111*, 1979/29.

MEXICO

Acervo Histórico Genaro Estrada, Secretaría de Relaciones Exteriores, Mexico City

Index

Page numbers in italic refer to tables.

www.ingramcontent.com/pod-product-compliance
Ingram Content Group UK Ltd.
Pitfield, Milton Keynes, MK11 3LW, UK
UKHW010120271125
465349UK00018B/231/J